Business Etiquette handbook

Parker Publishing Company

Editorial Staff

Business Etiquette handbook

Parker Publishing Company, Inc.
West Nyack, N. Y.

LIBRARY OF CONGRESS
CATALOG CARD NUMBER: 64-7753

Eighth Printing . . . . . . April, 1968

PRINTED IN THE UNITED STATES OF AMERICA

09585—B & P

WHAT THIS BOOK WILL DO FOR YOU

Here, in handy form, is a book that gives the answers to perplexing problems of business etiquette. It tells you the correct thing to say or do in dealing with your fellow employees and with the public. It will guide you safely through those awkward situations that crop up in every business office.

Knowing what is proper is more than a matter of avoiding embarrassment; your business career can suffer unless you master the art of courtesy. This book covers every situation from coffee breaks to a formal affair at The White House; it will help you at a meeting, on a business trip, at a company dinner, or simply in your office or plant on a typical day. It has information both for the newcomer and for the company president. And it reflects courtesy as it is practiced in the modern office, thanks to surveys and other careful research.

The business world has needed a source of this kind for a long time. We are confident that you will turn to it often, and that you will find it specific, easy to use, and accurate.

CONTENTS

Part 2 · Meeting the Public

•Part 1• Etiquette in the Office

•1• Getting a New Employee Off to a Good Start

Giving a new employee a friendly reception and a helping hand assures that he will become productive faster. It also helps him decide that yours is a good company, one with which he'll stay. But even if there weren't these very practical reasons for making a new employee feel at home and for helping him start on the right foot on his job, good manners would require it. Letting a new employee sink or swim in his new surroundings is as rude as it is costly.

This section explains how you can give a newcomer the kind of reception that will make him glad he came to your company, and that will shorten the time it takes him to master his new job.

Consider how the newcomer feels. A person's first day with a company, even his first week, is almost always a tense time for him. Even though he (or she) may have a great deal of experience from previous work, the need to meet new people and to cope with new responsibilities is trying. That's why the newcomer appreciates it so when his new co-workers give him a friendly reception and help familiarize him with the strange surroundings.

The formal company orientation. In most big companies, and in many smaller ones, the orientation of a new employee is not left to chance. His introduction to the company is commonly handled by the personnel or employment department. He is told the history of the company, who its officers and other key people are, what fringe benefits he will enjoy as a supplement to his salary or wage, what the company rules are, what his particular department does, and so on. He may be given a tour of the company's facilities; he may receive a company manual or handbook to which he can refer later when he has questions.

This type of orientation can be very effective, especially if it is handled in a friendly and personal way. It still remains for the new employee's immediate supervisor and co-workers, however, to help him feel at home.

Greeting the newcomer at the department level. A company-run or "front office" orientation, even a good one, is not enough. The real opportunity to give a new employee a courteous and helpful reception is when he comes to his department, the place where he will work. This is also the time when he will appreciate courteous treatment the most.

The new employee's department head may not be the man (or woman) who will be his immediate supervisor. If that is the case, the department head may handle introductions and show the new employee around himself, or he may delegate some or all of this task to the supervisor. What is important is that there be a definite procedure; the employee should not get the feeling he is being passed along to get rid of him.

In a small company, of course, one person would probably take the new employee through the entire greeting and orientation procedure.

There are basically three kinds of information that an employee should get at this stage:

1. Where things are
2. Who the people are he'll work with, and what they do
3. What his job is, and how it is done.

There is no set order for covering these matters. In many cases, however, the employee will understand his assignment more easily if he gets the other information first.

Show the newcomer around. A simple courtesy that is sometimes glossed over is to show a new employee his way around and let him get his bearings. It is of prime importance, naturally, that he be shown his work area or location and that he know where to keep his tools or other equipment and where he gets supplies he will need. Here are some other locations, and directions, that a new employee might be hesitant to ask about, yet needs to know:

- What is the most direct route from the parking lot to his work area?
- Where does he hang his hat and coat, and keep his lunch if he brings it?
- Where is the nearest water fountain? The nearest rest room?

- How does he get to the nurse or first-aid room if he has to?
- Where is the cafeteria, if there is one?
- Is there a fire extinguisher or other emergency equipment nearby?

There are probably several special locations you will want to show to a new employee in your department, depending on the work you do there and the job he or she has. Make every effort to *show* him places, instead of just telling him where they are; he will find his way again much more easily. If certain areas are restricted for some reason, be sure to tell him about those so that he doesn't get into trouble by accident.

Introduce a newcomer to people. One of the most inconsiderate things you can do to a new worker is to fail to introduce him to his co-workers. Someone must make it a point to see that he is properly introduced to the people with whom he will be dealing (for a detailed explanation of how to make introductions in a business office or plant, see pages 63-71). It will help if he is also given some idea of what the people do, as he is being introduced to them; this will make names and faces easier to remember, and give him a general idea of how his job fits in with others.

Give him clear and complete job instructions. In starting a new man off on his job, it is better to make your instructions too complete than to go to the other extreme and make them skimpy. The best path is in between; tell him enough so that he can go ahead with some confidence, but not so much that he is confused.

Here are some pointers on how to give a new employee his first on-the-job instructions:

- *Show him, as well as tell him.* Whenever possible, show how a thing is done, in addition to explaining it. Seeing a thing done is the best way to learn it; seeing also helps a newcomer remember it.
- *Be sure he understands one step at a time.* Find out, either by having him do it or by asking him questions, whether he understands the point you have just made before you go on to the next. The pause after each point, and the repetition of it, helps him learn, and helps him keep steps clear in his mind.
- *Try to give him reasons for what he is supposed to do.* It may take a little more of your time, but a new employee will appreciate it if you tell him why he is supposed to do each task, and do it a certain way. He will understand more readily, and be happier, when he sees

the logic behind his new duties. It may save you time in the long run, too, because he will be more apt to solve his own small problems when he knows why things work as they do.

· *Give him encouragement, not criticism.* A person approaching a job for the first time is almost certain to be nervous and more sensitive to criticism than usual. Show a new employee that you are there to help him do well, and that you will give him a chance. It is a small courtesy that means a great deal to him just then.

· *Give a definite assignment or goal.* It isn't enough to tell a new employee how to do his job; you should complete your instructions by giving him a definite goal, a specific assignment. For example, instead of saying, "Go ahead with this now, and see how you make out with it," say something like, "I'll let you go ahead with this pile of orders on your own, now that you have the hang of it. You should be able to finish by this afternoon. When you have done them all, tell me and I will go over them with you. Don't turn them over to Pat until I check them, even if it means waiting until tomorrow morning." This tells him what you want him to do, when you expect it to be done, and what he should not do. This is much more considerate than leaving him to guess or ask repeated questions.

Other information a new employee might be given at the department level includes:

· The hours of his particular department or shift (including lunch time, coffee-break, clean-up time, and so on)

· Whether he has to sign a time sheet or punch a clock, and where

· Any special procedures for getting or using materials or tools for his job

· Company policy concerning use of telephones or the like.

How should the supervisor treat the new employee? If you are to supervise, you must establish a cordial relationship with the newcomer. The faster he learns his routine and becomes a satisfied happy co-worker, the sooner *you* benefit by having one more dependable worker to help increase the efficiency and output of those under your guidance. Here are some rules to follow:

· *Be friendly but not familiar.* Your attitude should be one that makes the new employee feel he is welcome. Yet you must avoid a "chummy" approach. For one thing, this would invite a breakdown of authority. It might also embarrass the new employee, since he may be afraid to respond to a superior in such a friendly fashion, yet afraid that he will offend you if he doesn't.

· *Be understanding about initial mistakes.* Give a new employee a chance to show what he can do. Don't jump on him when he makes mistakes at first. Use his early mistakes as a means of showing how the job *should* be done; help him learn from his errors, in other words.

· *Have things ready for him.* One way you can show your consideration is to see that a new employee has a place to work at, that his work area is clean, and that he has the equipment he will need. If he is greeted by makeshift arrangements, and sees people scrambling to find him a decent typewriter or a tool that works, he will feel like an unwelcome intruder.

A newcomer appreciates help from his co-workers. Whether a person will feel welcome at his new company, and will enjoy his job and do it well, often depends on how he gets along with his fellow workers. They can make a big contribution to his morale and to his progress on the job if their reception of him is friendly and helpful. Here are a few courtesies you might observe as a "veteran" greeting a newcomer:

· *Offer to help or answer questions.* Sooner or later, a new employee working with you will want to ask you a question or seek your advice on a problem that crops up in his new duties. Yet, either from shyness or a reluctance to bother you, he may hesitate or find it awkward to ask you a question about his work. You can make it easier for him by offering to help or answer questions he may have.

Your offer should be a sincere one, of course; you should be ready to try to help when you can. However, you are not obliged, even by good manners, to give him all your time and neglect your own work. If a new (or old) employee takes advantage of your offer to help and makes excessive demands on your time, he is being inconsiderate. Your only choice in that case would be to say, nicely but firmly, that you have your own job to do and that he should see his supervisor if his instructions still aren't clear. This should rarely be necessary, since most people will not impose on your time.

· *Respect his sense of privacy.* Your curiosity about a new employee should not be allowed to get the best of you. Avoid "pumping" him, asking him personal questions; let him tell you about himself when and if he wants to. Nor should you unload on him your complaints about certain fellow workers or the job or the company or your personal life. He probably doesn't want to hear your problems. Also, it is discourteous to run down the company or your superiors, especially in front of a new employee.

Along the same lines, it is not good manners to draw a new employee aside and give him a run-down of others in the office or department. You would be doing your co-workers an injustice by influencing the newcomer's judgment of them. You are also being unfair to him; after all, most people want to make up their own minds about new acquaintances.

· *Don't impose on him as "big brother."* If you give a newcomer too much help by taking him under your wing, you may make him uncomfortable, and do him more harm than good. He may not want that much help; he may prefer to learn his own way. He may also feel that you are imposing yourself on him, yet be unable to tell you so nicely. And you could be making it difficult for him to make his own friends in his own time.

· *Don't make fun of a beginner or his mistakes.* It is only natural that a newcomer in any situation will be humiliated if he is laughed at or made fun of. Even though a new employee may commit ludicrous errors or have quirks or mannerisms you think funny, don't have the bad manners to ridicule him. Even laughter that is meant to be with him and not at him, or that is intended as friendly support, is dangerous, since you aren't sure that he will take it that way.

· *Invite him to lunch on his first day.* A good start towards friendly relations can be made by inviting a new employee to have lunch with you. If there is a group that usually eats together, inviting the newcomer along will help him to get to know several people at one time. If there is no regular group, perhaps a few employees could arrange to eat together that day. Even if an individual employee—probably the one with whom the newcomer works most directly—makes the offer, the new employee will appreciate the fact that he has someone to eat with. If the supervisor makes it a practice to take a new employee to lunch on his first day there, wait until the second day.

In addition to providing an opportunity to get acquainted, inviting the newcomer to lunch also gives you a chance to offer him some helpful advice. For example, you can tell him about the good eating places in the neighborhood and what their price ranges are; what shopping places can be reached during the lunch period; what points of interest (parks, museums, or the like) are nearby; and so on. If you eat in a company cafeteria, you can show him the ropes there—where different types of food are served, whether there are "specials," what to do with dishes and trays, and so on.

It isn't necessary to give the new employee the impression that you expect him to join you or your group every day for lunch. In fact, it's best if you don't try to hurry personal alliances and friendships. Word your first-day invitation so that it is clear you mean just that day, as a way to break the ice. If yours is a department or office in which everyone regularly eats together as a group, then of course your first invitation would be a permanent one. An invitation may even be unnecessary in this situation.

Ordinarily, the newcomer should expect to pay for his own lunch when he is invited to join co-workers. To avoid possible confusion and embarrassment, whoever does the inviting should make it clear that lunch will be "Dutch treat."

Some tips for the newcomer. Here are a few suggestions that may help you get a fruitful and congenial start on a new job.

• *Don't brag or show off.* It is a mistake to try to impress oldtimers by telling them how much better your old company handled things, or to point out mistakes you see them making. The only impression you will make is a bad one. If you see inefficiencies or know of a better method that could be used, the wisest course is to be patient. Once you have been there a while and have established a working relationship with the other workers and with your supervisor, your suggestions stand a much better chance of being accepted by them, instead of being resented.

• *Don't try to get too friendly too soon.* If you tend to be open and friendly, you would be wise to use some restraint in your first few days on a new job. Even though you immediately like some of the people you meet, it is prudent to wait at least a few days before you get on a very friendly basis with them. Not only will this avoid giving the impression that you are forward, but it will also prevent the forming of alliances that you may later regret.

• *What to do when you're invited to lunch.* In some companies, your immediate superior will invite you to lunch with him on the first day. If he does, let him take the lead in selecting the place at which you dine. Frequently, it will be in the company cafeteria. You simply follow the same procedures as does your host, paying for your own lunch when you reach the check-out register and attendant. He may prefer to dine with you alone, or suggest joining a particular group. In any case, let your conversation be guided by the supervisor or senior members of the group.

If your superior does indicate that he intends to pay for your lunch, simply thank him graciously. Don't create a scene by trying to insist that you pay your part of the bill; he wouldn't offer to pay unless he really wanted to.

Don't let the informal atmosphere of the lunch table trap you into being too familiar with your supervisor or department head. If he asks personal questions, it is to make conversation easier for you, and to learn something about you. It is not an invitation for you to ask *him* personal questions, or to get chummy. You should also curb any temptation you may have to try to impress him by boasting of your accomplishments with other companies. If drinks are included with lunch, be careful that you don't take more than you can handle, since it will loosen your tongue and might lead to embarrassment.

If your co-workers ask you to join them for lunch, expect to pay for your own. Let the others take the lead in conversation; "talking shop" is often against the unwritten rules at lunchtime. When lunch is over you might thank them for asking you to join them.

·2· Courtesy in the Office or Plant

Many things that you do in the course of a business day are basically matters of courtesy and of consideration for your fellow workers. This is so even though your actions are governed by rules.

It is not surprising that companies have rules about points of behavior that could properly be called etiquette (promptness, for example). Good business manners help things get done smoothly, just as good manners smooth the way in your personal life. A company cannot afford the inefficiency that would result if its employees were to ignore business etiquette and work on the basis of "every man for himself."

Your own interests as an employee are best served, too, when you know and practice courtesy during your business day. When you are considerate toward others, you are encouraging them to be considerate in return. That means you will work in an atmosphere of friendliness and cooperation; you will enjoy your job more. People will be more willing to give you assistance, or to get a job done for you in a hurry, when they know that you would give them the same consideration if positions were reversed.

One last but important point: in many cases, to ignore business etiquette in your dealings with others in your office or plant is to fail to act in the company's best interests. You will have difficulty making progress in the business world if you disregard the feelings of your co-workers and the interests of the company through discourteous behavior.

This section explains the common rules of everyday business etiquette in the office.

Points of Office Etiquette for the Individual

The need for courtesy is not necessarily limited to your dealings with fellow workers; it includes your dealings with the company as an individual employee. The major opportunities for exhibiting this kind of courtesy are spelled out below.

Be punctual. Most companies are fairly strict about requiring employees to be on time both for the beginning of the working day and for returning from lunch. If a company seems to condone laxity in punctuality it is apt to be because its employees are often called on to work overtime, or to work unusual hours. Still, as a general rule, punctuality is required in business.

Even so, punctuality remains essentially a point of etiquette. Just as you would be expected to be on time for a luncheon engagement, so your employer expects that you will be on time for your duties at the office. In social life, lateness is frowned on because it can inconvenience the hostess; in business, it can have even more serious consequences. One person being late can hold up several people who work with him. And if that one person is late often, he will sooner or later be resented by the others in the office who are more considerate and arrive on time. Your supervisor, too, is entitled to feel that if you will not make the effort to be at work on time you can't be very interested in the job, or in the extra effort that would be called for in a more important job.

If you find it difficult to put yourself in the company's place on the matter of punctuality, imagine your feelings if the company was rather lax on getting out pay checks on time.

Have a good attendance record. Your company can hardly expect every employee to have a perfect attendance record. Illness and other types of emergencies are not predictable, and they can happen to anyone. In recognition of this, most companies will pay for an absence that is not the fault of the employee, although they usually limit the number of days for which they will pay.

Excusable absences generally include those caused by:

- Your illness
- Serious illness in your immediate family
- Death in your family

- Weather or other natural disasters that make travel impossible
- Transportation strikes if you cannot find private means of transportation.

As an employee you have an obligation to be on the job unless there is a very good reason—one of those just listed—for being out. To feign illness so that you can take care of personal problems, or to stay home when you are only feeling somewhat out of sorts, is inconsiderate, if not dishonest. It adds to the workload of your co-workers, and it can upset the plans of an entire department or division. Nor can you consider yourself reliable if you cannot be counted on to be at work regularly.

When you must be out, you should telephone or otherwise inform your supervisor. Call soon after your place of business opens for work, so that he can make any adjustments in his plans as early as possible in the day.

Carry your share of the load. Naturally, you are paid to perform a certain job, and your company expects you to do so. What you may not have considered is the fact that the people with whom you work directly also expect you to carry your own work load. Loafing on the job may be hidden from your supervisor, but your co-workers will know about it, and will resent it, with good reason. If the job is to get done, someone will have to take up the slack you have created.

Be trustworthy. As an employee you have an unwritten responsibility to your company to protect its interests. There is a very basic reason for this. A business firm does not operate in a comfortable vacuum; it must compete with other companies. It would be at a serious disadvantage if its trade secrets—its plans for new products, its forthcoming advertising campaign, and so on—were made known to its competitors. The result is that company management expects employees to treat the company's internal operations and its plans for the future as confidential, or at least to protect them from competitors.

To illustrate how easily indiscretion on the job can backfire, suppose a secretary tells a salesman that he will not be able to see her employer next Wednesday because he will be in Milwaukee that day. Where her employer goes may be of no interest to the salesman, but it could mean a great deal to a competitor of the secretary's firm who hears the salesman mention it over the luncheon table.

The secretary in this case told the salesman more than was necessary. It would have been enough to tell the salesman that he could not see her employer next Wednesday, and to suggest another date. If she felt that an explanation was necessary she could have said simply that her employer would be out of town on that day.

The more you know about the company's operations, the more care you must use in discussing them. If you are the kind of a person who uses his apparent knowledge of "inside information" to impress others, you are a liability to your company, and are not trustworthy. If it becomes known that you are unable to use discretion in discussing company facts to which you have access, your job may be in jeopardy.

A secretary has a special responsibility toward her executive; she is in a position to know many things that he would not expect her to reveal. This includes personal information, as well as business information. The following suggestions are largely for the secretary's benefit, since this problem is a common one with the average secretary, but they may be helpful to anyone in a business office.

• *Be pleasant when you must be silent or noncommittal.* Even though you are turning down a request for information that you feel is obviously none of the other party's business, the best policy is to be polite. For example, you may have just explained to a caller that your executive is busy on a contract and can't be disturbed. If the caller should want to know what contract is involved, his question may be improper, but you gain nothing by telling him so. Instead, tell him pleasantly that your executive would prefer that you didn't reveal information of that kind. Or you might suggest that your executive will be glad to discuss the matter when the caller sees him at a later date. Or, if you don't know what the contract is, simply tell the caller this.

• *How to handle questions from other employees.* It is not unusual for a secretary to be in possession of facts or plans or news that her executive will not want her to discuss with other employees. The trouble is that it is often more difficult to keep facts from a fellow employee, especially a friend, than it is to keep silent with an outsider or stranger. You don't want to seem unfriendly or impolite, yet you know that your executive trusts you not to reveal confidential information.

Here are some typical situations involving co-workers, and suggestions for how to withhold information pleasantly but firmly:

• *The probing employee.* Some people ask questions out of habit, or because they are inquisitive by nature. They may want to know who is in talking to the boss, or when the new employee is coming and what he will be doing, or whether your executive has finished that report Mr. Brown asked for, and so on. It is not your job to feed the "grapevine," yet to fail to answer such seemingly innocent questions can seem unfriendly.

Often the best kind of answer in this type of situation is a very general one. For example, if someone has asked who is in your executive's office, you might reply "A customer who stopped in," instead of saying just who the customer is and why he is there. If the executive's caller is another employee, and you do not feel that you can politely refuse to mention his or her name, simply give the name and nothing more.

There is a strong temptation to resort to falsehoods in this kind of situation—"I don't know," "Mr. Berger has that file," and so on. This doesn't always work, because it is not easy to be a convincing liar. It also runs the risk of getting you involved in complications, if you later forget what your alibi was or if the other party repeats your statement to someone who knows it to be false. Apart from these practical reasons, dishonesty can hardly qualify as proper etiquette.

• *The employee with big eyes.* You may find that a certain employee drops by to discuss something, but seems to keep looking at important papers on your desk. Try calmly picking up the papers (perhaps covering them first with other papers from your desk) and tapping them on the desk as though to make a neat pile. Then you can either turn them over as though you are done with them, or put them in a desk drawer until your visitor has gone. If you are working with confidential material, it is a good idea to have a folder handy into which you can slide the papers when you aren't actually using them—and when you have a visitor.

• *The associate who asks you for information you aren't sure you should give him.* When you are uncertain whether or not another employee should be allowed to have something in your files, the safest policy is to politely stall for time. Ask the person if you can bring the material to him a little later when you are less pressed. This will give you a chance to ask your supervisor about it first. If you are busy at the time of the request, the other employee should not consider you rude for asking to oblige him a little later.

More difficult is the situation when a high executive asks for something, and your supervisor is not around (which is the reason the executive is asking you). A high-ranking executive's time is valuable; he should not be kept waiting on a pretext. Give him the information and any other help you can.

However, be sure that you tell your supervisor what happened when he returns. This will save him from being caught unaware if the executive should mention it to him, and will let him follow up if that is needed.

• *The employee who listens while you are on the phone.* Most people, when they sense that a phone call is either personal or of a confidential business nature, will either walk away from your desk or leave your office, unless you signal them to stay. If a visitor does not voluntarily leave you alone when you have a call that you must keep confidential, there are at least two methods of handling the situation without offending him:

• *Ask your caller if you may call back in a few minutes, because you have a visitor.* If the visit is an unimportant one, the visitor will often take the hint and indicate that he is leaving. The caller will also understand your situation, if the visitor does not leave and you must call back.

• *Ask the person on the phone if he will wait one minute.* Then say pleasantly to your visiting co-worker, "I wonder if you would excuse me while I take this call. I'll come and see you as soon as I am through."

Neatness is required in the office. How you keep house in your own home is your own affair. But in a business office, poor housekeeping leads to consequences that are undesirable for the company and for those who work there together. Untidiness inevitably creates some degree of inefficiency; papers can get lost, time can be wasted looking for something that on a neat desk would be immediately available, and so on. Untidiness can also offend your fellow employees, most of whom are probably more or less neat by nature. Office neatness and cleanliness is seldom your own individual affair, even though you might think so.

Here are suggestions for showing consideration through neatness:

· *Dust regularly.* Most offices have cleaning or maintenance service, but an after-hours cleaning crew will rarely touch a desk. This is a courtesy to the desk's occupant, who might want things left exactly as they are. It is therefore up to the individual employee to keep his or her own desk and area from accumulating dust and grime. All it takes is a touch, regularly, with a soft cloth. A secretary, of course, is usually expected to see that her executive's area is dusted regularly.

· *Don't spread out into space that isn't yours.* One consequence of untidiness is that you can find yourself needing more room to handle the disorder. This is unfair to others in the office, especially if space is at a premium. It is also inconsiderate to arrange your desk or other equipment so as to impede the free movement of your fellow workers.

· *Avoid over-decorating your desk or area.* When your desk, shelves and wall space are covered with mementos, photographs, trophies, humorous mottoes or other decorative effects, you are probably not beautifying the office; rather, you may be giving it a jumbled, untidy look. You may also be violating regulations against using nails in the walls, and so on. The proper atmosphere for a business office is one of neatness and efficiency, not hominess. "Pin-ups" are definitely out of place in a business office.

· *Be considerate with files and equipment you share.* If you share files, equipment or a supply cabinet with other workers, leave them in a neat condition, just as you would like to find them. When you see that some item in a supply cabinet needs replenishing, let the proper person know so that the item can be ordered. Don't be guilty of turning the contents of a supply cabinet upside down to find something and then just leaving it that way. This is a gross discourtesy to your fellow employees. So is the related act of leaving filing drawers in upheaval after tracking down a folder or letter you needed in a hurry.

· *Be especially neat when you use personal facilities.* Such places as the cafeteria and the rest rooms, and the locker or cleanup area if you use one, call for your best manners and your utmost consideration of your fellow employees.

In the *cafeteria,* lack of neatness is both unappetizing and unsanitary. Whatever the rules are in your cafeteria for keeping it neat, be scrupulous in abiding by them. Good table manners, too, are in order, of course.

A *rest room* can soon become unsightly and even offensive unless each employee does his part to keep it neat. Here are common courtesies you should observe:

Leave basins clean after using

Place paper towels in receptacles, not on the floor

Remove hair or bobby pins from a sink if you have let them fall there (they will clog it)

Don't flick ashes or drop matches on the floor

If you have a *locker or dressing room,* remember that others must use the facilities, too. If you share a locker with another employee, neatness is imperative, since a locker can become messy very quickly. Keep only essential items in the locker. Don't throw dirt-caked work shoes or boots in the bottom without at least an attempt to clean them. Try to avoid hanging wet clothing in a locker. If you bring your lunch, see that it is well wrapped or kept in a special container that will keep odors in. Don't leave food in a locker overnight; it invites insects and mice, besides creating a distinctive aroma.

If a shower is part of your daily cleanup at work, see that you don't strew wet towels around or leave a soapy puddle on the floor for the next man.

Smoking in the office. Each company has its own rules about smoking during business hours. You should familiarize yourself with these rules and follow them.

When smoking is allowed there are some basic courtesies you should observe. Always use an ash tray. Don't allow too many cigarette butts to accumulate in ash trays; this creates unpleasant odors and makes an office look unkept and unbusinesslike. A good way to empty an ash tray is to dump it carefully in a piece of scrap paper first, rolling up the paper neatly before you throw it into the wastebasket. Thus you prevent cigarette-ash dust and pungent, stale tobacco odors from permeating your office and desk area. A quick wipe of the ash tray with a tissue when you empty it will keep it bright and fresh-looking.

Of course, a lit cigarette should never be placed on the edge of a desk or any other piece of furniture. It should never be put out on the floor, under foot, or tamped against the side of a waste basket and then let fall into the basket. Waste basket fires are not unusual, and they always stem from carelessness.

If a woman smokes during business hours she should not walk around with a lit cigarette in hand. It is unladylike to do so. She should smoke at her desk, during a convenient lull in her work schedule, or at an associate's desk or her superior's desk (on invitation) when working together makes it natural to do so.

When smoking is permitted in conjunction with work, smokers should remember that non-smokers may find a smoke-filled atmosphere very unpleasant. A cigar smoker, especially, should refrain from his habit in the office unless he knows that no one objects to the strong smoke his cigars will give off.

•3• Working Harmoniously with Others

The observance of rules of etiquette in a business office helps make it possible for people to work together as a team and to enjoy their working hours. The following pages explain the basic courtesies that should be observed by people who work near and with each other in a business office.

Should you use first names in the office? Most modern offices are somewhat informal, and the use of first names among fellow employees is common. Even so, there are still situations where it is improper not to use title (Mr., Mrs. or Miss) and last name.

The basic and most important rule is simple: follow the practice that has been established in your particular office. There are some more specific rules that you should know about even in the most informal office, as follows:

· *Addressing your supervisor.* You should never address your immediate supervisor by first name unless you have been informed specifically that it is all right to do so.

· *Addressing executives.* You should never address a person of executive rank by first name, unless he or she tells you to do so. In some companies the degree of informality and the nature of the work make the use of first names between executives and lesser ranking employees a practical arrangement. In many companies, however, employees are expected to address executives by title, although the executive will usually address an employee by his first name if he knows it.

· *Addressing women.* It is a common sign of respect to address a woman as Miss or Mrs. even in situations where you might address a man by his first name. Most businesswomen, however, don't expect special treatment in this respect, and are accustomed to being addressed by their first name. The courteous procedure is to refer to a woman by title until you are sure that she would prefer that you use her first name.

- *Addressing older men and women.* It is not unusual for an older employee to prefer to be addressed by title by younger co-workers. It is an older person's privilege to expect this mark of respect. Even if others in the office refer to an older employee by first name, it is best to wait before you take the same liberty, if you are new in the office.

Daily greetings. In most offices it is customary to say "Good morning" when you arrive at your office in the morning. Depending on how the office is arranged, a single greeting may do for everyone, or you may greet people individually. If your office is on a first name basis, you would probably say "Good morning, Jim," or "Good morning, Nan."

On leaving the office you would probably say "Good night" to the same people you greet in the morning.

If you are uncertain about whether or not you should greet certain people—those from another office getting on an elevator with you, or a doorman or elevator operator, or even the company president—this is one form of courtesy that is universally acceptable. The simple act of saying "Good morning" to someone may be the beginning of a pleasant association that might not have otherwise arisen. Naturally, if someone greets you first in the morning, it is only proper to return the greeting pleasantly.

Controlling the urge to talk. While a pleasant greeting in the morning is proper, spending 15 minutes with each office friend discussing baseball or last night's dance is not. It means a late start for your working day, it distracts others in the office, and it may put your friend in a bad light with his or her superiors. Your own superior, of course, has a right to be similarly displeased if you regularly turn your "Good mornings" into prolonged conferences.

This need for restraint in personal conversations applies to the entire working day. Apart from being an injustice to the company, too much talking in the office is a discourtesy to your co-workers. It upsets their concentration; it creates resentment in those who do keep their personal conversations to a reasonable minimum; it can inconvenience them if your talking puts you behind in your work.

The office grapevine. A grapevine is a kind of word-of-mouth trail of office gossip.

There is a tendency to place great trust in a grapevine, but experience shows that this trust is not well founded. Although there is no doubt that a grapevine can spread factual news, it also thrives on rumors and half-truths, and seldom makes distinctions. It is good advice to be wary of pluckings from the grapevine, and of people who fancy themselves as privileged newscasters. The smart path is to regard grapevine news with caution, and, if you hear what seems to be very important news through this kind of source, to directly question your supervisor about it. It is not a good idea to be a "pipeline" for grapevine information, either; passing on unfounded rumors can lead to unfortunate consequences, and can involve you in embarrassing situations.

Don't forget that a rumor can have serious consequences when it gets outside the company. Even when you have no reason to doubt what you hear, avoid making public knowledge out of office affairs.

A company where the grapevine system is unusually strong is probably a company where top management does not make an attempt to keep its employees informed. The use of bulletin boards, a company newsletter or house organ, memorandums and so on would help prevent the spread of unofficial and probably inaccurate rumors.

The coffee break. The so-called "coffee break," a firmly established custom in millions of offices, takes many forms. In some cases it is actually a break from work, as the name implies. In other companies there is no formal stoppage of work; employees simply take coffee at their desks. Probably the majority of companies permit a coffee break only in the morning, but many have an afternoon break as well. In companies where fatigue is a factor, and where safety or concentration would be affected if continuous work stretches are too long, employees are given several breaks for rest during the day.

Most companies establish rules, to prevent the coffee break from being abused. Where there are definite rules, employees should observe them, of course. Where there are no formal rules, some common sense rules of etiquette can guide you.

• *When you go out for coffee.* In some offices employees go to a nearby restaurant, or to the company cafeteria, for their coffee and whatever they have with it. Two rules are important here:

1. Come and go quietly. Don't upset others in the office and give the office an unbusinesslike appearance by a noisy and boisterous manner when you are going for coffee, or returning.

2. Take only a reasonable time. If you stretch out your absence from your desk during coffee break, you are cheating your company and you are imposing on your fellow employees, who must make excuses for your absence or try to answer your phone or otherwise do your job until you come back.

• *When you send out for coffee.* Yours may be an office where an order is phoned in to a nearby restaurant or coffee shop and the coffee and pastry is then delivered. Sometimes coffee and lunch orders are combined. Here are two common-sense rules for this situation:

1. Have a system for handling the taking and placing of orders. There is no need for commotion and across-the-room questions and answers. Probably the best method is to have one efficient person do the ordering, and to have the others come to that person's desk to place their individual orders.

2. Be strict about finances. You are being inconsiderate and will eventually create resentment if you don't make prompt payment, or if you never have the right change.

• *When coffee service is available in your office.* Many companies arrange to have coffee (and tea, milk, pastries and so on) brought to individual work areas, either by their cafeteria or by a caterer or restaurant that will provide this service. The company will probably set up rules for using this service. In essence those rules will be as follows:

1. Keep the line short. Half the office should not be in a long line waiting for their coffee. Five or six at a time should be the maximum. Otherwise there will be congestion.

2. Have the proper change or a small bill ready, if possible.

3. Avoid making noise. Getting coffee should not be an excuse for merrymaking. If you must stand in line, whatever conversations you have should be quiet ones.

• *General rules for the coffee break.* Here are some rules that apply to the use of coffee in the office:

1. Be neat. Don't be guilty of having a desk covered with crumbs and coffee stains, or of leaving someone else's desk in a similar condition. If you use your own cup, wash it after use and keep it out of sight.

2. Observe common table manners. You should not talk with your mouth full, or borrow someone else's spoon or cup without asking permission.

3. Don't let the coffee break interfere with business. A coffee break is supposed to increase efficiency, but it can be harmful to business if not used with discretion. It would be very rude, for example, to rush out of your office while you had a visitor there, just so you wouldn't miss your chance to get coffee. Even if you explain where you are going, the visitor is left to wait with a feeling that he is being slighted.

One way to handle this situation, in an office that is not too formal, is to ask the visitor if he would like something from the coffee wagon, making it clear that he would be your guest. If he accepts the offer, it is best to arrange for someone else to actually get the coffee for you and your visitor, rather than go yourself and leave the visitor alone.

If a business caller comes to your desk while you are having your coffee, you should give him your full attention, which you cannot do unless you put aside your coffee. It is not polite to tell a receptionist to keep someone waiting in the company reception room until you have had a chance to finish your second breakfast.

• *When someone gets the boss his coffee.* If you are a secretary, you may be expected to get coffee for your executive in the morning. This should pose no more of a problem than any other part of your job, unless he is forgetful and doesn't reimburse you.

It is a breach of manners on the executive's part to expect his secretary (or anyone else) to advance money on his behalf. He should give her money in advance or else reimburse her promptly each day. Advance payment can be in the form of a weekly or monthly "kitty." The fund should be large enough so that if he buys coffee for business guests the fund will cover it.

If you are a secretary, or an executive's assistant, and find that you are out-of-pocket from buying coffee for your boss, your problem is a ticklish one. Probably the best solution is to suggest in a friendly way that he set up a fund. Make the point that with a fund you won't have to trouble him with reminders. Figure out beforehand how large the fund should be, so that if he asks the question you will have an answer ready.

Using company elevators. Men and women who work in buildings where elevators take them to their offices have certain obligations of courtesy to their fellow passengers and to the operator whose job it is to run the passenger service.

While men always remove their hats when a lady enters the elevator in a residential building, it is not always practical to do so in a crowded elevator in a commercial building such as a department store or an office building. If a man finds that the elevator is not too crowded and he can remove, or tip, his hat—especially if he recognizes and greets a fellow passenger—it is a courteous and appreciated gesture. But when the elevator is too crowded to do so conveniently he may keep his hat on.

It is expected that men will not smoke in an elevator. The confined area, lack of windows and poor air circulation would make for the discomfort of other passengers sharing the car. Therefore, it would be inconsiderate of anyone to light up a cigarette while waiting for an elevator and then to walk into the car with it. Not only is the discomfort to other passengers to be considered, but crowded conditions make lit cigarettes or cigars a danger to the clothes and person of the offender and anyone near him.

When you are waiting to board an elevator, it is courteous to step back to allow for those leaving the elevator. Men are not expected to observe the "ladies first" rule during morning and evening rush conditions.

Sometimes people at the back of a crowded elevator need to get out while those in front do not. Good manners require that two or three persons nearest to the front of the elevator step out momentarily, while those at the back come through.

Ordinarily, men step back to let women out first. They do this if the elevator is not crowded at the time, but when conditions are crowded it is far less awkward for men nearest the door to leave first, regardless of whether women are getting off at the same time.

If an operator has partly closed the door, but opens it again on seeing you coming toward the elevator, say "Thank you" or "Thank you for waiting." When the operator asks for floor numbers, the passengers should state the floors they want at once. It is a lack of courtesy to allow yourself to be so engaged in conversation that you have failed to indicate the floor you need—and then expect the operator to come to a sudden stop when you alert him at the last moment.

A business-like, impersonal attitude is required on the part of elevator operators. As a passenger, say a friendly "Good morning," or "Good evening," when you have the same operator each day, but maintain a courteous, impersonal attitude so that the operator can direct his or her attention to the responsibilities of his job.

Of course, it is unmannerly to push or jostle others in entering or leaving an elevator. If you are carrying packages, try to manage them so that other passengers won't be inconvenienced by them. A large pocketbook can also get in people's way unless you keep it under control.

Lunchroom etiquette. Company cafeterias usually have rules that employees are expected to follow in using dining facilities. These rules vary according to the type of service a particular cafeteria provides, but their purpose in each case is to assure the fastest and most pleasant service for everyone. You should observe the rules in your cafeteria or lunchroom carefully.

Below you will find some general rules that apply in most lunchroom or cafeteria situations. These are basic rules of etiquette that every employee should follow, so that everyone can enjoy his lunch time.

• *Be neat.* If the cafeteria is a non-profit one and does not provide table service for cleaning up after each group has eaten, it is especially important that you leave your table neat and clean for the next person who will sit there. If the procedure in your cafeteria is to keep food on a tray while you eat, instead of putting dishes and silver directly on the table, clean-up is simple. Still, you should take a last-minute look when you are ready to leave to be sure your place is neat.

• *Don't hog space.* Don't save a place for friends who are on a later shift. It is not fair to make people wait for a place to sit down while empty chairs are actually available. It is inconsiderate to automatically save seats for people who are usually there, but who could have made plans to eat elsewhere, or who could be absent. Again, this could inconvenience people who *are* there and need a seat.

• *Don't crash the line.* It is bad manners to expect friends on line to make a place for you ahead of them instead of taking your place at the end of the line. It should be obvious that if everyone took unfair advantage in this way there would be chaos.

• *Avoid dawdling.* When cafeteria conditions are crowded and people are waiting for a place to sit down, don't linger over your lunch longer than is necessary. To remain seated and chat idly while others are waiting to eat is a breach of good manners.

• *Wait patiently.* If you are standing and waiting for a seat it is extremely rude to "breathe down the neck" of someone who is having his lunch. To lean against his chair or otherwise stand so close that occasionally you bump the chair is an inexcusable display of bad manners.

• *Observe proper table manners.* Where people eat in more or less forced association in a company cafeteria, the need for the observance of common table etiquette is especially important. The basic rules—not talking with your mouth full, avoiding "boarding house reach," and so on—should be followed, even with your best office friends. The fact that you are not at home is no excuse for relaxing your manners.

Borrowing and lending. This is an area in which a breakdown of scrupulous courtesy can cause irreparable ill-will among those who must work together. In general, it's advisable *not* to borrow, if you can possibly avoid it. It may be very difficult for a gracious person to refuse to lend equipment, personal belongings and the like, even though he really would rather not. Though he lends you what you ask for with no outward sign of displeasure he may in reality, harbor resentment—particularly if you are an habitual borrower. There is always the chance, too, that no matter how careful you may be, you will break, tear or soil borrowed items unwittingly.

If you must borrow, be sure to make it a practice to return what you have borrowed as quickly as possible. Delays lead to forgetfulness and to accidents or actual loss of things—with the inevitable disagreeable feeling on the part of the individual who was kind enough to lend you his belongings.

As for borrowing money, the need for discretion is even greater. Don't borrow money, even very small sums, from co-workers if you can possibly avoid it. If you must borrow money, make certain that you return it as promptly as you can; it should not be necessary for someone who has been kind enough to lend you money to have to remind you of the debt.

However, if a borrower *has* been remiss, the lender shows far more courtesy and good manners by reminding him tactfully of the debt than by nursing a secret annoyance. Of course, it is the height of bad manners for the lender to complain about the debt to others as an oblique means of recovering the loan.

Observe the chain of command. Companies, like armies, have ranks of responsibility and position. The arrangement of people in the company from highest authority to lowest is often called the chain of command. It is an important rule of business etiquette that in your dealings with others in the company you not skip steps in the chain of command, or by-pass authority.

Probably this rule is most important when you are dealing with those above you on the ladder (this problem is discussed again at page 34), but it is appropriate to mention here that it applies to dealings downward and in a lateral direction, too. For example, it would be improper to give an assignment directly to a girl in a typing pool; you should deal with the person in charge of the pool. If you feel that a particular girl would be the best one to handle the assignment, the supervisor might be able to arrange for her to do it, but the choice is the supervisor's, not yours.

In the same way, if you are an executive, you should not give a direct assignment or order to someone else's secretary without her executive's permission. You may outrank her by far, but according to the chain of command she is not responsible to you. If she should oblige you in deference to your position she might well be criticized by her rightful boss.

The proper procedure would be to ask the other man's permission to use the services of his secretary. Most executives will cooperate when an associate has a work emergency. If you should have to press another man's secretary or assistant into service while he is absent, let him know about it when he returns. Naturally, he should receive your thanks, as should the secretary or assistant.

Don't be a chronic complainer. One of the quickest ways to become unpopular in your office is to be a complainer. People do not enjoy working in an atmosphere of discontent. Even though your co-workers may agree that you have a reason to complain they will resent it if you are forever telling them your troubles. This is true whether those troubles are connected with your work or with your personal life.

From the company's point of view, the griping of one employee can undermine the morale of an entire office. If you have a complaint about your job, or even about your supervisor or the company itself, your supervisor will want to be told. The chances are that he can correct a job problem, once he has the facts. If your quarrel is with him, he deserves to know about it; until he does, you can hardly expect him to change the situation. The longer you nurse a secret grudge the more difficult you make it to clear up the situation later.

Control personal phone calls, both in and out. Most offices have rules that either forbid or strictly limit personal telephone calls. There are several good reasons for such restrictions, and the rules should be observed by every employee. When you do place a personal call, or accept an incoming call, remember to keep your voice as low as possible, and to keep the conversation brief. Your fellow workers don't really want to eavesdrop on your personal life; it may even embarrass them to overhear you. Keep in mind, too, that they may be waiting for you to get off the line so they can place a business call.

Note that incoming personal calls are not an exception to these restrictions. If your company's rules are strict, then you will be expected to discourage friends and family from calling you at the office except on important matters. You are not freed from responsibility just because you didn't place the call yourself; time is still involved, and the lines are still being tied up. Nor is an executive getting around this rule if he gives his secretary a list of calls to make; he is still tying up an important line, and may be making it difficult for others to reach him by phone.

Control visits by friends or family. If you have either friends or family who are prone to pay you visits during the working day, remember that their presence can be disturbing to others. The best policy is to discourage such visits. When you have visitors, however, see if you can meet with them in a place that will minimize the disturbance. This is especially important when children are involved.

Eating at your desk. Companies lacking facilities for eating may permit employees to eat lunch at their desks. In most other offices there are rules against it.

If you are permitted to eat at your desk, good manners require that you be both neat and careful. Don't scatter crumbs or sandwich wrappers about; throw away napkins, coffee cups and stirrers, and so on. Protect your office furniture, especially your desk and its contents, from spills and stains. Some desk tops are easily marked by heat or moisture, so you should be especially careful with whatever you drink. These same rules apply when morning or afternoon snacks are available.

One rule is definite; you should not eat while you are serving or meeting the public. This gives an office a decidedly unbusinesslike atmosphere, and is likely to offend some customers.

·4· Etiquette Toward Superiors in the Company

Are you comfortable dealing with people above you in your company's chain of command? Do you know what courtesies are due them? This section explains the etiquette involved in dealing with your supervisor and others who are your superior in rank.

Reasons for deference to superiors. In every company, no matter how friendly and informal the atmosphere, there are differences in rank. The distinction between rank is a real one (or should be), because it is based on differences in authority and responsibility, and in value to the company. Just as social etiquette recognizes distinctions in social rank, business etiquette takes into account the differences in rank in a business organization.

As an employee in any company, large or small, you will be expected to show your superiors a certain degree of deference and respect. This applies to whatever non-working contact you have with them during the day—chance meetings, and so on—as well as to work situations. There is nothing in this that is demeaning or that infringes on your personal dignity; it is simply a recognition of the other person's position.

Examples of basic courtesy to superiors. It would be all but impossible to put down a precise set of rules; exactly what you do in any given situation will depend on the person you are dealing with, and on the particular circumstances. For example, your immediate supervisor probably expects little in the way of formalities of respect from you, because he works fairly closely with you and may not be far removed in rank. But a man on a higher plane above you will expect certain behavior from you in the form of formalities.

For example, you would probably not stand when your immediate superior entered your office or approached your desk. But if the company president, or someone else on a high executive level above you, were to approach you or enter your office, you would ordinarily stand to greet him. You would remain standing until he indicated that you should be seated or until he got what information or papers he wanted and left. If you were part of a group that was meeting when he entered, you would all stand.

Here are some other examples of how you might demonstrate your sense of respect for those above you in your company. You would address a senior as "Mr. Jones," until he says otherwise (as your supervisor might do). In fact, you should wait for a senior to make all overtures of informality and personal friendship. You would cut short a phone call, or a visit from another employee, rather than keep a superior waiting. You would allow him to enter a room or an elevator before you if you approached it at the same time.

These are only examples of the many situations in which your courtesy toward rank is ordinarily expressed. Some of the most important areas of relationship between you and your superiors are dealt with at greater length in the sections that follow.

Go through channels. A universal rule, although it is often an unwritten one, says that you should always follow the chain of command in dealing with people on different levels in your company. It is especially important that you not go "over the head" of your immediate supervisor.

To violate this rule is a serious breach of business manners. When you take information, or an idea, or a complaint, directly to your supervisor's superior (or higher), you place your supervisor in an awkward position. His boss knows something your supervisor doesn't know but should, something about his own area of responsibility. And the fact that you have bypassed your supervisor suggests that you lack confidence in his ability or willingness to handle the matter himself. As you might expect, a supervisor who learns that you have gone over his head will consider you ill-mannered, possibly even untrustworthy.

Even if the matter in question is a complaint against your supervisor himself, you should take it up with him before going to someone higher. The chances are your supervisor wants to correct any misunderstanding just as much as you do. But he may not realize that there *is* a problem or a misunderstanding, unless you tell him.

You are justified in going over your supervisor's head only if your problem is a very important one, and your supervisor will not or cannot help. This will rarely be the case.

Be loyal. One of the things your company pays you for is loyalty. Every company feels it has the right to expect that its employees will work for it, and not against it. In the same way, your immediate supervisor will expect a certain amount of loyalty from you—not blind obedience, but a willingness to work toward achieving his goals.

There is more to being loyal to your supervisor than simply doing as you are told. If you criticize him to others, you are not being loyal, even though you work hard for him. If you neglect to make him aware of information or ideas that could help him (or his staff or department) accomplish more or do a better job, you are not being loyal. The same is true if you fail to inform him of a problem, or potential problem. (This doesn't mean that you should try to tell your supervisor how to do his job; it simply means that you should think in terms of helping him.)

If you work for someone who you think is discourteous to you, or treats you unfairly, you may feel that you don't owe him loyalty. It is true that courtesy and loyalty are for supervisors, too; nevertheless, so long as you work under someone, your loyalty to him will be expected.

Respect the supervisor's time. One of the most important (and most appreciated) business courtesies you can extend to your supervisor is to respect his time. There are two types of demands you can make on his time, both of which can be systematically minimized:

- Amount (how much of his time you take)
- Frequency (how often you interrupt him)
- *How to spare your supervisor's time.* Here are a few suggestions for minimizing the amount of time you require from your supervisor:

1. Learn your duties thoroughly. A thorough knowledge of your job enables you to handle it on your own, without taking up your supervisor's time.

2. Learn what things are important, and what things are not. Then make it a practice not to bother your supervisor with unimportant matters.

3. Be prepared when you take your supervisor's time. Think out problems as far as you can before you take them to him. If you have your own conclusion or recommendation, give that to him

first, then give him the facts and reasons behind it. Have with you whatever files or correspondence you might need in discussing the problem.

• *How not to interrupt.* Constant interruptions make concentration on business problems difficult, if not impossible, for your supervisor. Here are suggestions for helping him in this respect:

• Make a list of questions, instead of taking each one to him separately. One long interruption is better than many short ones.

• Select a proper time for interrupting. Your supervisor is probably busier at certain times of the day than at others. Try to wait until he is not too busy before you approach him with your questions; he will appreciate it, and he will have more time to give you.

• Put questions in writing. If you give your supervisor a written memo on a problem he can give it his attention at a time that is most convenient to him. Many men prefer this system, since it reduces interruptions and gives them flexibility in the use of their time.

• *What a secretary can do.* If you are a secretary to a busy executive, you can perform a real service by helping him organize his working time, and by protecting him from interruptions and other time-wasters. An excellent source for these techniques is the *Complete Secretary's Handbook,* Revised Edition, by Lillian Doris and Besse May Miller (Englewood Cliffs, N.J.: Prentice-Hall, Inc., 1960). See also pages 105-120 of this book, where the subject of handling office visitors is discussed.

• *Does your executive have an "open door" policy?* Many men in supervisory positions try to follow an "open door" policy, meaning that their door is always open to employees who want to see them. If you take such a policy too literally, and run to your supervisor (or another executive) with every little thing that troubles you, you are guilty of violating the rules of business etiquette. The fact that an executive has an open door policy shows that he is making an effort to consider your point of view, and to respect your problems. You should return this courtesy by not imposing on his time without good reason; nor should you go through that door too often, even though it is open to you.

How to behave when you're criticized. Your supervisor is supposed to tell you what you are doing wrong, and explain how to do it properly; that's his job. If you have trouble accepting criticism, you are making your supervisor's job more difficult than it should be. In addition, you are denying yourself an excellent opportunity to learn and to improve.

· *When criticism is merited.* If you have made or are making a mistake, you should expect your supervisor to point it out. Here are some suggestions that will let you benefit from criticism:

1. Don't take criticism personally. Your supervisor is much more concerned with the mistake itself than with the person who made it; he hasn't the time to find fault with you as a human being. He points out mistakes to prevent them from happening again, not to ridicule you personally. If you keep that in mind, you will save yourself the anger or hurt feelings that you might otherwise experience.

2. Remember that criticism helps you improve. Learning what is wrong is just as important as learning what is right. When your supervisor shows you your mistakes, he is teaching you something. You should welcome criticism, then, because it will help you improve in your work.

3. Show your supervisor that you accept criticism constructively. No supervisor enjoys finding fault. By letting your supervisor know that you take his criticism in a positive way, you help him feel that you are both making progress. This is satisfying to him, and to you.

· *What about unjustified criticism?* A real test of your business manners comes when you are blamed for something that isn't your fault. What should you do?

If your first instinct is to bristle and deny it, or blame the person who is really responsible for the mistake, control it; you will only cause bad feelings. If your supervisor has made his own mistake in blaming you, he will hardly appreciate having it thrown in his face. If you are quick to blame someone else, that person won't be very happy, even though the blame is his.

Instead of protesting, then, swallow your temper and some of your pride. If the mistake is an unimportant one, why not let it go as though it were your fault? You might say something like this:

> That's true; there should have been three copies. I'll take care of it.

Here are some other suggested phrases for situations of this kind:

I think I know what may have caused that. Let me look into it.

. . . .

Yes, someone should have checked that order more carefully. Do you want me to call Shipping?

. . . .

I didn't set up that job, but I can straighten it out for you with Al.

. . . .

This type of reply is far better (and more considerate) than saying, "See Al; he did that, not me," or, "I never handle those orders," or, "I don't know anything about it."

Show a willingness to cooperate. Try to show your supervisor, by your attitude and your actions, that you are willing to do what he asks, as well as you can, without grumbling. By this simple courtesy you make his job easier, and you help create a working atmosphere of mutual cooperation.

Naturally, this is more than just a matter of courtesy; if you want to be successful in any business you must be willing to work hard and learn. But the fact remains that your supervisor will appreciate the cooperative spirit that tells him, "You can count on me to help."

How to handle conflicting orders. Suppose a man who outranks your supervisor gives you an order that conflicts with instructions your supervisor has given you. What should you do? Clearly, this is a situation that requires tact. Here are four pointers that will help you avoid embarrassment and trouble.

1. Don't argue, or create an argument between your superiors. If a man who outranks your supervisor asks you to do something, and you answer tactlessly, you can cause friction between the two men. Replies such as, "I can't do that; Mr. Gray told me to do it this way," or, "You'd better see Mr. Gray on that; I work for him," are apt to antagonize an executive.

2. If immediate action isn't necessary, you can acknowledge the order, and then consult with your supervisor at the first opportunity. If your supervisor doesn't want you to carry out the order, it is up to him to take up the matter with the other executive.

3. If the matter is an urgent one and your supervisor is not available for consultation, you must accept the higher-ranking executive's

authority. The safest policy is to indicate that you will do as you are asked, but to make it known in a tactful way that you will be violating your supervisor's instructions. If you can, try to explain *why* your supervisor gave you different instructions; the other man may then decide that your original instructions are more sensible, and withdraw his own orders. If he still insists that his orders be carried out, you have no choice but to obey.

Here is how such a situation might be handled:

> "That won't be any trouble, Mr. Brown. The only problem is that Mr. Gray gave orders not to quote any delivery dates until we had definite word from the factory about the strike."
>
> . . . .
>
> "I can do that for you, Mr. Brown, but I'd better mention that Mr. Gray told me not to do any work on that account until the Credit Department OK's it."

4. Regardless of what you do at the moment, be sure to tell your supervisor about the incident at the earliest possible opportunity. It is important that he know about it promptly, so that if further action is needed he can take it. If you should fail to inform him of what happened, he could be put in an embarrassing position. This is true of anything that happens in your office, but it is especially true when the situation is a potentially problematical one like conflict of orders.

Asking for time off. It is inconsiderate to take time off from your job except for reasons of sickness or family emergency. Those with whom you work count on you to be there regularly, and to do your share of the work. This is especially true of your supervisor, naturally. If you must take time off, however, there are at least two ways in which you can show your consideration for your supervisor. You can:

- inform him as promptly as possible of the fact that you will need time off (obviously, this is not possible with sudden illness)
- organize your work so that he will be inconvenienced as little as possible by your absence.

Asking for a raise. If you feel that you are not being paid enough for the work you do, you have the right to make your opinion known to your supervisor, and to ask for an increase in pay. Whether you win your case should depend mainly on whether you deserve an increase, and not on how you ask for it. Nevertheless, you can hurt your chances if you are rude or demanding in presenting your request.

Here are some approaches you should avoid; they miss the main point, and are offensive to many supervisors.

• *"I need the money."* A company can't pay according to need; it must pay according to merit and the employee's value to the company. Telling your supervisor about your personal financial problems may only embarrass him, and it doesn't give him a reason for paying you more.

• *"I've been here a long time."* Unless you have continued to improve on the job, and to learn, it won't help your case to point out how long you've been there.

• *"I should be making more than Frank; I've been here longer."* Don't use this comparative salary argument unless you can add ". . . *and I am doing a better job."* It won't help you, and it might hurt Frank; the statement implies that Frank is less than discreet about discussing his salary.

• *"If you want me to stay, pay me more."* The threat is only asking for trouble. It will antagonize the supervisor, and it will put you in an awkward position if your demand is turned down.

The best way to get a raise is to present solid evidence that you deserve it. Show specific accomplishments since your last increase; point out new or additional responsibilities you have been handling; show how you have saved the company money, or have improved a method with your ideas, or have increased the production of your staff or department; prove that you have been putting in extra time and effort. These are the positive reasons for an increase that carry weight with a supervisor.

Above all, don't have a chip on your shoulder when you see your supervisor about a raise. Be positive, but not belligerent or argumentative.

When you are leaving the company. Whatever the reason why you are leaving a company, beware the temptation to say, "I'm a free agent and can speak my piece about my supervisor and the company." Business etiquette, like social etiquette, is not something you practice only when you have to, or want to. Even if you are leaving because you are dissatisfied with your supervisor or with company policies, avoid a display of bad business manners when the time comes to leave.

· *How not to behave.* Suppose you have given your employer two weeks' notice (it is inconsiderate not to do so). Remember that you will still be a paid employee during that period. It would be unfair of you to do little or no work, openly criticize your supervisor or ridicule the company, or otherwise demoralize other employees. Your supervisor should be able to expect that you will perform your assignments as usual until you leave.

· *If you should be fired.* If you are fired, make a special effort to keep your temper. It will only make things worse if you fly off the handle and start an argument. Instead, concentrate on finding out why you were found wanting; there might be an important lesson in it for your future.

•5• Etiquette for the Supervisor

The authority to tell others what to do does not free you from the responsibility of treating your subordinates with courtesy and respect. On the contrary, as a leader you have the special responsibility of setting the right example. Courtesy toward subordinates is not just a moral obligation, however; your effectiveness as a supervisor will suffer if you neglect it.

Below you will find many of the common and less common situations where your ability to show consideration for your subordinates will be tested. In every case, you will gain rather than lose when you practice etiquette in your relations with people who work for you.

A request is better than a command. Barking orders is one way of getting people to work, but not the best. If you ask instead of command, your employees will respond to this sign of respect by working harder for you. By showing that what you want is willing cooperation, not subservience, you help your subordinates feel they are part of a team.

This does not mean, of course, that you should plead with your people to work. Your instructions must always be clear and definite, and there must be no question that you expect them to be carried out. You can accomplish this quite effectively without being dictatorial.

Courtesy demands that you set a good example. A supervisor should not place himself above the rules that he expects his subordinates to follow. If you discipline a subordinate for a rules infraction that you often commit yourself, he will resent it, and with good reason. You have privileges as a supervisor, but a supervisor who acts like a privileged character is showing his bad manners.

Show trust in your employees. If you take the attitude that your subordinates have to be closely watched or they'll take advantage of you, they will reciprocate by not trusting you, either. A much more pleasant and productive atmosphere will exist if you trust the people who work for you, and show them that you do. If they know that you have confidence in their readiness to do their best, even when you aren't looking over their shoulder, they will respond by *doing* their best.

When someone does take advantage of your trust, which sometimes happens, then you must discipline him. That shouldn't prevent you from showing every subordinate the courtesy of trusting him until he gives you reason not to.

Show your loyalty to them. How do you react when someone, especially a superior, questions you about a matter that seems to reflect poorly on the work or conduct of a subordinate? If your reaction shows that you are sure the employee was at fault and that you intend to discipline him for it, you are not being loyal to your subordinates. At the very least, you should suspend judgment in such a situation until the subordinate has a chance to tell you his side of the story. Rather than show your superior what a dynamic supervisor you are by promising drastic punishment to the guilty party, you should be prepared to show your loyalty by defending the people who work for you. You might simply say that you will look into the matter, and then take it up with the employee later when you can discuss it in private.

This is not to suggest that you should take the position that you or your subordinates can do no wrong; you should be big enough to accept blame when it is due. The point is that you should assume your subordinates are innocent until they are proven guilty.

Probably the most inexcusable discourtesy in this respect is to openly criticize a subordinate for something that you, as his supervisor, knew about and could have prevented. Using a subordinate as a "scapegoat" is both bad manners and irresponsible supervision.

Don't be careless with confidential information. Any person in a management or supervisory position will have access to information that, for good reasons, should not be made known to everyone. One courtesy your subordinates will expect from you is that you treat communications between you and them as confidential. Here are pointers on how and when you must watch what you say, and to whom you say it.

• *Don't discuss one subordinate with another.* You should never discuss with one subordinate the work performance or the personality of another, except where their working relationship makes it necessary. It is a discourtesy to the employee being discussed, and what you say might give the other employee an unfair advantage if they are in a competitive position for a promotion. It is also only natural that the employee to whom you reveal your opinions about his co-worker will wonder if you talk about *him* that way.

· *Never violate a confidence.* Whatever personal information you learn about an employee, through either his job application forms or your personal contacts with him, should not be revealed to others. If someone's salary has been garnisheed by a creditor, for example, you could cause him great embarrassment if you were to reveal this to anyone. Your subordinates should be able to feel that they can confide in you, if necessary, without fear that you will make public knowledge of what they say.

· *Keep company secrets, too.* There are supervisors who like to impress their subordinates by telling them about company secrets (and rumors) they have heard from higher management. This is a dangerous practice, and it violates a supervisor's responsibility to his company. You owe it to your company, as well as to your subordinates, to refrain from saying what shouldn't be said, and to protect confidential information.

Give your subordinates the information they need. It is bad manners to be careless with confidential information, but it is even more inconsiderate to deprive your subordinates of information they are entitled to have. The following paragraphs give specific examples of types of information your subordinates want and should have.

· *An employee wants his job clearly defined.* Make sure that each subordinate knows exactly what he is supposed to be doing. Give him all the information you can about how, when, where, and with whom he should work. Try to go beyond bare facts and give him enough background information to help him make decisions on his own when a problem arises. And be sure that he understands what the limits of his responsibilities and his authority are.

· *An employee wants to know how he's doing.* When a subordinate does something well, let him know that you notice it and appreciate it. Try to make clear just why the performance was a good one. When he does something incorrectly or poorly, you are being unfair to him unless you tell him that his performance was unsatisfactory; he can't learn from his mistakes unless they are pointed out to him. When you criticize, be specific and be constructive. And do it in private! (See below for more advice on how to give criticism.)

• *An employee wants to know what his job future is.* Your subordinates want to know what lies ahead, both for themselves as individuals and for the department and the company. Let them know what your goals are and how you plan to reach them. They should be able to see how they are contributing, and how they stand to gain if they do their job well.

Get their side of the story. Every employee likes to feel that he can talk to his supervisor when he has a problem or a question. If you discourage this, you may save yourself some time, but you will also frustrate the people who work for you.

Try to encourage your subordinates to come to you with questions. If you go a step beyond this, and show your interest in their progress by asking them how they are coming along, you will have their appreciation, and you will have better work, too.

An occasional employee will try to take advantage of your willingness to listen. You must make it clear to such a person that your time is limited, and that you can't afford lengthy discussions on matters that aren't connected with his job. This may take diplomacy, but it must be done. It would not be fair to your other subordinates to let your time be monopolized by one or two people.

Don't take a good employee for granted. Many supervisors spend most of their time and effort on problem employees. This is hardly fair to the majority of employees who get to work on time, work hard and effectively with little supervision, and do what is expected of them without complaining.

Show your appreciation of good performance by not taking it for granted. Make a point of spending time with the subordinates who help you the most by their dependable service. A pat on the back is a small courtesy that means a lot to most people.

The art of gentle criticism. The best criticism is the kind that makes the employee feel he has learned something, and makes him want to do better. You get this result only when you know how to temper your criticism with good manners, and a consideration of the other person's feelings. Here is how you can find fault with a subordinate firmly yet gently.

• *Be positive.* When you are reviewing someone's work, mention the good points first, complimenting him if possible. This will strengthen him for the negative points you are going to make.

· *Be specific.* When the time comes to point out a mistake to someone, don't be vague or ambiguous. Tell him exactly what he did or is doing wrong, and tell him exactly what he must do about it. You have gained nothing if he is left with a question in his mind as to what you didn't like, or how he is supposed to correct it.

· *Be helpful.* Instead of harping on the mistake, try to concentrate on what is to be learned from it, and on how to prevent similar mistakes in the future.

· *Be receptive.* Naturally, you can't afford to accept alibis from your subordinates; you have to get at the root of mistakes and find out exactly why they were made. But you will often find that a subordinate's explanation of how a mistake came about will suggest how a procedure could be simplified or improved. Knowing that you are willing to hear his side also makes it easier for him to accept your criticism in a positive spirit.

· *Control your anger.* It is dangerous to criticize when you are angry. You are likely to say things that will only make matters worse; you will dwell on the mistake and forget that there is something to be learned; you will create a reaction of anger and resentment in the employee, instead of a desire to improve. When criticism becomes personal, it tends to create more problems than it solves.

With this in mind, wait until you are calmed down before you discuss a mistake with a subordinate. Also, avoid the use of antagonistic or belittling words—"thoughtless," "stupid," "dumb," etc.—when you speak to him.

· *Do your criticizing in private.* Don't embarrass a subordinate by taking him to task in an obvious way in front of other employees. This is especially true if he is also a supervisor, and the other employees are his subordinates.

Use a private office or a conference room, where you can both feel free to speak. If a private room isn't available, and you must discuss it in his work area or another place where other employees are nearby, keep your voice low in volume and calm in tone. For a minor matter, of course, going into a private room would be unnecessary.

Learn to handle a personality clash. Every supervisor, no matter how capable, is apt to find that he must deal with problems that stem from a basic clash of temperament between two employees who work together. Personality clashes that you may have to handle are either those between you and a subordinate, or those between two subordinates. In either case, your business manners will be put to the test.

Handling a clash between you and a subordinate. If you seem to strike sparks with someone who works for you, here are some tips that can help you deal with the situation.

1. *Maintain a dignity that befits your supervisory level.* This means that no matter how angry you feel, you should not meet a subordinate's bad manners with equally bad manners. Refrain from shouting or other displays of temper or lack of self-control. If necessary, dismiss the subordinate until you have had a chance to calm down and analyze the problem.

2. *Find out what the real problem is.* The immediate unpleasantness may be only a symptom of what is wrong, not the problem itself. Here are some questions you might ask yourself, as a means of getting at the cause of the trouble between you:

   a. Does the subordinate get along with his fellow workers? Are you the only one who finds him difficult?
   b. Is it his work you object to, or is it strictly a personality problem?
   c. Could the tension between you be caused by differences in your educational or social backgrounds, rather than by your working relationship?
   d. Have you allowed your feelings toward him to influence what kind of assignments you give him, or to make you more critical of him than of others? (Have you been picking on him, in other words?)
   e. Is it possible that a misunderstanding is the root of the problem, and that a calm discussion might help clear it up?

3. *Make a sincere effort to overcome your differences.* Once you decide what the basic problem is, take steps to solve it. This is actually a two-step process; first you must resolve the immediate conflict, then try to eliminate the basic cause of tension between you and your subordinate. If you approach this second step with an open mind, and show him that you are willing to go as far as you can toward improving your relationship, he is apt to respond in the same way.

Handling a clash between two subordinates. A feud between two co-workers can disrupt an entire office and have a serious effect on efficiency and morale. It is important that you take prompt action to settle a clash between subordinates. Here is a practical approach.

1. If there is an incident, such as an open argument, handle that first. Use your authority to restore order and get people back to work.

2. Hear the arguers out. Give each subordinate a hearing and let him present his view of the disagreement. Encourage him to try to explain why his disagreement with the other employee came about, as well as give you his side of the specific argument.

3. Consider the two points of view and form an opinion as to whether one or the other is in the right, and decide what to do about it. If the blame is mutual, you might want to speak to them together and explain that you want no more disrupting disagreements. If one person seems chiefly responsible, it is usually best to deal with him alone. In a few cases you may be forced to change job assignments or keep the employees apart in some way; you may even be forced to discharge someone who is unable to work with others and creates a serious morale problem.

When you must fire an employee. It is unpleasant to have to fire an employee. It is also costly, in several respects. Whatever training the employee received is wasted. To find and train a substitute will take time and money. You also pay a price in the inconvenience of being short-handed, even for a short time. And the dismissal may have a demoralizing effect on the other employees. Nevertheless, if it becomes necessary to fire someone, you must do it.

Here are suggestions for handling a dismissal with a minimum of unpleasantness and cost.

• *Give the employee warning.* A sudden dismissal without some previous warning of trouble is rare. If you have done nothing about an employee's earlier infractions or poor work, and then suddenly decide that he has to be let go, you are being inconsiderate. Every employee deserves the benefit of initial warnings about unsatisfactory work or behavior; ample chance for corrections and improvements; even a chance for a transfer to another department where he might do better. He should also have your encouragement and advice when he first experiences trouble.

When other employees know that this is your practice, they also know that someone who seems to have been fired without warning actually had abundant notice, and every chance to improve. This is important, because employees are fearful and resentful when it appears that firings are handled inconsiderately and seem to come without warning.

· *Have good cause when you fire someone.* The power to dismiss an employee is not to be used capriciously. You must have a substantial reason before you can fire someone in good conscience. Again, the morale of your subordinates will suffer seriously if they feel that you will make up a flimsy excuse to fire someone you don't like. (If your subordinates are unionized, of course, the causes for which an employee can be discharged are probably spelled out in a contract.)

· *Don't humiliate an employee whom you are firing.* If it becomes necessary to dismiss someone, let him know about your decision in private conference. Climaxing a public disagreement in front of other employees by yelling, "You're fired!" is inexcusable melodrama that disgraces the employee before his fellow workers. In the privacy of your office or a conference room, tell him not only that he is being dismissed, but also why. Even in private, you should not get angry with him; make it clear that you take this action with regret and only after trying to prevent it. If his reaction is an angry one, avoid answering him the same way and creating an ugly scene.

· *Give him any last-minute help you can.* The reasons for an employee's dismissal may be such that you can still recommend him to another employer. Certainly you can see that he gets any severance pay or other company benefits due him. Your company may permit you to allow an employee who is on notice for dismissal to take time off to seek a new job. The employee who is leaving will appreciate any help you are able to give him—and your consideration won't go unnoticed by his fellow workers, either.

Good manners in dealing with your secretary. If you have a personal secretary, you probably spend a substantial portion of your working day with her. You probably know each other well, and know how to work well together. No matter how close your working relationship with your secretary is, be sure that you remember to treat her with courtesy.

Here are some important courtesies that secretaries appreciate from their bosses, as revealed in a survey of over two hundred executive secretaries in different parts of the country.

· *Remember to say "please" and "thank you."* It's never good manners to assume that because you have such a close working affiliation, you need not bother to use "please" and "thank you" in the daily course of your activities. "Please take care of this, Miss Kane," rather that a curt "take care of this," goes a long way toward making the work day more pleasant. Similarly, "thank you" to your secretary, spoken warmly and often, makes her work load seem lighter and her job more rewarding.

· *Don't blame your secretary when things go wrong.* When your secretary makes a mistake, point it out with a view toward preventing similar errors in the future, rather than waste time "placing blame." Remember that when you let your secretary save face (she does this for *you,* constantly, in many diplomatic ways) by getting down to the business of making corrections instead of "rubbing it in," you save time, energy, and avoid needless irritation.

· *Be open to suggestions.* The employer who treats his secretary like a machine will get, inevitably, machine-like reactions from her. Let her know that you respect her intelligence and value her opinion. An occasional, "We'll try it your way this time, Miss Ames," does wonders for her feeling of usefulness.

· *Don't "push" your secretary to work faster.* It isn't usually necessary to push a reliable secretary to work harder and faster; once she understands what has to be done, and when, she likes to establish her own pace. She's willing to accept the responsibility for getting it done promptly.

· *Don't discuss your secretary with others.* This is a courtesy that every secretary appreciates. In the course of the boss-secretary relationship the employer sometimes learns facts about the personal life of his private secretary. Just as an employer expects his secretary to keep *his* private affairs confidential, the secretary appreciates an employer who keeps what he has learned of her personal affairs confidential. Also, the thoughtful employer does not make personal comments about his secretary's appearance or her work, in the presence of others.

· *Be considerate in small things.* Often, it's the small irritations that are hardest to bear. When you *know* your secretary will probably have to stay overtime, do you wait until the last minute to tell her about it? Or do you give her the courtesy of letting her know as much in advance as you possibly can? When dictation or other work runs into lunch time, do you ask her if she has made a luncheon appointment? Even if she has not, she will appreciate your courtesy in having asked her, anyway.

• *Don't try to reform your secretary.* It's bad manners to carp on small habits and little things your secretary may do that are not quite to your liking. If her assets far outweigh her little liabilities, keep in mind that most likely she is putting up with you as she finds you, too. You would probably be surprised at the number of things in *your* personality that your secretary would like to change, if she could.

• *Respect her privacy.* Your secretary senses when to walk out so that you may talk on the phone in private or when to walk out quickly after introductions are made. She will appreciate it when you allow her a bit of privacy, too, when she has an important phone call, for example.

• *Maintain a sense of humor.* A kind word, a bit of fun, a little relaxation at the right moment can do wonders for both you and your secretary when the going gets rough. It takes little effort on your part, and it pays off.

Good manners toward junior executives. If you are a high-ranking executive with junior executives under your wing, your attitude towards them can make a significant difference in how successfully they develop. If you treat them with apparent discourtesy, you discourage them from doing their best. More harmful, probably, is the fact that you also weaken their image of authority in the eyes of their subordinates.

Here are specific ways in which you can demonstrate your consideration for your junior executives, and in doing so show that you are solidly behind them.

• *Give each man the prestige and status he has earned.* If a man has earned the right to certain privileges and status symbols, he expects to get them. It is a mistake to think that these things are unimportant; they matter to the executive, and their presence or absence is noted by his subordinates. Whether it is a larger office, or a listing in company directories, or a reserved spot to park his car, or just a name plate, see that a man gets it if his position deserves it. It is a small courtesy you can't afford to neglect.

Show by your actions, too, that you accord his position the respect it deserves. It is disrespectful to by-pass a junior executive and deal directly with his subordinates. It is disrespectful to fail to include him in meetings, or to leave his name off routing slips when information is being circulated to management people, or to otherwise suggest that he isn't very important to you.

• *Give him the authority he needs.* When a man is given a responsible job to do, he should also get the authority he needs to get the job done. If your junior executives have to come to you frequently for approval of plans, or if you frequently override the decisions they make, you are undermining their authority.

You should give every subordinate executive the degree of authority that his responsibilities require, and encourage him to use it. He will appreciate your confidence in him—and he will need it, if he is to become an effective executive.

• *Let him know he can count on your support.* One of the surest ways to smother initiative in a junior executive is to encourage him to make decisions, then blame or ridicule him when he makes a mistake. This is especially rude when it is done in front of his subordinates.

The only considerate policy is to stand behind your subordinate supervisors. Show them that you will back them up, both in their dealings with their subordinates and in your dealings with higher management. Do your fault-finding with them in private, and make your criticism constructive (see page 46 for advice on how to give criticism). They should feel that you will take their side until they are proven wrong, and that even then you will not humiliate or belittle them.

• *Don't get too friendly with your junior executives.* Familiarity may not always breed contempt, but there are other problems it can cause. It is difficult to take an objective view of the performance of someone who has become a close friend. It is even more difficult to criticize him, even though you may recognize that he needs it. And you are almost certain to create a morale problem when you show favoritism.

The rule about not getting chummy with subordinates applies to employees at any level below you, not just to junior executives. However, there is a special danger that a close friendship may develop between executives, even though they may be of different rank. There is not the same natural barrier between them that there is between an executive and a lower-level employee.

·6· When Men and Women Work Together

Women are employed in a great majority of business offices today. Their presence there sometimes brings up questions about etiquette between the sexes in a business atmosphere.

Do working women deserve special treatment? Ordinarily, women are extended special courtesies by men. But should they expect the same courtesies from men with whom they work as equals in a business office?

A survey of businessmen on this question showed that men do treat women in their office with special consideration, much as they would in a purely social situation, but with limitations. In straight business dealings they seldom make distinctions of sex. For example, a man might open a door for a woman in entering a conference room, but will not give her ideas any special consideration at the conference table. A man may pick up something that a female co-worker has dropped, or light a cigarette for her at the lunch table, but he will expect her to carry her own load when they are working together on a report.

When differences in rank are involved. A businessman can't afford to be deferential toward a woman when he is dealing with her as her supervisor on matters of business. If he is giving her an assignment, or discussing a problem on her job, or getting her opinion about a business decision—or criticizing her—he is acting in his role of authority, and chivalry would be out of place. He may treat her at such times much as though she were a man, and she should expect him to.

A woman who gets upset when she is even mildly criticized by her supervisor is a problem. She should try to realize that it is only through constructive criticism that she will improve and do her best work. If she cannot accept criticism, which is almost always meant as help, she is limiting her value as an employee. And she is being inconsiderate toward her supervisor, who may be forced to give her extra time that the other employees don't require.

When it is the woman who outranks the man, she will consider their working relationship as primary, and the difference in their sex as incidental. She will expect him to regard the situation in the same way; any deference should be to her position, not her sex. Certainly a man should not make the assumption that he will not like working for a supervisor simply because she is a woman. This is an injustice to her, and it places a barrier in the way of an effective working relationship. All a woman asks from men whom she will supervise is an open mind.

Sex appeal is not for the office. Seductive behavior or dress is generally out of place in a business office. But it is especially unwise for a woman to insinuate sex appeal into her dealings with men either above or below her on the company ladder. A male supervisor will resent it as an attempt to influence his judgment; a man working under her is likely to resent it because it puts him in an awkward position.

When a woman works as a man's secretary. A man's secretary plays an important role in his business life. She probably spends a good deal of time with him, and devotes most of her working day to his interests and needs; she gets to know him quite well, just as he gets to know her well.

In this rather special role, a secretary will find that certain points of business etiquette have special importance to her, and that certain attributes of behavior will be essential:

- She should be discreet and loyal. She should not give out information about either business or personal matters pertaining to her executive. She should not be critical of him to her friends in the office. She should act in his best interests when he is not there.
- She should have both the courage and the tact to question things that look wrong, instead of following instructions blindly. Most executives appreciate it when their secretary is alert and catches a potential mistake or sees a simpler or better way of accomplishing something. But if she is too blunt about it her questions will sound like criticism.
- She should never be "bossy," no matter how long and well she has served her executive or the company. A secretary who is too

officious and too outspoken can become more of a problem for an executive than a help to him. If she has authority, she should learn how to exercise it without fuss; if she has long experience, she should know how to make it useful without overstepping her position.

• She must not allow herself to become personally involved with her executive. Part of a man's confidence in his secretary is an assurance that she will not become emotionally involved. If he is uncertain about this he will not be able to confide in her as he might like to, and she will not be as useful or as helpful to him as she could be. A secretary-boss romance upsets the office work routine; it puts an emotional strain on the people involved; it can place them in an embarrassing position (the chances of keeping it secret are slim). And if something upsets the romantic relationship, the working one becomes awkward for both of them. (See also *Office romances,* below).

Office romances. Few companies would even try to restrict dating (or other social contacts) between employees. It is accepted that as long as an office romance does not affect standards of work and does not upset office decorum during the working day, there is no breach of office etiquette.

However, when employees conduct a romance on company time, they are guilty of poor manners and of questionable judgment. They are not giving their employer the time and concentration they are paid for. And by publicizing their interest in each other they are running the risk of embarrassment in the event their feelings change. It is best from every point of view not to bring private feelings and friendships into the office.

The husband and wife who work together. Some companies have policies about hiring related persons. For example, a company might not allow a husband and wife to work in the same department; some companies will not even have a husband and wife working at the same time anywhere in the organization. However, husband-and-wife combinations within a company are fairly common, even so.

The husband and wife who do work for the same company must be discreet in their conduct in the office. They should address each other according to the custom of the company. For example, if first names are not generally used, a couple would address each other as "Mr. James" and "Mrs. James." Before the public, particularly, Mr.

James would say: "Mrs. James will help you"—not "Mary will help you."

Of course, in a small community or business where the atmosphere is an informal one and everyone knows everyone else, a husband and wife running a business would seem needlessly stiff and formal if they addressed each other by their last name.

In a doctor's office, if a wife acts as the doctor's assistant she usually calls her husband "Doctor" in front of patients; she does not use his first name. He would address his wife as he would any assistant; for example, "Please prepare the patient for diathermy."

The male supervisor as counselor. If you are a male supervisor you may sometimes find yourself acting as counselor to employees, as well as supervisor. This may be true with men as well as women. However, when women are involved there are certain precautions you would be wise to take:

· Stay away from *personal* counseling, except to the extent that personal problems bear directly on the employee's work. You are asking for trouble if you try to advise employees on their personal life.

· Avoid too sympathetic a response to the employee's problems. This can lead some women to confide in you more than they mean to—which they may resent later.

· Confine any counseling sessions to company property, and to regular business hours.

Safety precautions for women employees. Where women are employed, their personal safety must be provided for, especially when they work after normal hours. This is more than a matter of courtesy; women are more vulnerable to robbery and other incidents, and therefore need special protection.

Here are some precautions (based on recommendations from the New York City Police Department) for safeguarding female employees:

· Don't allow a woman employee to carry large sums of cash to or from the bank or another office. She is a natural target for robbery. If it is necessary for a woman to do this job, discuss it with the local police department and work out a means of protecting her. This should be done whether regular or late working hours are involved.

• Don't let a woman work alone after office hours if the building is unguarded. Even if the building has a watchman or manned elevator, it's better to have someone else working in the same department, close by. If this isn't possible, someone should inform the guard that a woman is working alone, and where she is.

• Don't assign to a woman the responsibility of opening the office in the morning. It is a good idea to have two men, one of them a supervisor if possible, open the office.

Women can help themselves, too. There are things that women can do for their own protection when they work late:

• They can arrange for a friend or relative to call them at set intervals, just as a check. They can also phone home just before they leave the office, so that in case they run into trouble or delay they will be missed.

• They can try to avoid waiting for an elevator in the hall. If there are two of them, perhaps one can ring for the elevator while the other remains at the door of the office. They can then lock up the office and go down together.

• They should not take short cuts through dim or narrow streets, or through parks. They should seek out well-lighted and heavily traveled streets. It's a good idea, too, to avoid walking close to a building and its darkened doorways. Women who know they will be working late should try to park near the office and in a well-lighted spot; if necessary, they should be permitted to move their cars to safe locations before the end of the day.

·7· Making Proper Introductions

Introductions are a common and important event in every business office or plant. This section gives you the rules and tells you how to follow them with a minimum of trouble and a maximum of graciousness.

Some helpful hints about introductions. Knowing a few basic facts about introductions will help you to master the art of introducing people correctly:

1. Many, if not most, introductions involve people of unequal or different status or position. They can differ in rank, in age, or in sex, for example, or in all of these, but the result is the same: an introduction often consists of *presenting one person* of lesser importance or status *to another* of greater importance or status.

2. Generally, you mention or give the name of the more "important" person first. This is only a general rule, but a very helpful one.

3. Business introductions usually involve people who are meeting for a reason, or whose meeting has some business connection. Very often it is helpful, if not essential, to add a few words of explanation to your introductions, so that each person is made aware of his business connection with the other.

It should help you to remember that, in most business situations, it is more important to be cordial in making introductions, and to get names and titles straight, that it is to be absolutely correct in procedure. In other words, a natural and simple introduction that slightly violates the rules is better than a strained or awkward effort to be proper.

Fortunately, the rules are simple and logical enough so that you can manage to be correct and relaxed at the same time. Rules and examples are set forth below.

Who is to be introduced to whom? Here are the rules for deciding which person is to be mentioned first, or otherwise shown deference, in making a business introduction:

1. Introduce a man to a woman. The basic rule is that a man is presented to a woman, even though she may be much younger than he is. Socially, exceptions are made to this rule only in the case of church dignitaries, royalty, and heads of state; a woman would be presented *to* such personages, as a sign of respect. In business, other exceptions are sometimes made when the element of rank or authority is a strong factor. For example, when an executive is meeting his new secretary, his authority over her is so direct and so basic that it is logical to introduce her to him. But it would also be correct to follow the basic rule and present him to her, as man to woman. Another exception commonly made is that a woman who is applying for a non-executive position is often introduced *to* the executive who will interview her for that position. Here again, however, the basic rule can also safely be followed.

For examples of this rule, see "How to introduce a man to a woman," below.

2. Present younger persons to older ones. If other factors are equal, including sex, you would generally present a younger person to his or her senior in age. However, where two women are concerned, it is more tactful not to draw attention to the fact that one is older unless the difference in age is a considerable one. Also, a man is usually presented to a woman even though he may be older than she.

3. Present a person of lower rank to his superior. If two people are of the same sex and not widely separated by age, but one ranks higher in the company than the other, introduce the person of lower rank to his superior. This rule is especially pertinent if there will be a direct supervisor-subordinate relationship between the two people involved.

The basic forms of introduction. Here are acceptable ways of introducing one person to another:

(most formal)	"Mrs. Jones, may I present Mr. Crane?"
(less formal)	"Mrs. Jones, may I introduce Mr. Crane?"
	"Mrs. Jones, this is Mr. Crane."
	"Mrs. Jones, Mr. Crane." ("*this is* Mr. Crane" is implied; pronounce the names as though "this is" were spoken)

(informal) "Ann Jones, I'd like you to meet (or "this is") Bill Crane, from the Credit Department. Ann is my assistant, Bill."

Note that the first two examples often are pronounced as statements, not as questions. Note, too, that the second person in each example is being presented or introduced to the first. If you wish to make no distinction, use one of the simplest forms ("this is," or just the pronouncing of names).

If it should happen that you mention first the name of the person of lesser importance, there is no need to become flustered—simply alter the wording of the introduction: "Mr. Crane, I would like *to introduce you to* Mrs. Jones." You could also say, "This is Mr. Crane, Mrs. Jones," or even, "Mr. Crane, Mrs. Jones," using the same inflection in both cases.

If you have reason to believe that two men (or two women) might already have met, you may use this introduction:

"Frank Becker, have you met Ned Brown, from ABC Company?"

However, it is considered improper to ask a woman whether she has met a man; you would not say, "Miss X, have you met Mr. Y?"

Introductions by first name only are not acceptable and should never be made. Even if you have to ask someone what his last name is because you can't recall it, do so before you introduce him.

It is considered poor form to use these phrases of introduction:

"meet" (used alone, as, "Mr. A, meet Mr. B.")
"meet up with"
"shake hands with"
"I would like to make you acquainted with"

How to introduce men to each other. If you are introducing men who are about equal in rank and age, it is not important who is presented to whom, or whose name is mentioned first. Here are typical introductions:

Mr. Green, this is Mr. Purcell, who just joined our Trust Department. Mr. Green is with the Methods Department, Mr. Purcell.

Jack Winter, this is Paul Sommers. You will be working together on the Bryant account.

Ben Webster, have you met Frank Adams, our new trade editor? Ben will be handling production on many of your books, Frank.

If one man is senior in rank and especially if he is to be the other man's direct supervisor, present the other man to him. For example:

> Mr. Head, I would like you to meet Bob Newman, my assistant. Mr. Head is Manager of our Western Division, Bob.
>
> Mr. Strong, may I introduce John Bacon, who is joining Personnel Monday. John, this is our President, Mr. Strong.

When the only difference is one of age, introduce the younger man to the older, as mentioned above.

How to introduce women to each other. The rules here are the same as for introducing men, except that, as already mentioned, calling attention to a difference in age could possibly offend the older woman.

How to introduce a man to a woman. Usually, a man is presented to a woman (see page 62). This can be done as follows:

> Miss Larson, may I present Mr. Finch?
> (may I introduce)
> (I would like you to meet)
> (this is [spoken or implied])
> Betty Larson, this is Ken Finch, our new copywriter.

Group introductions involving men and women. In introducing three or more men and women, you try to follow the basic rule that men are presented to women. Here are illustrations that will show you how this is done in particular situations.

• *A man is being introduced to women.* Since a man is presented to women, you could say:

> Mrs. Bryan, Miss Ansel, this is Mr. Green. (You would mention first the name of the woman who is senior in age or rank, unless there is only a minor difference)

• *Men meeting a woman or women.* Again, the men are presented to the woman or women:

> Mrs. Bryan, this is Mr. Green . . . and Mr. Pinero.
>
> Miss Jones, Miss Tallman, this is Mr. Pinero . . . and Mr. Green.

• *A man meeting a man and woman.* Here you would present the man to the woman first, then introduce him to the other man:

> Mrs. Klein, this is Mr. Abbott. Mr. Abbott, Mr. Morse.

If it is two men meeting a man and woman, present the two men to the woman first, then introduce them to the other man.

Mrs. Klein, this is Mr. Abbot . . . and Mr. Ryan.
Mr. Morse (this is) Mr. Abbott . . . and Mr. Ryan.

• *A woman meeting a man and woman.* Introduce the women to each other first, then present man to woman. The simplest way is this:

Miss Collins, this is Miss Allen . . . and Mr. Neff.

However, if Miss Allen were Miss Collins' senior in age (or rank), you might do it this way:

Miss Allen, this is Miss Collins. Miss Collins, Mr. Neff.

Introductions to a large group. If you have to introduce someone to a fairly large group, handle it in the simplest and most natural way you can. If the person you are introducing will have a close connection with the people in the group, you should normally go through a complete introduction (see below). In other circumstances, especially at a large but informal gathering, you might introduce the person only to a few people nearest him, and let further introductions develop naturally from there. Or it might be advisable to simply present the person, by name, to the group, with the explanation that they will all have a chance to meet later. This last method would not be polite unless there were a reason why making introductions would be impractical at the moment.

In introducing someone to a group, avoid running through all the names without a break. It is better to introduce two or three people at a time, so that names can register and acknowledgments can be made. It is not necessary in a large group situation to single out all the women in the group and introduce them before you introduce any of the men; it is acceptable to take people in order.

Introducing a woman executive at a board meeting. If a woman executive is joining a board of directors or other executive group for the first time, the chairman will mention her name, and, although this is in effect an introduction, no one is required to stand. If a woman is brought to a meeting by an executive from her own firm, he can introduce her in this same way. Only the man nearest to the chair she takes will rise to seat her. If she is introduced to any of the men, it should only be to those in her immediate vicinity, who will rise to acknowledge the introduction.

Introducing members of your family to business associates. A man might introduce his wife by saying to a business associate or a fellow employee, "John, I'd like to introduce you to my wife. Jane, this is John Downing." Or he might say, "Mr. Downing, may I introduce you to my wife? Mr. Downing." This is somewhat more formal.

A woman might introduce her husband by saying, "Mr. Gray, this is my husband," or, "Miss Miller, my husband." To someone with whom she is on a first name basis she could introduce her husband in this way: "John, this is my husband, Paul. John Enright."

You would introduce a young son or daughter this way: "Mr. Gray, my son Ronald," or, "Mr. Gray, this is my daughter Grace." This form is used even when the "child" is a grown woman.

If you are introducing a sister or daughter who is married and has a different last name, you would say, "Joan, this is Mr. Gray. My sister, Mrs. Brockman." Or, if first names are to be used, you would say, "Mary, this is my sister, Joan Brockman. Mary Taylor."

How to introduce yourself. There are numerous occasions in business when you will have to introduce yourself. For example, should you come out of your office to meet someone who has been announced or who is waiting to see you, you might say, "Mr. Becker? I'm Mr. Pierce. Please come in." Or you could first ask him cordially to come into your office, then introduce yourself when he has done so.

If you are a secretary, and someone approaches your desk, you could say, "I'm Miss Cole, Mr. Pierce's secretary. May I help you?" If the visitor is someone who is expected, you might say, "Mr. Becker, I'm Miss Cole, Mr. Pierce's secretary. Mr. Pierce will be with you in a moment." You would then introduce the men when your executive was free: "Mr. Pierce, this is Mr. Becker, from the ABC Contracting Company."

If you should run into someone, perhaps at a dinner or meeting, whom you have met previously in a business situation, you should not ask him or her, "Don't you remember me?" Instead, say, "Hello, Mr. Becker, I'm Pierce (or Mr. Pierce) of the Millennium Company. You paid me a visit not long ago." Or, "Hello, Mr. Becker, I'm Miss Cole, Mr. Pierce's secretary."

Note that men frequently introduce themselves to other men in business by using only their last name, with no title (Pierce, instead of Mr. Pierce). But to a woman in business a man would always use his title, even on the phone: "Miss Cole, this is Mr. Becker, of the ABC Contracting Company."

In referring to yourself, the use of title (Mr., Mrs. or Miss) is correct only in business situations. Socially you would use your full name (Carol Cole or George Pierce); this would be true even though you may have originally been introduced to the other person in a business situation.

How to acknowledge an introduction. When you are being introduced to someone, give him the courtesy of your full attention. When the introduction is completed, you should acknowledge it verbally, and perhaps also by shaking hands, or bowing, or both, as explained below.

It is always correct, and is sufficient, to simply say, "How do you do, Mr. Fuller." It is proper to add something like, "It's very nice to meet you; we've corresponded so often," or "I'm so glad to meet you. John has been telling me about that new invention of yours." But such statements should be spontaneous and genuine. Don't use such stilted or stereotyped phrases as "I'm glad to make your acquaintance" or "Pleased to meet you." When in doubt, just say, "How do you do."

Another form of acknowledgment, used chiefly when meeting a group of people, is the repeating of the name of a person to whom you have just been introduced. You pronounce the name much as you would if it were preceded by "How do you do." This type of acknowledgment allows you some variety when you are meeting several people. Thus you might say: "How do you do, Miss Fairbanks" . . . "Mr. Green" . . . "How do you do" . . . "Mr. Stern" . . . "How do you do, Mr. Brown" . . . and so on.

Standing for introductions. A man stands to be introduced to a woman or a man. A woman is expected to stand for introductions to men or women considerably older than herself, or when meeting important state officials, clergymen, and their wives. However, she may stand for any introduction if she feels prompted to do so. It is generally accepted that an executive who is interviewing a woman or man about a position below the executive level would not have to stand to greet the applicant (although he could). However, he should not keep the applicant standing, especially if she is a woman.

Shaking hands and bowing. A man always shakes hands with another man to whom he is introduced. A very young man meeting a much older man might wait for the older man to extend his hand first, as a sign of deference. Women in business may or may not shake hands with each other; if one offers her hand, the other should respond in kind without hesitation.

In social circumstances a man is not expected to offer his hand to a woman unless she first offers hers, but in business it is not unusual for a man to offer his hand to a businesswoman he is meeting. Naturally, she would return the handshake in such a situation. If the man does not initiate the handshake, she may offer her hand or not, as she wishes. If she does, then he should respond without hesitation.

In acknowledging social introductions it is common to bow to the other person. (In this day and age, and particularly in the United States, the bow is a token one, a very slight and not-too-rigid inclination forward of the head and trunk for a man, of the head for a woman.) In business introductions the bow is much less frequently used, but is proper, nevertheless, for either sex.

A letter of introduction. Socially a letter of introduction can never be requested, but in business it is quite correct to ask banks, individuals and business firms for letters of introduction to their branch offices here or abroad. Many businessmen volunteer to give introductory letters to business friends who are going on a business trip.

A letter of introduction should give the full name of the person being introduced, together with reasons why he and the person to whom the letter is addressed should meet.

The reason for the two men to meet may be only that the writer of the letter knows they went to the same college or are members of the same club or share the same enthusiasm for some sport or hobby. Or it may be that one man can be of help to the other in business.

Whatever the reason, the writer gives the letter—unsealed—to the person he is introducing. The man receiving it may read it and may seal it then or leave it unsealed. When he delivers it, he should send it in with his card to the man to whom it is addressed, and sit and wait until it has been read.

When the letter is both a social and business letter it should be informal in tone, like the sample given on the opposite page:

Dear Walter:

My good friend Alfred Miller plans to be in Detroit next week and will present this letter to you.

Alfred was recently appointed to our State Board of Mediation and Arbitration, and is making a study of employee relations in large companies in highly industrialized areas. I have suggested that he speak to you while in Detroit because of your interest in industrial relations and the remarkable innovations in this field that you have introduced within your own company.

I know you will like Alfred. You may remember seeing him at Jane's wedding reception last year. I shall appreciate whatever you can do to help him, and I know he will be sincerely grateful for your assistance.

Jim tells me you are planning to be in New York next month. Can we meet for lunch one day? Cathy will want to see you, too, so plan to have dinner with us one evening.

Cordially,
Paul

The following is an example of a more formal, businesslike letter of introduction:

Dear Mr. Weaver:

This letter introduces a good friend of mine, Tom Babcock, publisher of a daily newspaper in our area.

Mr. Babcock is planning to construct a new building and I have told him of the magnificent new plant in which you print your paper. He is interested in inspecting it and will be in Auburn for three days next week.

I feel that your mutual interests will make your meeting worthwhile.

I shall appreciate whatever assistance you can give Mr. Babcock.

Very truly yours,
Walter Scanlan

·8· Office Parties and Gifts

In a company of any size there are times when the employees of a department or division decide a party for one of their group is in order. The usual excuses for these pleasant interludes are when a fellow worker becomes engaged or is married, leaves to have a baby, enters the service, or resigns, retires or is transferred. Luncheon parties are favored, principally because it is easier to get the whole group together then than after work.

Organizing the party. Generally, approval of the department head is sought before plans are made, because the lunch hour will usually run beyond the allotted time. Even though his approval is taken for granted, the courtesy of requesting permission must not be overlooked. After it is received, a committee should be appointed to work out the arrangements. A small committee of two or three is best for an affair of this kind; larger committees tend to become unwieldy. If need be, the committee can always delegate other members of the staff to perform certain tasks.

Remember that while party planning is rarely frowned upon by executives, employees should not take advantage of this and neglect their jobs while working out the details. Taking a few minutes of your working day to tell someone he's to plan transportation is acceptable, but spending a couple of hours working out the details is not. Your work comes first, and party plans should be made during lunch hours or after work.

Making reservations. To facilitate matters, make a reservation at a nearby restaurant for the number planning to attend. If the restaurant agrees, a great deal of time can be saved by circulating the menu ahead of time, having each individual write down his order, and then telephoning the order to the restaurant. In this way, lunch is ready to be served as soon as the group arrives. Orders for drinks can be handled in the same way, which eliminates the usual delay of ordering them and waiting for the order to be filled.

Whom to invite. Everyone in the guest of honor's department should be invited to attend. It is polite also to invite department heads and other supervisory personnel who may have worked with the employee who is being feted. However, there is nothing compulsory about attending these affairs. No one should be made to feel he has to be present or that a refusal to attend is unfriendly.

Paying the expenses. When ordering is done ahead of time, the committee on arrangements should collect the cost of each lunch, plus enough to cover gratuities to the waiters, the cost of a gift (if there is to be one), and the guest of honor's lunch.

If it is impossible to order lunch in advance and collect for it, then everyone at the luncheon should have an individual check. This prevents haggling over the bill and saves time. Either of the people next to the guest of honor should be delegated to pick up his or her check and pay for it. The cost can be pro-rated afterwards among those attending the luncheon.

Seating the guest of honor at an office party. Place the honored guest at the center or head of the table. If the group is large enough, have the restaurant set up a T-shape table and the crossbar of the T can be the head table. Place cards may be used in seating the others or they may choose their own seats.

How the guest of honor behaves. Gracious acceptance of the thoughtfulness of his co-workers should mark the behavior of the honored guest. It is distressing to see people with so little poise or sense of gratitude that they act bored or as though the whole idea were silly. Just before the party breaks up the guest of honor should stand and briefly but sincerely express his thanks to his co-workers.

Buying presents. Constant requests for money with which to buy gifts can be a nuisance to employees, as well as a budgetary strain. There have been instances where people have thought the number of collections had got so completely out of hand that they refused to contribute to anything. On occasion management sees fit to refuse permission for a gift collection.

To begin with, a gift is not always necessary. The type of luncheon party described above, which everyone underwrites, can be given in place of a gift. A gift isn't called for when an engagement is announced, an employee resigns or a temporary employee (no matter how well liked) finishes her job and leaves.

Collecting for a gift. When gifts are collected for individually and two occasions come up at once, the best thing to do is take up one collection and divide the amount in two.

A revolving gift fund is another method of keeping collections under control. With this system everyone in an office pays a small amount (as little as five cents) either weekly or on pay days. Then when a gift is to be bought, the money for it comes out of this fund.

One thing that should never be done is to purchase a gift and then raise the amount it cost. Collect the money first and then buy what you can afford with the sum collected.

How much to spend for a gift. Length of service affects the size and cost of gifts in most offices. On the average, however, $20-25 is spent for a retirement gift; $10-15 for a wedding gift; $10 for flowers; $5 for a baby present. From $3.50 to $5 is spent for a corsage, a memento frequently given to a girl who has received a promotion.

Presenting the gift. At a luncheon, the gift may be put on the table at the guest of honor's place, or someone can make the presentation during the luncheon, whichever seems better suited to the occasion. If presentation of the gift is made in the office, place it on the recipient's desk before he arrives in the morning or while he is out to lunch, so that it will be a surprise.

The card that goes with the gift. A small plain white card signed "Your fellow employees," "Your friends at the office" or something similar may be enclosed with a gift. Or a commercial card may be purchased and circulated for everyone to sign before being attached to the gift. When flowers are ordered, the florist will sign the card the way you ask him to.

Expressing thanks for a gift from co-workers. The individual receiving the gift is expected to show it around the office. A note of thanks is proper. Although a man's co-workers present their wedding gift to him rather than sending it to the bride-to-be, she is the one who must write the note of thanks. If the gift is from all the employees (as would be the case in a small firm) address a note to the company. When it is given by the staff of a department or division of a large company, address a "thank you" note to the head of the department, who will either circulate it or put it on the bulletin board.

•9• Social Relations Within a Company

Participation in Employee Recreation Programs

Most companies of any size encourage their employees to take part in a planned program of recreation. Such pastimes as bowling or bridge occupy the winter months, with golf and tennis and other outdoor sports being offered in the summer. Taking part in these activities provides not only relaxation but also an opportunity to meet co-workers with similar interests.

Avoid business discussions. One important point to remember is that any problems you may have in your job are not to be discussed during these recreation periods. The purpose of such a program is not to provide a captive audience for the complainer, but to give everyone an opportunity to relax and get to know co-workers in an informal atmosphere. Anyone who imposes his personal business problems on the other members of a team he belongs to is being rude—and he runs the risk of saying too much for his own good on the job.

How to be a good team member. Another point of etiquette to remember if you join a team is to take your responsibilities as a member seriously. Don't join one of the groups and then show up only when you want to or have nothing else you want to do. This shows lack of consideration for others, and inconsiderateness is the basis of bad manners. But care must be taken that seriousness as a team member doesn't lead to neglect of one's office duties. For instance, bowling on the department team is a fine idea, but devoting hours of a work day to planning and organizing each match or to discussing everybody's game is carrying the recreation program beyond its boundaries.

Friendship Among Co-Workers

Friendly relations among the employees of a company—from the highest to the lowest ranks—sustain morale and make each workday pleasant. But most authorities agree that while an amicable relationship with co-workers is ideal, it is wiser not to let office friendships develop into intimate ones.

When a close friendship develops. Over a period of time it is more than likely that you may build up a close friendship with a fellow worker. When someone's companionship is important to you, you will naturally want to see that person outside of working hours. When this occurs, make a conscious effort not to spend time at the office discussing with your friend the things you did the night before and the plans you have for next week. Maintain an impersonal relationship in the office.

If romance blossoms. Should a close friendship become romance, discretion is even more important. A couple in love who work in the same office can easily become the office joke if they don't discipline themselves. After all, the romance may founder, and should that happen, you'll be all the happier that everyone didn't know about it.

Friendship on the executive level. As with lower-echelon employees, it is considered dircreet for executives in the same company to avoid close friendships with each other. It is believed that in certain instances such friendships between executives can adversely affect their business judgments and decisions.

Social Gatherings of Company Personnel

Sociability among co-workers. The temptation to invite a few people from the office to your home can be a strong one. Perhaps a group of you have a good time together during the lunch hour, or possibly one of the girls is so humorous—making everyone in the office laugh—that you think she'd be lots of fun at a party.

When you gather them all together away from the office, however, the result can be deadly—no fun, no laughs, just a dull evening. Also, there's the possibility of discovering that one or two of your fellow workers are less attractive after they've had a drink or two, and incidents can occur that result in strained feelings.

Even if none of these things happen, a small social group within a large office inevitably isolates itself from the rest of the staff. Its members become cliquish, with their own jokes and topics of conversation. The effect on the general office morale is anything but good.

Sociability between senior and junior executives. An invitation to lunch, an occasional drink together after hours, a game of golf once in a while, usually constitute the somewhat impersonal social relations between senior and junior executives. However, a senior executive will from time to time invite a few of the younger or newer men in the firm to his home so he can get to know them better and meet their wives if he hasn't already done so.

Extending strictly social invitations is the prerogative of the senior officer, and under no circumstances should a junior executive be first to do the inviting.

Should a high-ranking executive entertain you and your wife, it is a polite gesture for you to reciprocate but it is not necessary that you do so. When a junior executive does entertain his superiors, he does so as naturally as possible. Whether he plans a formal or informal dinner party doesn't matter. What does matter, though, is that he does not try something his household cannot handle. For instance, when Mr. and Mrs. Junior Executive have no household help, it would be foolish for them to try to entertain in the same formal manner as someone with a chef or a cook and a waitress. A simple meal, well prepared, and served either buffet style or at the dining room table, is in much better taste than a pretentious one that doesn't turn out right because it's too much for one person to handle.

Plan a company dinner you can manage with ease. Do things as nicely as you can. The really important thing is that a host and hostess be gracious and, without appearing anxious, do everything possible to make sure everyone enjoys himself.

Sociability between executives and employees. Employees should be their most pleasant selves when invited to visit executives of the company. But no matter how friendly a party gets, remember next day at the office not to act in an over-familiar way. You might be on strictly formal terms with your superior at the office but the party may have been so gay and chummy that he was calling you by your first name and urging you to call him by his (something you wouldn't normally do). Don't keep it up the next day at work; go back to addressing him as you always have.

If you are a secretary visiting your executive's home, be particularly careful not to adopt an intimate tone when speaking about him to his wife. Equally unacceptable is talking about him as though he were a naughty little boy whose every action at the office has to have your approval.

·10· Business Gifts and Cards

Sending gifts to clients and customers—particularly at Christmas time—is a traditional practice with a large number of business people. Most do it because they enjoy giving presents and look on the custom as a form of public relations.

Occasions when a gift is appropriate. There are numerous occasions when a businessman feels called upon to send a gift. He may want to express his thanks to a secretary at a branch office who did some work for him, or to out-of-town hostesses who entertained him while he was on a business trip. He may want to say "good luck" to a business associate who is ill, or to one who has moved to new quarters, opened a branch office, or is celebrating a business anniversary.

Flowers, plants, candy and books are all pleasant ways of saying "thank you" or "good luck." They are gifts that do not make people feel obligated and that can be accepted without embarrassment.

Christmas gifts. Many companies give gifts at Christmas even if they do so at no other time. A company that does distribute Christmas presents must be sure they are carefully selected and in good taste. Gifts for an individual might include desk and personal accessories. Some companies prefer to send a gift the man's family can enjoy, perhaps fruit-of-the-month or cheese-of-the-month or even flowers-of-the-month. A Christmas floral arrangement or a box of greens, holly, and pine cones for holiday decorations are welcome gifts. One manufacturer gives presents of gay Christmas gift wrappings made by a division of his company. If the personal tastes of the recipients are well enough known to the donor, tickets to future sports, theatrical or musical events can be given. It is best not to give a gift to charity in someone's name unless you are very sure it is an organization in which the individual takes an interest. Gift selection services are used by many companies. A selection service sends a card and a catalog of gifts to a list given them by the company; the recipient picks out the gift he wants and it is sent to him. This is not only a time-saver, but insures that the gift is something the recipient will really enjoy. Of course, it is an impersonal method of gift giving.

Keeping a Christmas list. A list of the gifts given out each year—and to whom—will prevent duplications. A card file or one of the small books designed for this purpose and found in any stationery store will serve as an efficient reminder.

Gift giving at the office. Exchanging gifts with people you know at the office is permissible but is best done away from the office. If you don't see a fellow employee outside the office, then the exchanging of gifts is hardly warranted. There is no obligation to give gifts to fellow workers, except when you are requested to bring a small gift for an office party grab bag.

It is never considered proper for an employee to give a gift to a man or woman who ranks him in a supervisory or managerial capacity. An executive may give his secretary a Christmas gift, but he does not expect her to give him one in return. Of course, if the entire office staff presents him with a gift on some special occasion, the secretary will want to join in with them.

"Thank you" notes for business gifts. It is correct for a wife to acknowledge a gift sent to the home by a business associate of her husband's. Whether or not she knows the giver personally does not matter. The husband in turn mentions the gift with his thanks next time he sees the man who sent it, or he adds a brief note in his own handwriting to the next business letter he sends him.

Letters of thanks are not necessary for presents exchanged with friends in the office. A verbal thank you is sufficient. The one exception is a wedding present, and the thank you note is always written by the bride.

The trend away from gift giving. Mainly because of the few individuals who have turned a generous and friendly gesture into one of self-aggrandizement, there has developed in recent years a strong reaction to business gift giving. A great many executives feel the giving of gifts has no place in business. Many firms forbid their employees to accept gifts from people with whom they do business and have informed suppliers and salesmen that gifts are neither necessary nor desirable. Others forbid employees to give gifts to customers or clients.

How to request that gifts not be sent. A number of companies are taking the time and trouble to write letters to suppliers and salesmen informing them of their desire that gifts not be sent to employees. The request should be made in a courteous manner, and the following letter is an example of the way to handle such a demand:

> Gentlemen:
>
> With the approach of the holiday season we feel it is appropriate to express to our suppliers appreciation of their service and cooperation throughout the past year.
>
> We also take this opportunity to remind you of our company's policy prohibiting the acceptance at any time of gifts and gratuities by our employees.
>
> The best expression of your good wishes is your continuing attention to our needs. We sincerely hope our satisfactory business relationship will continue for many more years of mutual benefit and progress.
>
> Cordially,

When receiving gifts is forbidden. The wise businessman will never try to circumvent a company ruling that forbids employees to accept gifts from people it does business with. If you disregard the ruling and send a gift anyway, the person receiving it may well be put in an embarrassing position. Many companies insist that gifts be returned to the donor. Sending a gift to someone's home may seem like the clever way of getting around the ban, but it is a rude disregard of a company's policy and may only serve to get the recipient in trouble. It certainly doesn't build good will for the giver of the gift.

When giving of gifts is forbidden. Many companies inform their salesmen that the giving of gifts to their customers does not meet with approval. When this is the case, a salesman who wishes to send a gift to someone with whom he does business must do so at his own expense. He cannot ask his company to reimburse him, when giving gifts is not in agreement with company policy.

Christmas Cards

The exchange of Christmas cards among employees is looked on by most companies, and the employees themselves, as an expression of good will and friendliness.

Who should get them. If you decide to send Christmas cards to friends at the office, make up your mind to send a card to everyone in your company (if it is a small one) or in your division (if you work for a large organization). Avoid favoring a few with best wishes for the season. Some people solve this problem by sending only one card addressed to the company (or the division).

Mailing Christmas cards. Christmas cards should not be sent to office addresses, but to the homes of the recipients. It is for this reason that most companies distribute printed or mimeographed home address lists to employees just before the holiday season.

Not only should Christmas cards not be addressed *to* someone at his office they shouldn't be mailed *at* the office. Mail room facilities are jammed up and mail room help overtaxed if even a small percentage of the employees in a company send their personal Christmas cards out via the office mail box.

Signing Christmas cards. A married man or woman may sign cards to casual business acquaintances with only his or her name. But if the card is going to someone you consider a friend, even though he or she has not met your spouse, sign both your names.

Whose name comes first? Usually the person signing the card puts his or her name last, as a matter of courtesy. When the names are printed or engraved on the card, there is no hard and fast rule as to which name comes first. It is not considered good form to use "Mr. and Mrs." on a Christmas card unless the greeting is a very formal one, such as, "Mr. and Mrs. Preston Hawks wish you a Merry Christmas and a Happy New Year." A card may be signed "The Preston Hawks" or "Preston and Cynthia Hawks."

When a businessman sends Christmas cards from the company rather than from himself and his wife the cards might read:

"The Bolton Company
sends best wishes
for the Holiday Season"

or

A Merry Christmas
and
A Happy New Year

The Bolton Company

·11· In Case of Illness or Death

When illness, injury or death occur at work, the shock frequently leads to confusion rather than the prompt action that is called for.

Emergency telephone numbers. Even the smallest company should have the telephone numbers of a doctor, the nearest hospital, and the police posted in a place accessible to everyone.

Telephone a doctor first, when illness or injury occur. Should a doctor not be immediately available, telephone the police and ask them to summon an ambulance, if one is needed, or to locate a doctor.

Both a doctor and the police should be called when sudden death occurs.

Notifying the family. Unless there is no other choice, news of serious illness or injury or death should not be conveyed to the employee's family by telephone. A member of the firm should go to the employee's home to give the news in person and to offer his services during the next few hectic hours.

When an executive dies. A private secretary or an assistant to an executive can be of invaluable assistance to the family when an executive dies suddenly. Here is a list of details that must be attended to when death occurs, things a secretary or assistant might be able to do:

1. Notify a mortician and instruct him as to the deceased's family's wishes.
2. Notify the deceased's insurance company.
3. Insert a death notice in the newspapers. If funeral arrangements are not complete at the time this is done they can be added later. If the deceased was well known, inform the city editors of the town's newspapers of his death. When a funeral is limited to personal friends, the words "Funeral Private" are included in the obituary. If the family does not wish flowers to be sent, the words, "Omit flowers" are added to the obituary.

4. When a church funeral is to be held, make arrangements with the church as to date and time.
5. Telephone or wire invitations to whomever the family would like to have act as honorary pallbearers. Be sure to give them the date, time, and place of the funeral.
6. Notify close business friends and associates when and where the funeral is to be held. This may be done by telephone or by sending them the personal card of the nearest relative with this information written on it.
7. Notify any organizations to which the deceased belonged of funeral and burial plans.

Newspaper notices placed by companies. Many companies notify the business world of the death of a very important employee by inserting a formal notice in the newspaper. Such a notice is placed in what is called display space, not on the obituary page, but it is bordered in black. The following are examples of notices of this kind.

It it with profound sorrow that
we announce the death of our
beloved friend and founder
ANDREW B. CHRISTOPHER
on May 9, 19__
Out of respect for his memory
all trading will be suspended
for Monday, May 13, 19__.

A. B. CHRISTOPHER & CO.

The staff, employees and fellow directors
mourn the passing of our esteemed
colleague and Honorary Chairman of the Board

DR. KENNETH L. PETERS

FAIRHAVEN MANUFACTURING COMPANY

BOGERT & PEABODY CO., INC.
ONE ROCKEFELLER PLAZA
NEW YORK, NEW YORK

Announces with deep regret the death of

PHILIP WEAVER
Chairman of the Board

When an employee or a member of his family dies. It should be the duty of the Personnel Office to notify the secretary or the president of the company upon the death of an employee or someone in an employee's family. The employee's division or department head, if any, also should be notified.

The following is a simple, dignified sympathy card that the president's office can send to the employee or his family in behalf of the company. Be sure to address the envelope in long hand.

Our sympathy

is extended to you in your sorrow

CRANDALL CAN COMPANY

A letter of condolence may be sent, instead of a card, to the bereaved family or to an officer of the company for whom the deceased worked. Letters of condolence should be brief, sincerely sympathetic, and tactful. Don't dwell on—or even mention—anything that might cause pain to the reader, such as a long and painful illness suffered by the deceased.

A handwritten letter of condolence is preferred, but as with all other correspondence, including personal letters, if your handwriting is almost impossible to read, use a typewriter. Here is an example of a business letter of condolence:

Dear Mr. Martin:

It was with real regret that we learned of the death of Joseph Smathers.

He was a man with whom my company had business dealings for over 30 years. His integrity, discretion, and ability made our association one that I have valued highly through the years. I will feel his loss personally, and I know he will long be missed by everyone in the textile business.

Please convey my deepest sympathy to the other officers of your company upon the death of a respected associate and a fine friend.

Sincerely,

Here is a sample of a letter to the widow of an employee:

Dear Mrs. Cartwright:

It was with a very real sense of loss that I heard today of the death of your husband. I valued his friendship for many years. I don't believe I've ever known another man who was so loved and respected by all who knew him. It was a privilege to know Jack, whose place in our company can never be taken by anyone else.

My heartfelt sympathy goes out to you and your family. If there is any way in which I can be of assistance in the weeks ahead, please do not hesitate to call on me.

Sincerely,

Sending flowers. Upon the death of an employee or a member of an employee's immediate family (wife and children), or of a customer or client, a spray or wreath of flowers may be sent to the funeral chapel or to a memorial service in a church. Management usually sends flowers, but when the company permits it, the members of the employee's department will send an additional floral piece. The florist will have a plain card on which can be written a brief message, such as, "Deepest sympathy," the company name, and the department or division.

Flowers should not be sent when death occurs in an Orthodox Jewish family; instead, a gift of fruit or candy is appropriate.

In some instances, the family of the deceased requests that flowers be omitted. Frequently the family suggests that instead of flowers contributions be sent to a particular charity or association in which the deceased was deeply interested, or to an organization conducting research in the disease of which the individual died.

Mass cards are sent to Roman Catholic families by Catholics and non-Catholics. They are available at any Roman Catholic church and it is proper to make an offering to the church at the time you request the mass card.

Acknowledging flowers and letters of sympathy. Printed or engraved cards of thanks are not in the best of taste unless the deceased was so prominent that literally hundreds of people sent flowers and letters of condolence. When such is the case, it is considered proper to reply to all but close friends with such a card. Otherwise, a handwritten note of thanks is proper. Acknowledgments may be brief, but should be warm and personal.

Dear Mr. Moran:

Thank you so much for your kind letter of sympathy. It has indeed been a comfort to know that Jack was so well loved and appreciated. Thank you also for the lovely flowers [or "for the donation to the Heart Fund in Jack's name"].

Your thoughtfulness has been most touching and sustaining.

Sincerely,

Personal mourning. However deep one's sorrow, it is not good form to display one's feelings at business. Mourning publicly is embarrassing to your co-workers and business associates, making them feel awkward and inadequate even though they sympathize with you.

If you are a business woman, a simple black or grey dress or suit such as you might wear at any time is acceptable, but black-bordered handkerchiefs and deep black stockings or entirely black attire only draws attention to you and your private emotions. It is always poor taste to display in public—particularly in the impersonal atmosphere of business—emotions and feelings that have no place there.

A black band on the left sleeve is the traditional symbol of mourning for males. In addition, men in deep mourning wear white shirts, and black shoes, gloves and ties. In business, though, a man has no more wish to attract attention and sympathy than does a woman in mourning. For this reason, most men no longer wear the traditional arm band to business but confine their mourning attire to black tie and socks worn with a dark suit but not necessarily a black one.

•12• Special Etiquette Problems in Various Sizes of Office

The common rules of etiquette as they apply to business situations are followed in offices of every size, for the most part. Yet the size of an office (meaning the number of people who work there, more than physical size) does tend to have a bearing on how people behave toward each other. The differences are especially noticeable—and important—to someone who is just taking up duties in an office that is much smaller, or larger, than the office to which he or she is accustomed.

This section discusses etiquette problems peculiar to offices of a given size, or that are more pronounced in certain offices because of size.

The Small Office

The atmosphere in a small office tends to be more informal and relaxed than that in a larger organization. This can be pleasant, but it is also deceptive; an informal working environment can place more demands on your sense of etiquette than the more formal atmosphere of a larger office does.

Overfamiliarity in a small office. When the same few people work together every day in the confines of a small office, there is the danger that relations between them will become too personal, too casual. This is a mistake in any office, large or small, but the problem is magnified in the small office, where people have no choice but to work closely together.

The more personally involved fellow workers are, the more delicate the problem of etiquette becomes, in spite of the casual atmosphere that may prevail. Who eats together, who gets what kind of gift on festive occasions, who does special favors for whom, all are public knowledge in the small office, and all must be delicately handled.

There is no rule that says you can't be friends with people in your office. You are wise, however, to avoid becoming too familiar with co-workers; in the small office you must be especially careful.

Another aspect of this problem arises when people of different rank become too familiar. The saying is still true; familiarity does tend to breed contempt. A supervisor makes his position difficult when he allows himself to become too friendly with people working under him. Again, the small office is conducive to this situation, and therefore calls for special awareness on the part of those working there.

The problem of first names. In the small office, where the atmosphere is usually an informal one, employees are most often on the first-name basis. However, in offices where the principal activity is face-to-face contact with the public, employees are generally required to use last names (preceded by Mr., Mrs. or Miss) in addressing each other. This is generally true even in a small office.

Naturally, if the employer or managing executive in a small office insists on a certain degree of formality, employees must comply. The executive in this situation has two responsibilities:

- he must make clear to every employee what the policy is concerning the use of first names (and other aspects of employee behavior), and
- he must consistently set the proper example.

For more on the use of first names, see page 21.

Discretion is more important in the small office. Although discretion is the rule in all business organizations, it must be more carefully exercised in the small office. Here, since the atmosphere is more informal, important policy decisions are more likely to be common knowledge among staff members. Even the office boy may know about plans for expansion, additions to the executive staff and the like. This places a greater responsibility on each employee. He must be constantly on guard to make sure that these company matters are not being told to the wrong people.

Distractions are magnified in the small office. If you work in a small office you must keep in mind that any noise or activity on your part can distract the entire staff. Here are areas where you must show extra care:

• *telephone conversations:* prolonged "small talk" or speaking too loudly or making too many personal calls are even more inconsiderate actions in the small office than in the larger one.

• *personal conversations:* one of the hardest temptations to overcome is the urge to chat with your neighbor in the office once in a while. In the really small office, a two-party conversation soon becomes a conference, since the others can't help but overhear and become involved.

• *distracting habits:* if you have a habit of drumming your fingers, or whistling or humming, you must remember that in a small office such distractions can be maddening to your fellow employees.

• *visits from family or friends:* you should make it clear to your family and friends that, because of the size of your office, visits during the working day are not a good idea. If visitors do come, see if you can't speak with them somewhere where your co-workers won't be distracted.

Special dining etiquette for small offices. In many organizations where a small number of people work, a certain area is set aside for lunchroom facilities. In places such as banks and schools, this often consists of a small kitchen and an equally small grouping of tables and chairs. The lunchroom cannot possibly function without the full cooperation and consideration of each user.

The problems in this type of a lunchroom are more specialized than the usual ones. Since there are generally cooking, refrigeration and storage units in these lunchrooms, some common sense rules for use of the facilities should be established. Below are some of the more important rules for those who use small lunchrooms of this type:

1. Never use a co-worker's cooking utensils without his permission. If he says you can, make sure that you clean them thoroughly before returning them.
2. Do not store foods with permeating or offensive odors in the lunchroom refrigerator.
3. Make sure that you leave the area clean for your co-workers on later lunch shifts.

4. Don't bring foods that may cause you to monopolize the stove because of the lengthy preparations they require.

5. Be considerate by not using more than your share of the storage space in the lunchroom.

For a discussion of the actual etiquette of eating with one's co-worker see "Lunchroom etiquette" on page 27.

The Medium and Large Size Office

Larger offices are generally more formal. As offices get larger, they generally tend to become more formalized. Employees are less likely to make acquaintances in sections other than their own.

The more formalized atmosphere generally frees the large office from the problems of overfamiliarity that exist in the small office. But there are many other problems of etiquette inherent in larger offices. These are discussed in the following pages.

Cliques in the large office. The tendency to form cliques is stronger in larger offices. In the large office's impersonal atmosphere, people with similar interests are drawn together. In time, a kind of unofficial club or society comes into existence.

Cliques are not beneficial, either to the company or to the people who belong. A clique is almost certain to lead to jealousy and to dissension between employees who are "in" and those who are "out." The chosen members are prone to regard "outsiders" as fair game for uncomplimentary discussions. There is also a great temptation for the group to play politics in the office, particularly when a promotion is in order.

These things impair the morale and the efficiency of an office. They also violate the basic premise of etiquette, which is consideration for others.

There are practical reasons, too, for refusing to become associated with a clique. Management is inclined to take a dim view of them, and this can harm your career. Also, while you may gain associates by identifying yourself with a clique, you simultaneously cut yourself off from others in the office.

Supply problems in a large office. It is easy to get the feeling that supplies are unlimited in a large office. The truth is that because so many people depend on the same source, it is often more difficult to keep a large office properly supplied. Be sure that you don't inconvenience others by taking more than you need; when something runs short, it will take time to replace it.

Behavior toward VIP's in the large office. When you work for a large company the chances are that you will have dealings with high-level executives, or will greet and be greeted by them during the day. Even in companies where informality is the rule, such men are entitled to a certain degree of respect.

· *The use of first names.* There is among executives of high rank a certain freedom as to the use of first names. The vice president of a corporation might call the president "Jim" if they had known each other for some time. On the other hand, an office boy would not think of calling the president, or a vice president, by his first name. The best thing for anyone to do (newcomer and old-timer as well) is to let the executive take the lead in the use of first names.

The use of the more formal "sir" in addressing people of high rank is gradually fading out and giving way to the less formal "Mr. Blank."

· *Saving the busy executive's time.* You should give priority to a high-ranking company official when he comes to you for information or asks you to do something. Whether the request is direct or comes through your supervisor, handle it promptly.

If you are in conference when a high executive wants to see you, what you do depends on who you are talking to. If it is a co-worker, excuse yourself immediately and find out what the executive wants. If you are talking with someone from outside the company, consider why he is there. If he is a customer, the executive will probably want you to conclude your business rather than inconvenience a customer. If the visitor is the one who expects to gain from the conference, he will not mind waiting while you talk with the executive. In many cases you will have to use your own judgment; if you feel that an interruption is necessary, be sure that you offer your apologies to your visitor.

Of course, no ranking executive should abuse his right to priority by making unnecessary or improper demands upon the time of employees not under his supervision. Unless he has a special reason for doing otherwise, he should go through channels in his dealings with people in the company.

· *The executive has precedence.* When people of different rank in a company approach a door, an elevator or a lunchroom line, the general rule is that rank should be given precedence. This is a simple rule to follow if the persons involved are of the same sex. If a man and woman are involved, the rules are somewhat more flexible, tempered with common sense.

If the woman is the higher one in rank, both her position and her sex give her the privilege of going first. Very often the man will let a woman pass first even though he outranks her somewhat. However, if he is much higher in rank than she is, the problem becomes more pronounced. A satisfactory solution would be for the woman to offer to let him be first, but for him to indicate pleasantly that he expects her to precede him. Thus she will have shown her deference to his position, while he will have recognized her as a woman. However, if he is much higher in rank than she is, he is not being rude if he goes first; the situation is a business one, not a social one.

It should be noted that a woman who works directly for a man—a secretary, in particular—will commonly give her boss precedence in situations of this kind. She will not expect him to defer to her simply because she is a woman.

Etiquette in the company parking lot. People tend to forget their manners when they take the wheel of a car. This can lead to frayed tempers and bad feeling, and worse, when employees are trying to get in or out of a company parking lot. In a large company, especially, where hundreds of cars can be involved, it is essential that each driver be considerate of the others.

Several of the rules that follow will sound obvious—because they are good, common sense rules. These rules were adapted from those drawn up by one large company whose parking lot had become the scene for an unpleasant and often dangerous half-hour struggle twice a day. With a few rules of etiquette spelled out and then enforced, the situation was greatly improved.

Here are the rules:

1. Drive slowly when entering or leaving the parking lot.
2. Follow direction signs in the lot.
3. Do not park in reserved areas, which are usually plainly marked.
4. Park within the white lines or any other space marked off for *one* car.
5. Don't forget to close your windows, switch off your lights and motor, and remove your key from the ignition switch.

6. Respect the paint on your neighbor's car by opening your door gently.
7. If you should happen to damage a car in any way and the owner isn't present, be courteous enough to leave a note with your name, address and telephone number in a place where he can see it.
8. Lock your car doors to minimize the possibility of theft.
9. Don't use your high-beam headlights in the parking area; they will blind the driver ahead of you.
10. At quitting time, when several lanes of cars are trying to leave via the same exits, be polite and take alternate turns.

Etiquette for car pools. In large companies whose many employees come from far and near, car pools will usually spring up, formed by people who live in the same area and want to share commuting expenses. Either the members take turns driving their cars, or one member drives regularly and the others pay him their share of expenses. In either case the arrangement can lead to disagreements unless the members of the car pool observe rules of etiquette.

· *General rules of etiquette for the car pool.* Here are some basic rules:

1. Be punctual. Driver and passengers must realize that to hold up the others is impolite and can cause them to be late. It is best to have a definite agreement on what the latest time is that the pool can leave, and to stick to it.

2. Let others know of a change in plans. It is inconsiderate to neglect to notify the others of a change in plans. Naturally, this is especially true when you are the driver, but it applies to passengers as well. Even if by agreement the group will leave at a given time if you don't arrive, it is polite to tell someone that you won't be there and save the group the wait and the uncertainty. For this reason it is best if each member has the phone number of the others.

3. Don't offend through personal habits. In the close quarters of an automobile, personal habits are accentuated, especially offensive ones. This makes it essential that you show extra care. To smoke a cigar, for example, would not be considerate unless you knew that no one in the pool would object. Insisting on a window seat or on some other preferred treatment will only create ill will.

• *When you are a passenger.* As a rider in a car pool you have certain responsibilities toward the driver:

1. Respect the driver's property. Do not drop cigarettes or cigarette ashes on the upholstery. Close car doors gently. In short, treat the car you ride in as if it were your own.
2. Be prompt in payment. If yours is a pool where payment is involved, don't make the driver have to ask you for it. This can be an embarrassing situation for both of you. To avoid it, pay the driver promptly on the day agreed upon.
3. Don't ask the driver to be your private chauffeur. Even if you are paying for your ride, don't ask the driver to go out of his way to help you do any of your special errands. Of course, in an emergency this rule can be relaxed.
4. Help, or at least offer to help, the driver with emergency repairs. It is extremely inconsiderate to sit in the car while the driver is changing a tire or doing some other emergency work.

• *When you are the driver.* If you are the driver in a car pool, you have special responsibilities, too:

1. Drive safely. The lives of your passengers are in your hands. Drive with prudence and remember that unnecessary sudden stops or jackrabbit starts can make the ride an uncomfortable and uneasy one for your riders.
2. Keep your car in good repair. Regular maintenance will prevent breakdowns that can greatly inconvenience both you and your riders. Don't leave broken windows, doors and the like in disrepair—an open window can defeat even the best car heater on a cold winter's day!
3. Make sure you have adequate insurance. Even if insurance is not compulsory in your state, make sure that you are protected against any liability that might arise out of an accident.
4. Make definite financial arrangements with your riders. If cash payments are involved in your car pool, each member should know exactly what he has to pay and when you expect him to pay it. Some people feel that it is polite to appear casual or reticent about these matters; actually, it is inconsiderate to be anything but clear. It only embarrasses your passengers when a mixup occurs because they weren't sure of the rules.

·13· The Office Memorandum

The memorandum, or memo, is used in business offices as a means of internal communication for two reasons. First, it serves as a written record; it prevents misunderstandings, and it saves the receiver from relying on memory or checking back on what was said or meant. Second, a memo can be sent to someone without interrupting him with a phone call or personal visit.

The memorandum and the note. Memos and notes are fairly distinct in some companies, while in others there is little or no distinction. Where a distinction is made, a memorandum is more formal. It is usually typed in a certain format and size, and is intended to be filed. A note in this case is simply a handwritten message of no permanent value—arrangements for luncheon, reminders of an appointment, notice that a phone call came in, and the like. If standardized paper is used for notes, it is often a small message form on which standard information or queries can be checked off ("Called," "Will call again," "Please call him," "Please see me," and so on). Some executives use note paper with an identifying phrase such as "From the desk of John Jones" printed on it.

Most of the material in this section pertains to memos, since they are somewhat standardized in many companies.

The format of a memo. There is no one way to write or arrange memos, but within any one company there should be consistency. Without it, there is likely to be confusion. A format is also a work saver; a secretary can type a memo more easily from notes when she is familiar with a definite style, and even writing up a memo is both quicker and easier when there is a format to follow.

The sample below shows a typical memorandum style.

September 10, 19__

TO: James R. Jameson, Personnel Department

FR: Alex Cooper, Methods and Systems Department

RE: FORMAT FOR MEMORANDUMS

> This will show you the style we follow in writing memorandums for interoffice use. The style is designed for speed both in typing and in reading. Memos are typed on 6 x 9¼" paper, punched for insertion into binders.
>
> The best reference line is one that conveys the essence of the memo, yet is brief. This helps the receiver when he reads the memo, when he files it, and when he has occasion to find it again.
>
> Supply has copies of this sample memorandum available now, if you would like to order them for the people in your department.

Typewrite a memo. Since the memo is almost always filed, it should be typewritten. Typing a memo provides it with two important qualities:

1. *It gives the memo the needed formality and clarity.* For example, if the memo is one that gives the recipient instructions on how to perform a certain task or assigns a task to him, it should be typed. This gives it authority and avoids misunderstandings.

2. *Typing gives the memo permanence.* Typewritten documents do not fade or smudge the way handwritten ones do.

Write a note longhand. Because notes do not usually have to be filed and generally refer to an immediate, transitory situation, they are usually written in longhand. This saves time, and since notes are generally more personal than memos the reader will value the personal touch of your handwriting on the note.

Routing memos. A memo containing subject matter that is pertinent to more than one individual is often routed, instead of sending a separate copy to each.

When routing is necessary, certain problems of etiquette and office management arise. Should they be distributed alphabetically? By rank? By convenience of location? By job priority? There is no definite answer to these problems. A great deal depends on the individual needs of your organization. The four basic routing methods are discussed below.

1. *Alphabetical routing.* This method has two basic advantages. First, it is easy to do. The person sending the memo does not have to search through office, building, or state location files. He doesn't have to find out individual ranks within the firm. There is no need

to find out who has to see the memo first. All he has to do is decide who should see it and then arrange their names alphabetically in the "TO" notation of the memo. The second advantage is that alphabetical routing makes no rank distinction. No one in the office can have his feelings hurt because he thinks that John Doe in the next office is "a privileged character." This seems a small advantage, but it is often necessary so that harmony can be maintained in the office.

The disadvantages of alphabetical routing are two. First, no allowance is made for location; if the memo is passed along strictly by alphabet it may have to follow a tortuous path. Also, alphabetical routing makes no distinction of job priority. The person who should see the memo first may see it last.

2. *Routing according to location.* The main advantage of routing according to location is that it saves time. A memo can be sent to all the recipients in one location and then sent to another location for distribution there. This is a logical system that is best used when the memo is general and gives no specific job assignments or instructions.

Locational routing has two major drawbacks. Here, as in alphabetic routing, no attention is given to job priority. Also, routing according to location may involve more work than alphabetical routing. The person sending the memo has to find out where each of the recipients is located, if he doesn't know, and then he has to route the memo accordingly.

3. *Routing according to rank.* Routing according to rank, from top to bottom, is fairly easy to do. All that is necessary is a list of company employees and their respective ranks in the organization.

The faults of this system are that it makes no job priority distinction, and pays no attention to location. A better way to keep executives informed and to show deference to the executive position is discussed below in the section called "Informational routing."

4. *Routing by job priority.* The advantage here is that the person who must act on the memo's contents first sees it first. There are no delays in following the directions in the memo.

The disadvantage of this system is that no attention is paid to the location of the recipients.

Routing by job priority is one of the best routing methods possible when it is combined with informational routing (see discussion of informational routing below). This combination not only allows the person who has to act first to see the memo first, but allows executives to keep in touch with company operations as well.

As you can see, the four basic routing techniques all have their advantages and disadvantages. What is an advantage for one firm may be a disadvantage for another. The most important thing for you to do is to *choose one method, flexible to your needs, and stick to it.*

Informational routing. Occasionally, memos must be routed to certain executives who are not directly affected by their contents. This is called informational routing. The name of each executive who is indirectly affected is included in the heading of the memo, often with the letters "FYI" (meaning "for your information") next to his name.

September 28, 19__

TO: John Adams, Personnel
Philip G. Olsen, Production
James R. President, FYI
I.M. Treasurer, FYI

Send memos through appropriate channels. A basic rule in business etiquette demands that you never go over the head of your immediate supervisor without his knowledge and consent. This means you should direct a memo to a higher executive only if your superior knows about it and approves of your action. If you have any doubt, it is best to direct the memo to your supervisor and let him convey the information to the higher party.

Reply to memos. Some memos are sent with no expectation of a reply. A memorandum intended only to convey information would be an example. Included would be memos intended primarily for someone else but routed to you (or a copy sent) to keep you informed. A memo setting forth a policy or announcing an activity or forthcoming event doesn't usually require a reply unless your compliance or participation must be made known.

When a memo does call for an answer, remember that it is a business communication and deserves prompt attention. Where a brief reply is in order—"yes," "no," or "will do," for instance—then a verbal answer, especially by telephone, is often used, unless the matter is not important enough to merit interrupting the other person's day with a call. A method used in many companies for brief, non-urgent answers is to write the reply on the memo itself and return it to the sender. This method does not interrupt him, gives him a written answer, and results in just one paper to file if he wants to keep it. If a speedy reply is needed, however, the telephone is best.

With any but the simplest reply it is best to give it in writing in the form of an answering memo. A memo is also used to confirm an answer that was first given orally because of urgency. A memo of reply should be typed on the same size paper as the original, for purposes of filing.

• Part 2 • Meeting the Public

·14· The Guest in the Office

The way in which a caller is received in an office makes an indelible impression on his mind. It helps shape his opinion of the efficiency of a company and the caliber of the people employed there. Businesses do project images, which often start with the impression clients and customers have of a company's employees and their attitudes.

A company should make some provision for the comfort of its visitors. It is also of the utmost importance that the first person a caller meets—whether it is the switchboard operator, a receptionist, a secretary, or a plant guard—be polite and considerate and make every effort to be helpful. The employee whose manner toward visitors is rude and snippy, or condescending, or self-important, can do unbounded harm to the prestige of a company.

Making adequate provision for guests. Callers are in effect the guests of a company, whether they have an appointment or arrive uninvited. Therefore, some space should be set aside as a reception area for visitors, with adequate facilities for their comfort and convenience. This space where guests are received—whether it is part of a secretary's office, or space adjacent to a switchboard, or a room all by itself—should provide comfortable seating, good lighting, and up-to-date picture, news and business magazines. Ash trays should be generous in size and sufficient in number.

If possible, the receptionist or a secretary should empty and wipe the ash trays and straighten the magazines after each visitor has gone, so that the place looks tidy for the next person who has to wait. At the very least, this cleaning and straightening up should be done several times a day.

A telephone in the reception area is an aid for visitors whose business keeps them out of the office and calling on others all day. But this is a feasible convenience only when the calls go through a switchboard and your operator can make sure all the calls are local ones or the charges have been reversed. Many companies have pay phones installed as the simplest and safest solution.

A coat closet or rack—or at least a coat tree—frees the caller from the nuisance of sitting with his hat and a folded-up overcoat perched on his lap.

A washroom off the reception room is a convenience that guests appreciate, but if you can't provide one, at least don't make it necessary for callers to have to request a key in order to get into the nearest company washroom. The doors to the washrooms nearest the reception area should be kept unlocked.

Etiquette for the Receptionist

The receptionist is expected to present to the visiting public a pleasant countenance and a friendly manner. Ideally, she should have an outstanding memory for names and faces, so that she can greet callers after their first visit as friends of the firm and not as strangers. She should know a good deal about the business and the way work is handled and who performs various tasks; she can then intelligently answer questions put to her by the public and also refer to the right person callers who are doubtful as to whom they should see.

Smoking at the desk. A majority of companies prefer that their receptionists do not smoke. At best, smoking is an untidy habit and one that many people find unattractive. If your company does permit its receptionist to smoke on duty, be sure you rest the cigarette in an ash tray or put it out completely before speaking to visitors.

Eating at the desk. A receptionist's personal habits should be as circumspect as possible, in order to avoid offending the sensibilities of the majority of visitors. Chewing gum, munching candy or food of any kind, and drinking beverages are all taboo. Never eat lunch at your desk, no matter what emergency arises.

Rising to meet callers. A receptionist is not expected to rise and greet callers. You make an exception when the visitor is a dignitary you recognize, such as a clergyman or a political figure, or is a member of your employer's family with whom you are on particularly friendly terms.

Greeting the caller. Until midday, "Good morning" is the accepted greeting; "Good afternoon" serves until six o'clock; after six, visitors should be greeted with "Good evening." "How do you do" is an acceptable greeting at all hours of the day.

A voice that is neither too loud nor too high makes a pleasant impression, but a voice so affectedly low that people have difficulty hearing it is irritating.

When a visitor does not immediately offer his card, and is a stranger to her, the receptionist courteously asks his name, whom he would like to see and whether he has an appointment. "May I have your name, please?" is a more polite inquiry than an abrupt, "Name, please?"

The caller without an appointment. A receptionist should never act as though a visitor who doesn't have an appointment is an interloper. This is not only rude but senseless. Nor should the receptionist take it on herself to decide whether a caller has what she considers a legitimate reason for visiting her company. Any visitor—expected or unexpected—must be made to feel welcome.

The receptionist's primary concern should be to find out what the caller without an appointment wants or who he wishes to see. Perhaps he just has a message or papers to leave for someone; possibly he wishes to ask a question about the company that the receptionist can answer.

Some companies insist that the receptionist find out the reason for the visit before announcing the caller. If this is so, she inquires courteously: "Can you tell me what you wish to see Mr. Clements about?" Or, "May I tell Mr. Clements what you want to talk to him about?"

If the caller refuses to tell the receptionist the purpose of his call, she may tell him politely that she is not free to announce him without also explaining the reason for his visit. If he persists in his refusal, the receptionist should recommend in a pleasant manner that he write to the man in question for an appointment.

When company policy does not require that she find out the reason for his call, the receptionist merely finds out the visitor's name and who he wishes to see and then announces him over the telephone. If the man is not free the receptionist must convey this message as courteously as possible. She can say, "I'm sorry, Mr. Michaels is not available this morning." Or perhaps, "I'm sorry, but Mr. Michaels is not seeing visitors this afternoon." Or, "I'm sorry,

Mr. Michaels is not free at present. Could you stop in some other time?" If she has been given a definite explanation—such as that Mr. Michaels is in a meeting, is out, or is getting ready to leave on a business trip and hasn't the time to see anyone—the receptionist may repeat it to the caller.

The caller with an appointment. When the caller informs the receptionist that he has an appointment, she should thank him and ask him to be seated. If she has a list of visitors expected (and each secretary should give her such a list daily) she refers to it to verify the appointment and then announces the caller.

If there is to be a delay, the receptionist informs the visitor. When the reception room is a large one, she should go to where the visitor is seated and tell him the man he wants to see will be free in a few mintues. Under no condition must she call this out from her desk. Of course, if the room is small, and the visitor is seated nearby, she may speak to him from her desk.

Announcing the caller. When the receptionist telephones an office to announce a caller, whether the secretary or the man himself answers the telephone she merely says, "This is the receptionist. Mr. Root is here to see Mr. Michaels." She will then be told whether Mr. Michaels can see Mr. Root, and, if so, whether she should have the visitor wait or to send him right in. Usually, she allows relatives and known friends to go in unannounced.

Handling the crank caller. Patience helps with crank callers, who usually have a complaint they are anxious to tell someone about. (A sense of humor is helpful, too, but keep any humorous reactions to yourself; a crank doesn't think his problem is funny.)

Actually, there is no reason for being rude to cranks, however troublesome they are, or however weird the stories they have to tell. Listen to the complaint with as much patience as you can muster and then refer the caller to an officer of the company who specializes in handling this kind of problem (such as the public relations man). If the crank caller wants to see a specific individual in the company, refer him to the man's assistant, if he has one, or say that the individual he wishes to speak to sees people by appointment only and that he should write for one.

Cranks are usually so filled with antagonisms and hatreds that the slightest thing can trigger off an explosion. They must be handled with delicacy and courtesy, but also with firmness. Don't argue with them, and never lose your temper. But don't waver. Once you have decided how to handle the situation, stay with that decision.

Handling the unwanted caller. The unwanted caller is the one nobody wants to see. The fact that you know this doesn't mean you can be rude to him. Treat him as courteously as you would anyone else, unless he becomes seriously annoying, in which case someone in management should explain to the unwanted visitor that he isn't winning friends in the company with this behavior and that it would be a good idea if he didn't turn up so frequently.

Unfortunately, many men avoid this task by saying to the receptionist or secretary, "I don't want to see that fellow again. Tell him I'm out next time he comes."

Of course, the day you are telling someone Mr. Smith isn't in is just the day Mr. Smith will dash out of the office asking about some missing papers. It is wiser, therefore, simply to tell the unwanted caller that he must make an appointment with the man he wants to see. Suggest that he write for an appointment as the man in question has taken on added responsibilities and is only seeing callers with appointments.

If your suggestions seem to fall on deaf ears and the unwanted caller continues to appear, try to treat him pleasantly and continue to recommend that he write for an appointment. Even if he becomes angry, maintain a cordial attitude.

Should the unwanted caller decide to wait in the reception room, no matter how tactfully you have tried to get rid of him, the best thing to do is to ignore him. He may think that by waiting he can thwart the receptionist and catch the individual he wants to see on the way out or in. But the chances are that he will tire of waiting and leave without further ado.

How to address a visiting dignitary. Even the average office may be graced by a visit from such dignitaries as political, church, or government figures. It adds immeasurably to your poise if you can address such a person properly and unhesitatingly.

A list of dignitaries and the proper way to address them is included among the tables in the back of this book.

When the caller has to wait. Show the visitor where he can leave his hat and coat. Male visitors feel uncomfortable if a woman helps them off with their coats, but it is a polite gesture to help a female visitor remove her coat and to hang it up for her.

Indicate where the caller may sit, and point out conveniences that are available. If the visitor is a close friend of the executive he is calling on, or is of sufficient importance for you to feel he merits special attention, ask if there is something you can do for him while he is waiting. If he wishes to make a telephone call or look up a telephone number, you might offer to dial it or look it up for him.

Don't feel you have to entertain the waiting caller by talking to him constantly. If he seems to want you to talk to him, by all means do so, but avoid expressing opinions about any controversial subject or answering any but the most general inquiries about the business, particularly when the questioner is a stranger to you.

Any waiting period for a caller with an appointment should be brief. Visitors will understand unforeseen delays such as a long distance telephone call or a hurried meeting with a superior or subordinate in order to fill him in on some new development. But it is every bit as rude to keep a caller waiting more than a minute or two as it is for him to be late for his appointment.

Introducing callers to each other. There is no reason why waiting visitors should be introduced to each other. It's entirely possible that people who are waiting together will strike up a conversation, but the receptionist isn't expected to make formal introductions.

Substituting for the receptionist. A receptionist should never leave her desk for any length of time without arranging for a substitute. And she should brief the substitute as to who the people in the reception room are waiting to see.

When the Secretary Receives Visitors

One of the most important aspects of a secretary's work is the way in which she handles visitors. She is a reflection not only of the company's public relations image—as is the receptionist—but of her executive's personal image. She is a key figure in building good will both for him and for the company through her attitude of considerateness regardless of the relative importance of each caller.

Smoking at the desk. In most modern offices smoking at the desks is allowed. But because smoking is an objectionable habit to many people, if you do smoke be discreet. When a visitor approaches your desk and you are smoking, either put out your cigarette or place it in an ash tray to one side of your desk while you are talking to the caller. Do not smoke while you are conversing with him.

Never put lighted cigarettes any place but in an ash tray. If you rest them on the edges of desks and cabinets, unsightly burns can be the result.

Rising to greet guests. Unless your desk is hidden from view, there is no need for a secretary to rise to greet guests, unless she wishes to do so as a mark of friendship or honor.

When the visitor has an appointment. If her executive is free, the secretary can call on the intercom to say Mr. Jones has arrived for his 10:30 appointment. However, if her executive is occupied with another caller or is on the telephone, the secretary places a note before him explaining that Mr. Jones has arrived and is waiting. If the person already in the executive's office is a co-worker, or a personal friend or relative, the secretary can announce the caller on the intercom and need not use a note.

If he can't immediately wind up what he is doing, or has fallen behind schedule in his appointments, it is courteous for an executive to leave his office to greet the man who is waiting for his appointment and explain that he needs only a minute or two more to finish up what he is doing. If the executive does not or cannot perform this courtesy, the secretary can smilingly make the same explanation to the waiting caller.

When the executive is not in his office. On occasion an executive will have been called out of his office just before a visitor arrives. When this happens the secretary should apologize for her executive and explain the circumstances.

You can say, "Good morning, Mr. Smythe. Mr. Rogers was called into the plant about ten minutes ago because of a production problem. He should be back any minute now. Do you mind waiting?"

If an unexpected emergency will keep the executive out of his office for more than a few moments, you might explain it this way: "Good morning, Mr. Smythe. I'm so sorry, but Mr. Rogers was called to the office of the chairman of the board a little while ago. I'm not sure when he'll be back. I tried to reach you, but your office said you had already left. Can you wait?" The visitor can then decide whether to wait, come back later or make another appointment, or even see someone else—the executive's assistant, for instance, if he has one.

When the visitor has to wait. If the visitor has to wait, the secretary invites him to be seated and gets on with her work. If the guest is particularly important, she may ask if there is anything she can do for him. She makes no effort to "entertain" waiting callers, but responds pleasantly to their small talk, just as a receptionist does. If direct questions are put to her about the business, she avoids them adroitly, pretending complete ignorance of the topic, if need be, or changing the subject.

When the secretary tells a receptionist a caller will have to wait, it is courteous for her to come out to the reception room and explain to the visitor the reason for the delay. If this is not possible—if she is taking dictation, for example—the receptionist will have to explain the delay. When the executive is ready to see the visitor, the secretary can either call the receptionist and tell her to send the caller in, or she can go out to the reception room and escort him in herself.

Announcing a caller. If the secretary is told to send the guest right in, she may do one of two things. If the caller is known to her employer, and has visited the office before, she may nod to him and say something to the effect that, "Mr. Michaels is free. Won't you go right in?" However, if it is the caller's first visit, or he is an infrequent caller, the secretary should accompany him to the door of her employer's office, open it if it is kept closed, step to one side and say, "Mr. Michaels, here is Mr. Roper."

When older people or dignitaries or women are announced in a business office, it is considered proper to mention the guest's name first. For instance, should a church dignitary visit your executive, the polite announcement would be: "Bishop McLaughlin, Mr. Michaels." (Refer to the chart in the back of this book for the proper titles by which to announce officials and dignitaries.)

Members of the executive's family are allowed to enter his office unannounced, unless there is a guest in the office. In this case, the secretary announces their arrival on the intercom right away.

Canceling an appointment. Occasionally there is reason for canceling an appointment, but this should not be done lightly. Only a matter of absolute necessity makes the cancellation of an appointment excusable.

If an executive is called away and knows he will not be back in time to keep a scheduled appointment, his secretary should telephone the individual who is due for the appointment, explain the circumstances, and offer to make another appointment.

Should you have to call and change the time of an appointment for any reason, be as gracious as possible. Perhaps you could say, after introducing yourself: "I am sorry to have to ask this favor. But would it be possible for Mr. Springer to come to Mr. Michaels' office at three o'clock today instead of two o'clock? Mr. Michaels has been asked by the president of our company to attend a very important luncheon meeting which will probably last until well after two o'clock."

When the executive is behind schedule in his appointments. If he is badly off schedule, it might be best to try and cancel one appointment, so he can catch up. The next best thing is to point out to him that he will have to make up time and ask him to cut short the next one or two appointments. If he is agreeable to this, you can let him know when the allotted time is up for each one.

Interrupting when a visitor is present. Should your executive have on his schedule a meeting at a specific time and a visitor is in his office as the hour approaches, the secretary may enter the office, apologize for the interruption and remind him that an appointment is coming up. The time of the appointment should not be mentioned. A vocal reminder is better than a note because then the visitor is alerted to the fact that he should depart.

Allow enough time for your employer to end his talk with his visitor unhurriedly and still reach his appointment promptly.

When your executive does not want to see the caller. When you are certain your executive is not interested in seeing a certain individual, be polite but definite in refusing him. You can say something like this:

"I wish I could be of help, Mr. Gray, but right now Mr. Michaels will see only those directly connected with a new project. He will be involved in this for some time, and I think the best way to reach him would be by letter."

Some people have a flair for turning people down in such a way that they feel they've been honored rather than refused. Try to cultivate this manner by treating even the unwanted guest solicitously. Never try to raise your own sense of self-importance by acting in an unpleasant, rude manner.

When the callers are office personnel. Many executives today maintain an "open door" policy for memebrs of their company. Naturally, executives on the same level are free to come and go as they please, unless the executive has a visitor from outside the company. When lower echelon personnel indicate that they'd like to see your executive, try to first find out why. You can sometimes prevent someone from going over his immediate superior's head and thereby causing ill feeling, or you can point out that your executive is not the right one with whom to discuss this matter. If you feel the problem merits your executive's attention, make an appointment for the employee and explain the problem to your executive so that he will have some idea of what to expect.

If the employee will not tell you his problem, do not refuse him an appointment as you might an outsider. Set up an appointment for him and inform your executive that Charles Cole, the new young salesman, or John White in the mailroom, has asked to see him but is reluctant to tell you why.

The secretary will interrupt her executive whenever a company employee comes in with an emergency work situation.

When the caller has no appointment. In a majority of cases, it is left to the secretary to decide how the caller without an appointment will be handled, since she knows her executive's business needs and his schedule. It is her job to protect him from unnecessary interruptions.

First she must find out what the visitor wants. If he doesn't volunteer the information, she must politely ask for it (see page 107).

If she feels that her executive will want to see the caller, she asks the caller to wait and goes into her employer's office (unless he has told her to handle such situations over the phone or intercom). She gives the executive the visitor's card and states his reason for calling. When the executive is with someone, whether a company employee or another visitor, she does not interrupt him, but waits until he is free. The caller without an appointment must, of course, expect to wait.

The executive may be free at the moment and consent to see the caller but if he has an imminent appointment the secretary should remind him, saying, "You have ten minutes until Mr. Grant arrives for his three o'clock appointment." She lets her employer know the minute Mr. Grant comes in.

At times callers without appointments refuse to state their business. The secretary then politely asks them to write for an appointment. She can say, "Unless I know what you wish to discuss with Mr. Michaels, I cannot announce you. This is a rule laid down by Mr. Michaels. I would suggest that you write him, telling him what you want to see him about and asking for an appointment." If the caller is persistent, she should be firm but treat him courteously.

When her employer has an assistant, the secretary usually turns unknown and uninvited callers over to him; or she may refer the caller to another person in the firm.

She might say, "I think Mr. Gray in our Accounting Department would be more familiar with your problem than Mr. Michaels. Do you mind if I telephone Mr. Gray's secretary and find out if he can see you now?"

If she can arrange the meeting immediately, she should give explicit directions for reaching Mr. Gray's office, or she can accompany the visitor there. Should Mr. Gray be unable to see the caller until another time, she passes that information on, telling him the date and time if a future appointment is arranged.

Etiquette for the Person Being Visited

Rising to greet visitors. A man should rise to greet any visitor, male or female, from outside his company. The exception is with a job applicant below the executive level. But many men rise anyway, especially if the applicant is a woman, as they consider that drawing fine lines of distinction between greetings for one level of employee and another is actually rude.

When a co-worker visits the office frequently, it is not necessary to rise in greeting. Nor does a man stand each time his secretary comes into the office. He will rise to greet female executives on the same level as himself or co-workers of higher rank whose visits are infrequent. In the latter case, he remains standing until told to be seated or the caller leaves. A senior officer need not rise to greet male or female junior executives or anyone below him in rank.

When an executive has a constant stream of visitors, it is impractical for him to rise and greet each one. It is a good idea for someone who sees many people in the course of a day to leave his office door open most of the time so that he can entertain callers and still continue to handle problems and questions that are brought to him by people in his company.

A woman who receives guests is not required to stand in greeting, but it is a courteous gesture to a visitor from outside the company or to a co-worker who is considerably older or of much higher rank.

Should you be on the telephone when a guest enters, indicate a chair to the caller; when you finish your conversation, rise and greet him.

Shaking hands with a guest. A man always shakes hands with male visitors. Although socially a man would wait for a woman to extend her hand, in business a handshake between a man and woman is a customary greeting. A woman offers to shake hands with the person she is calling on as a mark of cordiality, although she will usually wait for older men and women, or more important ones, to extend their hands first.

Seating the guest. The person being visited indicates where his guest should sit and takes his own seat simultaneously or after the guest is seated.

Leaving the office to greet a caller. Coming out of your office to greet a visitor before he is ushered in is a spontaneous gesture you would most likely make only for people of whom you are particularly fond, or perhaps haven't seen for some time, or have been looking forward to meeting, or who are of some eminence.

Occasionally a man will leave his office in order to personally inform a caller that he is tied up with another visitor and will have to keep him waiting for a few minutes.

Are shirt sleeves permissible? Most companies condone men working in shirt sleeves within the privacy of their offices; however, those who do so are expected to put their jackets on when receiving a caller, unless the visitor is a very old and good friend, or when they leave their office to go elsewhere in the company. Companies with a formal business atmosphere—banks, brokerage houses and such—look with disfavor on anyone at the executive level working in shirt sleeves, even in his own office.

In more informal offices, or in offices to which plants are connected and virtually all the callers are customers or suppliers, it is considered perfectly correct for a man to work, go from office to office, and receive callers in his shirt sleeves (provided he doesn't wear suspenders).

The attitude towards shirt sleeves is as much regional as it is a point of etiquette. In southern and southwestern states where temperatures are very high, men leave off their jackets. A white, long-sleeved shirt, buttoned at the cuffs and neck, and worn with a tie is acceptable in its place. In northern cities this attire is frowned upon as too informal, even during the hot summer weather, and no matter how high the thermometer goes a man is expected to wear a jacket to business.

Smoking when there is a guest in the office. If you are a smoker, naturally you won't hesitate to smoke in your own office. However, if your caller is very elderly, and particularly if it is a woman, it is courteous either to refrain from smoking or to request permission to smoke.

The polite guest will usually refrain from smoking until you either offer him a cigarette or cigar or tell him to smoke if he likes.

Seeing a guest out. Men stand when a visitor is leaving their office and usually shake hands if the visitor is a man. Frequently the man being visited escorts the caller to the door and shakes hands with him there. If the caller is a woman the man always escorts her to the door and opens it for her.

A woman is not required to stand when a caller leaves, unless the guest is elderly or prominent. However, it is a courtesy for her to do so. When she walks a male guest to the door, she lets him open it. But she performs this task for another woman.

If the callers are co-workers, the senior officer present is allowed to leave the room first. However, should he stop to talk on the way out, junior executives may ask his permission to leave.

When relatives and friends visit the employee at the office. There's no excuse for relatives and friends stopping in to visit with you at the office. Of course there are special occasions when someone brings you the wallet or keys or eyeglasses you absent-mindedly left at home. But these errands shouldn't be excuses for lengthy chats. Keep the visit brief. You may introduce members of your family to nearby co-workers, but don't take your relatives on a tour of the office during working hours, introducing them to everyone on the staff. Never take them into the office of a senior executive unless he invites you to do so. Should a relative be accompanied by children, the little ones mustn't be allowed to run around at will and play with typewriters and other office machines. If they aren't prepared to stay quiet and in one place, usher them out as fast as you can. Don't give them a chance to become nuisances.

There may be times when you will want to show off the view from a new office, or the handiwork of an interior decorator, or perhaps a painting newly acquired by your company. By all means do so, but invite your friends and family to come during lunch hour or after the office closes for the day.

Visits by former employees. No matter how friendly ex-employees remain with former co-workers, they should not fall into the habit of dropping in for a chat whenever they are in the neighborhood. When a situation of this kind develops, a supervisor or officer of the company may take the individual aside and explain that social visits during the business day are frowned upon by management and should be confined to lunch hours and after hours.

When relatives and friends visit the executive at the office. An executive's family has no more reason for office visits than does the family of the lowliest employee. Most executives are well aware of this. However, there are instances where an executive's family develops the habit of dropping in at the office any time they are in the area. This can be a problem for the secretary, especially if active children are involved or frequent requests for the secretary to perform personal services. It is ill-tempered and rude ever to complain to your executive about his family and a problem of this kind can only be met with patience and good humor.

An executive should never encourage office visits from friends who are out of work, retired, or have a lot of free time on their hands. When such a visitor seems prepared to pass the time merely chatting, say politely that while you'd enjoy spending the entire day with him you have to get to work. Make some remark, such as, "Give me a ring for lunch next week," or "Let's meet at the club for a drink some day soon after work," thereby leaving the way open for another visit but not on company time.

Dealing with the caller who outstays his welcome. Some people never get the idea that an interview or a meeting is over, and to a busy executive this can be an annoyance. Instead of showing displeasure, the person being visited should make it politely obvious that he considers the purpose of the meeting has been accomplished or the discussion is at an end.

He can say something like this: "Our talk has been most helpful and has cleared up most of our questions. I'll get to work on this right away and get in touch with you early next week." Or perhaps, "This has been a valuable meeting for both of us. Thank you so much for coming." If a remark of this type doesn't budge a caller, the only thing to do is rise in a gesture of dismissal, saying, "Thank you for coming. Your help has been invaluable to me."

If it seems necessary to make an excuse, it should be enough to refer to a very full schedule.

When a guest has been waiting long. Occasionally you may be away from your office or tied up in a meeting when an expected visitor arrives. Go up to him as you return to your office, greet him and shake hands, and apologize again for his having to wait (presumably your secretary made a prior apology on your behalf), take him by the arm and lead him into your office. This courteous behavior on your part should help to soothe any annoyance the caller had been feeling over having to wait so long.

As you escort the guest into your office, you might say to your secretary, "Please see that we are not interrupted for the next 15 minutes." However, the guest will understand if you have to confer briefly with your secretary.

Sharing business space. When an office is being shared by two or more businessmen or business staffs, consideration for others is a prerequisite to pleasant relations. People who share office space or who rent desk space in an office must try to make as little disturbance as possible so that everyone can concentrate on his own work.

Loud or angry discussions in person or over the telephone are to be avoided. In fact, all telephone conversations should be carried on as discreetly and quietly as possible. The same is true for personal conferences.

In the same vein, you should be careful not to show an untoward interest in the work the others are doing, the papers on their desks, or the mail that comes for them. Make every effort not to eavesdrop on their conversations or phone calls, even if you are close enough to hear.

It is not necessary to introduce a guest to others sharing the office, unless they are to do business together or you feel they have some mutual interest that would make it worthwhile for them to know each other.

If you have occasion to answer the telephone for someone with whom you share an office, be courteous and write any message down with care. "He's not in" or "They're not here" makes the person on the other end of the telephone wonder what kind of people he's dealing with. Nor is it polite to leave a message saying, "A woman called this morning" or "You got an out of town call this morning. He'll try and call you again later." Think what your own feelings would be if your office mates answered your phone and took your messages in this manner.

Etiquette for the Caller

When the caller steps into what is obviously a reception room, he should remove his hat. If the entrance is a lobby, then he need not remove it. He should put out a cigar or cigarette or empty his pipe and put it in his pocket before entering the reception room.

Being on time for appointments. A business appointment is something to be kept, and on time. A minute or two shouldn't matter, but it is unforgivably rude to show up late by more than that for a business appointment. If something has happened to delay you, telephone and explain you'll be a few minutes late. Otherwise, your lateness can be attributed only to carelessness or lack of regard for the person with whom you have the appointment.

Behavior of the caller who has to wait. The caller keeps his hat off while waiting. Cigar and pipe smokers are advised not to light up while waiting in a confined area. The odor of cigar and pipe smoke is distressing to a great many people and is a difficult one to get rid of. If you must smoke, smoke a cigarette, but remember to put it out before you enter the office of the person you are visiting.

The visitor without an appointment. When you don't have an appointment but ask to see a particular man, you must expect to be asked why you want to see him. This is not rudeness or idle curiosity on the part of the receptionist or secretary. A busy executive expects to hear more than, "There is a man outside to see you." He prefers something like, "Mr. Greene of the Soft-Sell Company would like to see you for a few minutes about a new machine he believes will interest you." Or, "Mr. Baxter of the Zing Advertising Agency is here about the brochure you want to send out."

Never use the name of a mutual friend or business acquaintance as an entering wedge unless the person has given you permission to do so.

The proper thing for the caller with no appointment to do is to answer the questions put to him by a receptionist or secretary as courteously as possible. You can forestall some of them by presenting your business card immediately and briefly stating your business. Most receptionists and secretaries will go out of their way to help someone who is polite and not overbearing and who doesn't try to keep from them information they need to know.

If you don't know whom you should see, ask the receptionist or secretary to suggest the right person.

The visitor's appearance. Regardless of the informality of the office you visit, everyone working there will be dressed for business. As a visitor you should be dressed accordingly. Sports and casual clothes are as out of place as evening dress. Anyone who looks as though he or she had just come off the golf course, or left a cocktail party, is not properly dressed for a business visit. Job hunters, in particular, should make every effort to look well groomed. Women should wear neat, tailored clothes, including a becoming but simple hat, immaculate gloves, and shoes and a handbag that look as though they had been polished or brushed. A man's suit should be neatly pressed and conventional in style, color and fit. A dark conservative tie and a clean white shirt, neat socks to match the tie, and well polished shoes are the proper accessories. Both men and women should wear a minimum amount of jewelry.

Most businessmen who have achieved executive status are highly sensitive to the way people look, as are all personnel interviewers. Be sure you give an impression of cleanliness, careful grooming, and alertness.

Behavior during a visit. When the person on whom you are calling offers you a chair, thank him and seat yourself; don't sit before you've been invited. If you are carrying a coat and hat your host will usually offer to take them from you, but if he doesn't you can say, "May I put these things here?" and deposit them on a nearby chair. If you have a briefcase or folder, keep it on your lap or on the floor next to your chair; never place it on your host's desk. A woman should keep her handbag on her lap or on the floor and not on the desk. Should you need a pen or pencil or a paper clip or sheet of paper in the course of your visit, don't use one you see on your host's desk unless you first ask permission.

Don't slouch in your chair, or twist yourself into knots. Sit up straight, with both feet on the floor. Slouching is disrespectful, as well as unbusinesslike.

Keep your eyes off papers on the desk and the appointment calendar. Even if it's impossible for you to read anything from where you sit, gazing at these things gives the impression that you're trying to snoop.

Smoking when you make a call. If the person you are visiting invites you to smoke or offers you a cigarette or cigar, accept the invitation if you wish. If he doesn't voluntarily give you permission to smoke, you may ask it or you can refrain from smoking. The latter is the more advisable course to take. It is still considered good form for a woman not to smoke while she is on a business call (particularly when she is jobhunting), even if invited to.

Superior officers visiting a fellow employee need not ask permission to smoke, although many will do so as a courteous gesture.

When the visit is over. Don't prolong a business call; when the time comes to leave, do so without dragging out your leave-taking. Simply thank the person you've been visiting for seeing you or for giving you a few minutes of his time. As you leave the office and the building, it is polite to smile or nod to people you spoke to on the way in, such as the receptionist and the secretary, and to say "thank you."

When you join a conference. If you have been invited to join a meeting or a conference in another office, it isn't necessary to tap or knock on the door before entering.

Visiting a co-worker. If the company is a large one, offices can be some distance apart. In order not to waste your own time, and because it is polite, telephone the person you want to see and make sure he is in his office and available.

Even when you are expected, ask the secretary's permission to enter an executive's office. You can say, "I'm expected. Shall I go right in?" The secretary will either say "Yes, go right ahead," or will announce you first if she knows that is what her employer prefers. Possibly someone else stopped by while you were on your way and it would be impolite for you to go right in and interrupt.

Should you find the secretary away from her desk, knock on the door and open it. Don't knock and wait for someone to come to the door and open it, or even to call, "Come in." That kind of formality is not necessary in a business office.

If the person you are calling on is speaking on the telephone, you can wait outside until he finishes, or, if you know him well enough, take a seat in his office but at some distance from the telephone. If he is dictating, he will probably motion you to sit down and wait while he finishes. Never interrupt him, whether he is dictating or telephoning, unless it is a matter of the most extreme urgency.

If he has someone else in his office he will conclude the conversation if you are expected. If you are not expected, excuse yourself, leave the office and call him later.

Many large offices provide cubicle space for executives and staff members below a certain level. These afford little enough privacy, so if you visit someone in an office of this type and he is on the telephone wait outside until he hangs up. If he has a visitor, tell him you'll drop back later or ask him to call you when he is free. Never be rude enough to walk right in and stand there waiting for the conversation to end.

Conversation in an office of this type must be conducted in quiet tones if everyone else in the area is to remain undisturbed at his work.

·15· Telephone Manners

The way in which a telephone call to a company or an individual is answered by the switchboard operator has an important psychological effect upon the caller. A cheerful voice and inflection, plus careful enunciation, make the caller feel immediately that he is dealing with an efficient, dynamic company. Just the opposite impression is given by the voice that sounds bored and tired and that slurs its greeting so that the caller isn't sure he's made the right connection.

Answering the telephone. You are expected to make a connection promptly when a call comes in. This is more than a form of courtesy; prompt telephone service suggests to callers an efficient company.

The telephone greeting. Give the greeting that conforms with the time of day and then the policy of the company—such as, "Good morning, The Palisades Company," or, "Good afternoon, Bryant 9-8000." Knowing that he has the right number, the caller merely has to ask for the individual he is calling. When your company requires a special greeting on holidays, sound as though you mean it when you answer a call with, "Merry Christmas; Palisades Company."

If you work in a small office—perhaps a one-man company—and answering the telephone is part of your job, give the company name and your own. For instance, "Briarwood, Incorporated—Miss Dunn speaking." You may precede this with "Good morning" or whatever is appropriate to the time of day. But when the name of the company is a long one, it might be best to omit the greeting and just give the company name and your own.

The case of the vanishing operator. Don't annoy callers by doing a disappearing act the minute you answer the call, then coming back on to ask who the caller wants, and disappearing once again just as he is telling you. No one likes to be left talking to himself.

Also, when you ask someone *why* he is calling, listen until you've heard the answer—even though it is a long, complicated story. It only irritates callers if you ask them the reason for the call and then seem not to be paying attention because you are answering other calls.

Frequently company policy requires that the switchboard operator ask the name of the person calling. A very busy switchboard operator is permitted to use the somewhat brusque, "Who's calling?" or "Who's calling, please?"

Should a caller refuse to give his name, the operator may connect him with the secretary of the man he has asked for and leave it to her to find out the reason for the call.

Having the caller hold the line. When the caller gives you the name of the person he wants to speak with, thank him and connect him.

If the line is busy, tell the caller, "Mr. Brown's line is busy. Will you wait?" If he answers in the affirmative, say, "Thank you." Return to him every minute to keep him posted; no one likes to feel he's holding on to a line that's been forgotten. You can say, "Mr. Brown's line is still busy." And don't forget to say, "Thank you" when he says he will continue to wait.

When Mr. Brown hangs up, say, "Mr. Brown's line is free now. Thank you for waiting."

Should a caller decide not to wait when Mr. Brown's line is busy, be sure you get his name, number and extension. Write them down, and say, "Thank you. I will tell Mr. Brown you called."

Handling problem calls. When you plug in a call from someone who seems vague about what he wants or who he wants to speak to, or who is obviously a crank caller, don't cut him off abruptly while you answer other calls. The problem here is not to let a caller of this type take up so much of your time that the switchboard lights up like a Christmas tree while he tells his tale. Listen to him closely to see if you can help him by referring him to a certain department or individual. If you must interrupt him to answer another call, say, "One moment, sir. I have another call to answer." If you decide it is pointless to connect him with anyone, suggest that he write a letter to the company, explaining his problem.

Telephone Etiquette for the Secretary

The manners which you as a secretary display in handling telephone calls are actually an important form of public relations. The courteous secretary whose voice has a smile in it and who sounds genuinely interested in what the caller has to say enhances both her executive's personal image and the company's image. However mysterious it seems, telephone wires carry accurate reflections of your personality and your emotions. The listener knows instantly—no matter how you try to hide the fact—whether you are sincere or are masking irritation; whether you really want to help him, or find the whole problem boring.

Answering the telephone. Answer promptly when the telephone rings. Give your employer's name, followed by your own. For instance, "Mr. Weaver's office—Miss Martin speaking." If the caller is another secretary, saying Mr. Baker of the Corrugated Carton Corporation is calling your employer, say to her, "One moment, please," and then inform your employer of the call. By the time your employer picks up the telephone, Mr. Baker should be on the line.

Screening telephone calls. The whole point in having a secretary answer telephone calls is to save her employer time, possible embarrassment or annoyance, and involvement in unnecessary detail. He doesn't expect you to put every call through to him, but when you do announce a call he would much prefer that you tell him who is calling him and why, rather than saying "There's a call for you on extension 21."

The switchboard operator's somewhat brusque "Who's calling, please?" is not smooth or polite enough for use by the secretary. But even this brusqueness is preferable to the rude "Who is this?" that some secretaries use to find out who is calling.

You should politely ask, "May I tell Mr. Allen who is calling?" Or "May I ask who is calling?" If you don't recognize the name of the caller, you can say, "May I ask what you wish to speak to Mr. Allen about?" Or, "May I know the reason for your call?"

When the caller won't give his name. Most callers will volunteer their names as well as the reason for their call, because they realize the secretary is under orders to find these things out. Every so often, however, someone will insist on withholding this information. You can handle such callers in two ways. You can say, "I'm sorry, but Mr. Allen is not available at the moment. Would you mind calling back?" Or you can simply tell him that you are not permitted to put through a call without first finding out who is calling. If he still insists, suggest that he write for an appointment.

When someone telephones you to arrange an appointment with

your executive, you must find out as much as you can about the man and his business before you set it up. No reasonable person expects a secretary to give him part of a busy executive's day without proof that he has a valid reason for requesting it.

Taking messages. When your employer is not at his desk when a call comes in, you can take the message for later delivery. If he is at a company meeting and the call is important, type out a brief message, bring it in to him and wait for him to tell you whether he will leave the meeting to take the call or would rather call back later.

A pre-printed message form like the following (on colored paper so it won't be overlooked) is handy.

To ______________________

Date ______________ Time ________

WHILE YOU WERE OUT

Mr. ______________________

of ______________________

Phone ______________________

	TELEPHONED		PLEASE CALL HIM
	CALLED TO SEE YOU		WILL CALL AGAIN
	WANTED TO SEE YOU		RUSH

Message ______________________

____

____

____

Operator

Offer to help. When your employer is not available, offer to help the caller in any way that you can. He may only want to check on something you can verify for him. However, be wary of giving out confidential information over the telephone unless you are sure about who is on the other end of the wire. An unscrupulous competitor may not be above describing himself as an employee of the company and asking questions about confidential matters.

Handling complaint calls. A complaint call isn't necessarily a crank or a nuisance call. An individual can have a perfectly sound reason for complaining. Poor handling of telephone calls from people who have a complaint is bad public relations, because it leaves customers or clients with an impression of having been treated rudely. This can prompt them to call the president or some other company officer with a complaint of rudeness on the part of an employee added to the original complaint.

Never interrupt a complaining caller and don't give in to the urge to be defensive because he is complaining. Don't bluster or argue with him. Instead, listen sympathetically and reassure the caller you will help in whatever way you can. Take down notes of what he has to tell you, being sure to get such details as names or invoice numbers right. If you can't answer the problem yourself, tell the caller what you plan to do and why. Be clear and concise. If you have to investigate before you can give the caller a reply, tell him so. But try to give him a specific time for your return call—say tomorrow morning or in an hour. Be sure to make that call, even if someone else takes over the problem. You can explain to the client or customer that the matter is now out of your hands but that someone else (whom you should name if possible) will handle it.

If you must put someone else on the line after listening to the caller's story, don't just hand the telephone over to a fellow employee. Fill him in first, as much as you are able to. This will save the complainant the additional aggravation of having to tell his story all over again.

At the conclusion of your conversation thank the caller for taking the trouble to telephone and inform you of the problem.

Transferring calls. It's annoying—even infuriating—to telephone an organization and have whoever answers the telephone listen for a second or two, then interrupt in order to transfer the call to someone else. One businessman was transferred in this way three different times, ending up, much to his annoyance, with the first person he had talked to. Even the most reasonable caller is bound to feel a little annoyed at being shunted from one person to another—none of whom seem to listen to him.

The polite thing to do is to listen to what the caller has to say and then decide who is the right person to handle the call if you are not. Ask permission of the caller to make the transfer. For instance, after listening to a caller, you might say, "I think Mr. Jones in our advertising department will be able to answer your questions. May I transfer you to him?" Or, "May I transfer you to our Billing Department? I believe Miss Carter, our head bookkeeper, can help you." Or you can ask the caller to hold the line while you make sure the person to whom you plan to transfer the call is actually the right one. If this will take time, offer to call back as soon as you find out who should handle the call. Nothing so annoys a caller as to be transferred from one department to another, each time having to repeat his story.

When you do have occasion to transfer a call, don't jiggle the plunger rapidly to attract the operator's attention. Too rapid a movement of the plunger can fail to light up the light on the switchboard. Depress the plunger slowly and rhythmically and when the operator answers say, politely, "Please give this call to Miss Helen Smith in Accounting."

Wrong numbers. When you receive a call that isn't meant for you, be polite to the person calling. Showing your annoyance is rude and uncalled for; the person making the call has as much right to be annoyed as you have.

Instead of a harsh, "What number do you want?" or "Who do you want?" say, "This is Eldorado 9-9999" or "I believe you want Miss *Helen* Smith in Accounting. I am Miss *Betty* Smith in Advertising. I will have the call transferred."

When you get the operator, don't scold her for giving the call to you; the caller can hear this. Just tell her who the call is for.

When you make a call and find you have a wrong number, don't vent your annoyance on the answering party, who has been inconvenienced as much as you have. When you suspect you have a wrong number, ask "Is this Eldorado 9-9999?" Or "Is this the Latham Company?" When the answer is no, say, "I'm sorry, I have the wrong number," and hang up.

Calls for visitors in your executive's office. When a telephone call for a visitor comes in, ask the caller if you may take a message. If so, type it on a sheet of paper and hand it to the visitor as he leaves. However, if the person making the call says he or she must speak to the visitor at once, go into the office, catch your executive's eye, apologize for the interruption, and tell the guest the name of the person who wants to speak to him. He can either take the call there or ask you to tell the caller that he will call back.

If there are several people in your executive's office, hand the individual being called a typed message that there is a telephone call for him and the question: "Would you like to take the call on my phone?" The visitor can then leave the conference room and take his call without disturbing everyone else.

Holding the line. When your telephone has no "hold" button and you have asked a caller to hold the line until your executive can get back to his desk, be discreet in your remarks while the caller is holding on. Everything you say will be picked up by the telephone.

When you have more than one telephone line. If your employer is talking to someone on one line and a call for him comes in on another, explain that your employer already has a call and ask the second caller if he will wait. If you consider the second call more important than the first, type on a slip of paper the name of the caller and the fact that he is holding the other line and place it before your employer.

Don't put the second call on hold and just leave it there. Keep the waiting caller informed. You can say "Mr. Allen is still on the other wire, but he's just about finished with the call." Or you may want to suggest that Mr. Allen return his call, if the conversation is still going on.

When you have more than two telephone lines, don't let more than one individual wait. Tell any other callers that you will have to ask your employer to call them back.

It is discourteous to keep a caller waiting unnecessarily. As soon as your employer's line is free, put the waiting call through; don't make the caller wait while you file a few papers or ask your employer a question in between calls.

Placing calls. When your executive asks you to place a call for him, you should do it immediately. Dawdling is discourteous, and, in a business office, can have serious consequences. When you are given an unfamiliar number, repeat it to be sure you have it right.

When you reach the secretary of the man you are calling say, "Is Mr. Cartwright there? Mr. Weaver of the Everight Agency is calling." Then put your employer on the line, for the person making the call should never keep the answering party waiting for him.

Personal telephone calls. If your company permits employees to make and receive personal telephone calls, try not to take advantage of this freedom. Tell your friends frankly that they should telephone you at work only when it is urgent that they do so. When you do make or get a personal call keep it brief; the office isn't the place for long conversations about little things, interspersed with giggling. Other people don't find it entertaining, and may even be embarrassed to listen to your personal conversations with friends. Also, no one who wants to ask you a business question should have to wait while you carry on a personal conversation over the telephone.

Try to avoid accepting a personal call while you are in your executive's office. If possible, leave word with whoever answers your telephone when you're not there that you will return any calls that come in for you. If there is no one else who answers your phone and a call does come for you, tell the caller that you are busy and will call back.

When personal calls are forbidden. Many companies, particularly large ones, frown on personal telephone calls and request their employees not to make them. The feeling is that personal telephone calls disrupt office routine and add unnecessary expense to the overhead.

When personal calls are not allowed, a pay telephone is usually provided for emergency and other important calls. Anyone who uses a business telephone to make personal calls where they are forbidden is guilty of the worst kind of rudeness—the kind that implies rules are only for those stupid enough to abide by them.

Telephone Etiquette for the Businessman

Telephone calls and ringing telephone bells are the bane of many a businessman's life. For this reason the handling of telephone calls is usually turned over to the secretary, with the average businessman rarely placing a call himself and receiving only those his secretary thinks he will want to take.

Making and taking your own calls. The latest trend encourages men to answer their own telephones and make their own calls. Those who go along with this idea claim it saves their time and patience to handle telephone calls themselves. Men who oppose this idea claim that it wastes time, rather than saves it, for them to place their own calls and to answer every incoming call, a number of which can be handled by the secretary alone.

Some companies adopted the policy of having men handle their own calls only because so much time was being wasted by secretaries maneuvering to give their employers status by putting him on the phone after the other fellow. Secretaries are not wholly to blame for this childish nonsense. The question of who gets on the telephone first is a matter of foolish pride with many businessmen.

The following simple common-sense rules of courtesy can solve this problem:

> *Inter-office calls.* The junior in rank should be on the line first, regardless of who initiates the call. If the two men are of equal status, the one who is making the call gets on the line first.
>
> *Local calls.* The one making the call should be on the line first.
>
> *Long distance station-to-station calls.* The one making the call should be on first.
>
> *Long distance person-to-person calls.* The one receiving the call should be on the line first.

Announcing oneself. The man who makes his own telephone calls announces himself to a woman as "This is Mr. Jackson of Linwood and Sons." To a man he would say, "This is Jackson of Linwood and Sons."

A woman introducing herself over the telephone says, "This is Miss Terhune of Smithfield Brothers."

Answering the telephone. When a man answers his own telephone he says, "Herrick speaking." Or he may mention his department, such as, "Accounting, Mr. Herrick." Or "Payroll, Herrick speaking."

A woman answering her own telephone says merely "Miss Collins" or "Miss Collins speaking." If she is part of a division or department, she might say, "Advertising, Miss Collins."

Telephoning for an appointment. If you are asked what day and time suit you best, when you ask for an appointment, don't reply that you are free to come any time. That leaves the situation right where it was. The proper answer helps the person with whom you are speaking to arrange a time that best suits you. Say, "I can come in any morning between ten and eleven." Or, "I can come only on Fridays after two o'clock."

Don't use the name of a mutual friend as a means of getting an appointment unless you have asked for—and received—permission to do so.

Receiving a call on another person's telephone. Occasionally an important telephone call will be referred to you when you are visiting in someone else's office. Your host will usually invite you to use his telephone or you may ask permission to use it. If you wish, you may say you will take it outside at the secretary's desk. Try to keep your conversation brief; your associate is waiting to resume your discussion.

If you have no need of a telephone in your work, and calls for you come in on someone's else's telephone, discourage all but important calls. Otherwise you are going to be a nuisance to the individual whose phone you use. Again, keep your conversations brief and to the point. Don't tie up the phone for long periods of time, chatting with your friends.

Making a call on someone else's telephone. If you have occasion to call long distance—perhaps to your home office or factory—from an office you are visiting, reverse the charges or ask the operator for the charges so that you can pay for the call—or at least offer to cover the expense. If the call is a local one it isn't necessary to offer to pay for it, but you should not make a practice of telephoning from someone else's office.

Placing and receiving telephone calls when you have a guest. Anyone who has a visitor in his office should avoid making calls, unless they are pertinent to the business being discussed.

As for incoming calls, when the individual who is your guest is very important, or the subject of your discussion is involved, tell your secretary not to put through any but the most urgent telephone calls. But usually a businessman will continue to take the calls that come in for him even when he has a guest, because the alternative is a long list of calls to be made afterwards. If calls do come in, excuse yourself to your guest and make the telephone conversation as brief as possible. Don't continue your conversation with your guest as you pick up the receiver; finish what you are saying first and then pick it up.

Should a telephone call of extreme importance, or of a private nature, come in while someone from your office is visiting you, courteously ask him to leave: "This is an important call I've been waiting for all morning. Will you excuse me? I'll be in touch with you later."

Telephone interruptions. Should you be interrupted while you are speaking on the telephone—and this should occur only in an extreme emergency—try to finish your call. If you can't, apologize to the person on the other end of the wire and say you will call back.

When a call is disconnected, whoever put in the call should ask the operator to connect him with the number again.

Should you pick up an extension telephone and discover you've interrupted a conversation, quickly say, "I'm sorry," and hang up.

•16• Credit and Collection Etiquette

Courtesy in the personal interview. If you are the credit granter, the main purpose of the credit interview is to gain the necessary information so that credit may be extended to your customer. There is, however, a secondary goal that you must keep in mind; that is, to sell the customer on your credit service. The way to do this is through courteous, friendly and understanding treatment during and after the interview. Never let your desire to gain information make you forget that you are dealing with an individual who is entitled to all the courteous respect you can give. Discussed below are some of the ways that you can make your customer feel at ease during the interview and sell him on your service as well.

· *Making the atmosphere pleasant.* The applicant shouldn't feel that he is on trial. Help him to feel at ease with a pleasant word or two before getting down to business. Ask the routine questions first and save the more searching and intimate ones for later. This gives the applicant a chance to get used to you and it relaxes him so that he can answer the later questions more readily. In asking the questions, avoid the extremes of obvious boredom or rapid fire delivery.

· *Be familiar with the applicant's case.* If you can, review the credit application before the interview. Know the reasons prompting the application. Memorize the applicant's name, so that you can address him correctly without groping.

· *Privacy is a must.* It is good etiquette as well as common sense to hold a credit interview in a private place. As a matter of etiquette, no one should be made to talk about personal matters when there is a chance of being overheard. Common sense tells you that the applicant will be more cooperative in answering questions in an atmosphere of complete privacy than if there are people milling about and a telephone constantly interrupting the conversation.

· *Allow sufficient time for the interview.* Plan your schedule so that you will not have to rush any of your interviews. In trying to win a customer for your business, it is crucial that you make him feel that satisfying his need is the most important thing you have to do. It is discourteous to the applicant and detrimental to your business when you rush an interview. The customer feels that you don't care about him and is rightly offended. In turn, you must depend on his complete and correct answers to conduct your credit dealings successfully. If you rush him, he may not answer your questions in the way you would like.

One word of caution: Don't extend an interview needlessly just because you have some allotted time left. Remember that the object of the interview is to secure credit information. Remember also that the applicant's time is valuable and he may not care to prolong what for him is essentially a difficult situation.

• *Clarity is very important.* One of the easiest ways to cause hurt feelings, strained tempers and to spoil business opportunities is through misunderstandings. It is imperative, therefore, that you make sure all you say is understood by the applicant and that you fully understand everything he says. If there is a chance of misunderstanding, clear it up immediately.

Do not ask vague questions. Make sure that your questions do not suggest answers to the applicant. A question like "Your car is paid for, isn't it?" may tempt the applicant to answer "yes" when he really should say "no." This question could better be phrased in this fashion: "Is your car paid for?"

You must be just as precise in your interview notes as you are in your questions. Never leave anything for later clarification. "Later" may find you calling the customer to get an answer he remembers giving you during the interview. This is bad business manners.

Explaining the terms of the contract. Make sure that you have fully explained the terms of the contract to the applicant and that he understands them completely. This prevents future hard feelings and collection problems. Tell him exactly when payments are due and exactly what the amounts are. Let the customer know his responsibility in fulfilling these terms, and tell him what the consequences can be if he fails (fine for late payment, repossession, and the like). This will often eliminate the need for costly and embarrassing collection letters; most people pay their bills promptly once they know exactly what payment is expected, and when.

Discretion in the choice of credit bureaus. Occasionally when a loan is large and the application and interview information is insufficient to permit credit extension, it is necessary to call upon the services of an outside credit bureau. Or perhaps you do this as a matter of course in your business. Whatever the reason, choose an agency whose activities during the credit check will not embarrass your customer. Make sure that they are discreet throughout their credit check. To find out about credit bureaus and cooperatives in your area, the best source of information is your local Chamber of Commerce.

Don't give the applicant false hopes. When you are in the early part of the credit check, it is inconsiderate to give the applicant too hopeful a picture of his chances of receiving credit. This doesn't mean that you should discourage him by making him believe he has no chance at all. However, by giving the applicant too optimistic an outlook you encourage him to take for granted that he will get credit. He may build his plans around this sure thing and then, if you must deny credit, he may be seriously embarrassed. For the sake of your customers and your business, don't give any applicant false hopes.

When you must deny credit. One of the most difficult things to do is to tell someone that you cannot extend him credit. If handled incorrectly the situation can both perplex and alienate the customer. Here are some ways of handling a credit denial.

- Express sincere regret and tell the customer that you and your company would like to serve him in the future.
- Maintain your composure even if the customer loses his temper. Treat him with respect and speak softly and soon he'll be agreeing with your decision.
- Never, under any circumstances, imply to a customer that it was any weakness in his character that caused the denial of credit.
- Don't divulge your sources of information. If you dealt with a credit bureau and discovered that Joe's Hardware Store had found your applicant slow in payment, it will serve no purpose for you to blame your refusal on that store.

Combining Courtesy with Collection

Essentials of effective collections. The effective collection strategy is planned with two purposes in mind:

1. Getting the customer to pay, and
2. Keeping the customer's goodwill and business.

To accomplish the first purpose without regard to the second is relatively easy, but to accomplish both requires a high degree of skill and diplomacy. Before you can decide on the tone you will use throughout the collection effort, you must consider the different reasons for late payment, and judge your customer accordingly.

Delinquent accounts generally fall into these categories:

1. Customers who overlook bills simply because of negligence or poor business methods.

2. Customers who disregard due dates because of the smallness of the account.

3. Customers who are temporarily slow, but who usually pay on time. They pay on time when the due dates of your bills coincide with their own financial state, and make you wait when these periods do not coincide.

4. Customers who are chronically slow.

5. Customers who are temporarily slow because of current financial difficulties.

6. Customers who are crooked or deliberately fraudulent.

The person who extends credit cannot maintain good will and business if he treats a forgetful customer in the same manner as one who is deliberately fraudulent. For this reason, you should never presume guilt on the part of any of your customers. Approach collection with the idea that your customer has merely been forgetful. If the customer's later actions prove you to be wrong, you can adopt more forceful methods.

In the following sections of this chapter, procedures for collection are presented in the following groups: (1) reminders; (2) letters for the early stages of collection; (3) letters for the middle stages of collection; (4) letters for the late stages of collection; and (5) final action when collection effort has proven futile.

The second bill—a reminder. When it is assumed that the customer's failure to pay is due to forgetfulness or carelessness, it becomes necessary to bring the status of the account to the customer's attention. For this purpose a mild and inoffensive reminder may be used. The best way to tactfully remind a customer of his overdue account is to send him a duplicate bill or statement and reminder. The reminder may be a typewritten or rubber-stamped phrase on the face of the duplicate statement such as:

Past due
Please remit
Account past due. Please remit.
Please give this your attention

Since the reminder stage will be your first collection contact with the customer, it is important that you (1) make it clear that you expect payment and (2) make sure the customer cannot possibly take your request for payment as a slur on his honesty.

When a reminder or two doesn't work, it becomes necessary to take further action, usually in the form of collection letters.

Etiquette in collection letters. Collection letters proceed in a logical sequence from a gentle inquiry as to why the customer has not paid his bill to a demand that he pay promptly. Both courtesy and good business sense say that you should begin by giving the customer the benefit of the doubt. In the early stages of the collection effort you usually don't know the customer's reason for not paying his bill on the due date. If you adopt too demanding a tone in your first letter to a customer who was merely forgetful, you are likely to create hard feelings and lose a valuable customer.

Below are illustrations of the various types of letters used in each stage of collection.

• *Early stage procedure.* In this stage of the collection series you are inquiring why the bill has not been paid. Is there a legitimate reason for the delay? Or is the customer just stalling for as long as he can? Does the fault lie with your goods or services? Are the customer's finances strained?

The following is an example of the kind of letter that can be used at this stage of collection. It can be modified to suit your needs.

Dear Mr. Blank:

Could there be something wrong with the merchandise covered by the above sum? Or perhaps you have a question as to the correctness of the charge?

If so, you have only to tell us about it—on the back of this letter, if you wish—and we shall be glad to go into the matter thoroughly with you.

If everything is satisfactory, but you just haven't got around to sending in your check, surely you will want to forward it to us now.

Very truly yours,

· *Middle stage procedure.* This letter of the collection series will depend largely upon the reply to the first one. If the customer responds with an actual grievance, or if circumstances beyond his control make payment impossible, your reply should take on an appropriately personal character. If there is no reply, however, the customer is most likely trying to avoid payment and needs more urgent prodding. To the customer who is a poor risk you might send a very strong letter. To induce payment from the medium or good risk you might appeal to such motives as pride, duty, justice and fairness, or self-interest.

For example:

Dear Mr. Fisk:

We are going to make an extra appeal for payment of your account, because we must have your full support if our relations with each other are to be profitable to both of us.

You know that we are interested in having your business, and that we are eager to be of assistance to you. However, you place us in a difficult position when you do not pay your bills, because this defeats our efforts to be of service to you.

We feel that you want to work with us, so we have hesitated to put our request for payment in the form of a demand. Yet we do think that we are not unreasonable in asking for and expecting your check at once.

Very truly yours,

· *Late stage procedure.* If the customer has not replied to the reminders and the early and middle stage letters, you can assume that he is unduly negligent, irresponsible, or has no intention of paying. A late stage letter must impress upon him the urgency of the situation and it must demand payment. If his record has been bad, you are not wrong in threatening to bring suit or to turn the account over to a collection agency (see page 144).

But even a demand letter can retain customer good will by restraint in phrasing and an attitude of fairness, and by showing the customer that your firm has been patient and considerate.

You will notice that the example below, while firm in demanding payment, still gives the customer the benefit of the doubt.

> Dear Miss Thompson:
> Thus far in our efforts to collect your account, we have proceeded on the assumption that you have the will to pay and intend to do so.
> We shall not change this attitude unless you force us to. Although you have ignored the letters we have sent you during the past (days, weeks, months), we are still not convinced that you do not intend to pay this bill.
> It would be to your interest to call on us while we are still in this frame of mind—say, within the next three days.
> Very truly yours,

When the threat of force is necessary. You may want to send the delinquent more than one demand letter, forestalling as long as you can the need to threaten to call in a collection agency or a lawyer. You can add a sense of urgency by using registered mail, or by sending a telegram.

When the customer ignores all your requests, then you may have no alternative but to turn the account over to a collection agency or lawyer for further action. But you should continue to consider the customer's side, even though he probably won't be a customer after agency or legal action. Specifically, you should give him fair warning of what you plan to do. Many customers will want to prevent a lawsuit and a warning will prod such people into action.

Caution should be exercised in threatening to resort to force. It is a serious mistake to tell a customer that he is getting his last chance to pay before the account is turned over to an agency or attorney for collection, and then later to write the customer with the same threat.

Below is an example of a courteous but firm letter giving the customer fair warning.

> Dear Mr. Jones:
> Ninety percent of the accounts we collect through attorneys are handled that way because customers will not answer our letters.
> We are forced to sue because friendly requests bring neither payment nor explanations.
> Your account of $....... is long past due. We assume that the amount is correct, for you have never questioned it.

You have disregarded our letters about it; but in spite of that, we really cannot believe that you do not care. There must be some other reason. Perhaps you cannot pay it all. But don't you think in fairness to yourself, as well as to us, that you should mail us a check for all you can spare and tell us frankly how you are situated and when we can expect the rest?

We would prefer not to use the services of our attorney, so before sending the account to him we will wait another ten days for your explanation and check.

Very truly yours,

Discretion in the choice of a collection agency. Just as there are credit bureaus that are a notch above the average, so there are collection agencies that employ more courteous methods than others. Although in all likelihood you will do no future business with the customer once you have turned his account over to an agency for collection, courtesy still demands that you exercise discretion in your choice of a collection agency.

As with credit bureaus, the best source of information on collection agencies operating in your area is your local chamber of commerce.

•17• Business Cards and Public Announcements

Business cards are carried by all business people who call on other companies, clients or customers. Never order them unless you are given permission to do so.

The proper size for a business card. The business card is usually 3½″ x 2″ (larger than a social calling card). However, many companies use cards of a different size or shape, so their card will be distinctive.

What appears on a business card. On the executive level a business card usually has the man's name in the middle of the card and his title and the firm name in the lower left hand corner, either one above the other. Sometimes the address is in the lower right hand corner. If the business is in a large city the street address and city can be used, but the name of the state is left out. Some very prominent men omit their title from the card and simply their name and the name of their company appear on it. A telephone number is rarely put on an executive card.

Executives use a conservative type style, such as Block or Roman —never Script—engraved or printed in black or gray on quality parchment or white pasteboard.

Initials and abbreviations, while not correct on social calling cards, may be used on business cards. However, the word "Company" should be written out unless the abbreviation is part of the registered name of the firm. Unlike a social card, the title "Mr." does not precede the name.

Below the executive level, the firm name is usually imprinted or engraved in the center of the card and the individual's name, title, and department in the lower left corner. The address and possibly the telephone number may be in the lower right hand corner. Occasionally, the man's name and title will be centered and the company name will be in the left-hand corner and the address on the right.

The cards used by salesmen, or to advertise a company, frequently carry a trademark or emblem or an eye-catching design. The printing or engraving may be done partly in color. A calendar or advertising matter often appears on the back of the card. The telephone number is always on a card of this type. Doctors and dentists frequently put their office hours on their cards.

A woman's business card. The business cards used by a woman are the same as a man's, with the exception that her title—Miss or Mrs.—precedes her name. To be perfectly correct, a married woman should never use "Mrs." in conjunction with her given—or first—name. For instance, if Joan Banks is vice president of an advertising agency and is married to Robert Banks, the laws of etiquette require that she be Mrs. Robert Banks, never Mrs. Joan Banks. This poses a problem—although a somewhat artificial one—for a career woman who uses her married name. If she insists on being absolutely correct, the only thing to do is to use her maiden name in business—say Miss Joan Thomas—and be Mrs. Robert Banks the rest of the time. She can use plain Joan Banks on a business card, but this leaves anyone she calls on in the dark as to whether she is to be called "Miss" or "Mrs."

A woman doctor uses either her maiden name or her married name combined with her first name and her title. For instance, when Dr. Jane Harrington marries Frank Smith she does not become Dr. Frank Smith, but she may call herself Dr. Jane Smith. On her business cards she can be either Jane Harrington, M.D. or Jane Smith, M.D.

Sending a business card with a gift. Business cards should not be used for enclosure with a gift, even though the gift is going to a client or customer. The giving of a gift is a social gesture, and therefore a social card should be enclosed. This rule is honored more in the breach than in the observance. However, presidents or board chairmen of large companies often have a special card printed for enclosure with Christmas gifts. It mentions the company name and the name of the executive sending the gift, but in no way resembles a business card.

The exception is the card enclosed with a gift sent to a new business. In this instance a business card is perfectly correct.

Public announcements. Newspaper space is often taken to make formal announcement of some occurrence a company considers of unusual importance and wide interest.

Written in a style as formal as a social engagement or wedding announcement, these notices appear in regular advertising space. Announcements of this type serve as notification to the general public of such information as a company's new address or the address of a newly opened branch office; a change in the company name; the addition of a partner or other executive officer to the staff; the death or retirement of a top executive, and so on.

The following are examples of special announcements of different kinds (for announcements of the death of an important executive, see page 84):

We are pleased to announce that

on April 20, 19__

we will occupy the 13th floor

of 100 Broadway, N.Y.C.

Our friends and business associates

are cordially invited to visit our

new and larger offices.

JAMES & ALLEN

Members: New York Stock Exchange
American Stock Exchange

We announce the retirement of

MR. SIMON M. BLOOM

as a General Partner of our firm

BLOOM & CO.

April 20, 19__

PIERPONT SMITH & CO., INC.

announces that it has become

a Member Corporation of

the New York Stock Exchange

April 20, 19__

WE ARE PLEASED TO ANNOUNCE

THE FORMATION OF

TREVOR & CO.

BARTON TREVOR
JOHN Q. MACKENZIE

48 Powell Street

April 20, 19__ BArtlet 6-2222

ON THIS, OUR TWENTY-FIFTH ANNIVERSARY, WE WISH TO THANK OUR MANY FRIENDS FOR THEIR CONTINUED EVIDENCE OF CONFIDENCE.

THE JOHN B. POSNER COMPANY, INC.
506 Eastern Causeway Seattle, Wash.

·18· Charitable Donations

Businesses of every kind are under great pressure to cooperate in the hundreds of annual drives to raise funds for various causes. Virtually all large companies set aside money for this purpose—usually a fixed percentage of the net profits. Executives receive letters from groups of every description, asking for financial support. Some try to give a small amount to each solicitor; others give larger amounts to a carefully selected number of organizations in which they take a deep interest. Many companies urge their employees to support accredited charitable organizations, either through local community drives or collections in the office or plant.

Evaluating requests. A committee of evalution serves a good purpose when a company receives many requests for donations or for permission to solicit funds among its employees. Good choices for such a committee are the company treasurer, the assistant to the president, and the public relations officer. All requests for financial contributions are turned over to this committee, which should have complete responsibility for approving or turning down the pleas.

Major considerations in deciding which organizations to support are these:

1. The purpose of the organization making the plea.
2. Its leadership.
3. The reputation of the organization and its leadership.
4. What the organization has accomplished in its field.
5. What benefits the community in which your business is located derives from the organization.

Investigate when you are doubtful. A great many frauds are disguised as charity drives, and no one need feel guilty if he investigates a group that is soliciting money or if, for reasons he considers sound, he turns down a request for a donation.

Refusing a request. Whatever the reason for refusing a plea for a donation or permission to solicit among your employees, make the refusal a courteous one.

When a request is obviously part of a mass mailing, no reply need be made if you do not wish to contribute. But should the request be in the form of a personal letter, then a reply is necessary, either to accompany a check or to refuse the request.

Here are sample letters of refusal:

Dear Mr. Downing:

Your letter in behalf of the Save the World Federation reached me this morning. As you know, I am vitally interested in the work this group is doing, and want very much to support it.

However, this year I have pledged to our community hospital all of the money I would ordinarily give to several organizations. For the present, then, I can give only a token contribution to the Federation, and enclose a check for $10.

Next year I will be in a position to give the organization firmer financial support, so please keep me in mind. In the meantime, I wish you success in this year's drive.

Sincerely,

Dear Mr. Morton:

Your letter of May 21 requests permission to solicit our employees during your fund-raising campaign for the Society for the Aid of the Underprivileged.

We have respect for your cause and for the work you have been doing over the past several years, but it is the policy of our company not to permit collections to be made on the premises for any cause, however worthwhile. Requests of this nature are so frequent that despite their individual merit we have had to deny them categorically.

Very truly yours,

Dear Mr. Scott:

Your letter of November 10, requesting a contribution for the League for Human Understanding, was referred to our committee which evaluates solicitations for funds.

I regret to inform you that the report of the committee is that the League for Human Understanding is not eligible under present company policy to be a recipient of company funds.

Very truly yours,

Coin boxes and posters. A company will frequently permit coin boxes or posters in behalf of a fund drive to be put up in its building. They are best confined to the company cafeteria or lounges and should not be placed in public corridors or reception rooms.

Personal solicitations. A company is well advised to forbid receptionists or secretaries to allow an unknown individual to solicit funds. All such solicitors should be required to submit to the president of the company a written request for permission to solicit employees.

Mixing charity with business. It is not good form to use a business relationship as an entering wedge for a plea in behalf of a favorite charity. No matter how well-meaning the businessman, or how worthy the cause he espouses, for him to pressure a business acquaintance into contributing to his favorite charity is rude; it amounts to blackmail. Also, unless authorized to do so, an employee should never solicit for a charity or cause on company stationery.

Solicitations by employees. When it comes to solicitations or the sale of tickets for employees' pet projects, management usually examines each request carefully and gives permission to particularly worthwhile projects. Should you have occasion to request such a favor, accept management's ruling with good grace. If you are refused permission, don't sneak tickets to your co-workers in the washroom or cafeteria. It would be a display of very poor manners for you to try and circumvent such a ruling.

•19• Etiquette for Sales and Service Personnel

Unfortunately, a lot of people in service and sales work are afraid that being polite, kind, and helpful makes them seem inferior to those they serve, so they adopt a haughty, overbearing manner. Good manners never make anyone inferior; in fact, they are the only way to combat effectively the petty irritations inherent in work with the public at large.

General Rules if You Sell or Serve

Politeness heads the list. Politeness is the most important requirement for a sales or service career—and that means a politeness so ingrained, so genuine, that it is impervious to the rude and boorish individuals who frequently take advantage of the discipline under which sales and service people work.

When politeness is combined with enthusiasm and sincerity, success in sales and service jobs is assured.

Personal appearance. Cleanliness, neatness and simplicity of apparel are essential in presenting an attractive picture to the public. Women should avoid elaborate hairdos, heavy makeup and strong perfume; hands and nails should look well cared for, and no nail polish at all is better than chipped nail polish. Shoes should be conservatively styled. Avoid wearing flats and spike heels as well as open toes and open backs. Keep jewelry to a minimum. Clothes of conservative color and cut are advisable. If you wear a uniform, wear a slip under nylon or other sheer fabrics. And be sure the uniform is neatly pressed and in good condition. Unless you are in real danger of catching a cold, don't wear an odd sweater or jacket over your dress or uniform.

Men in sales or service work should wear suits of dark color and conservative cut. Shirts and handkerchiefs should be white and clean; socks should match the suit or tie in hue. Keep shoes well polished and don't let them run down at the heels. Uniforms should be clean and in good repair.

Immaculate hands, nails and hair also are important aspects of grooming when a man deals with the public.

Personal habits. Eating, drinking, chewing gum or smoking are prohibited while you are working. Should you sneeze or need to blow your nose, do so as discreetly as you can and, if possible, out of sight of the public. Avoid touching your hair and face while on duty. Comb your hair only in private.

Brush your teeth after meals whenever possible, and use a good mouth wash. Clean breath is of the utmost importance when your work involves close contact with others.

Try to remember names. It's a gracious gesture to address by name people you see frequently. It is also good business for anyone dealing with the public to make every effort to remember the names of customers.

Personal remarks. Use discretion in speaking to customers. Personal remarks in a derogatory vein are taboo. A pleasant or flattering remark is permissible, but it is best to confine your remarks to whatever is necessary to present the service or merchandise you have to offer.

Responsibility for inside information. People in service jobs often can't help acquiring confidential information about the people they deal with or the company they work for. It is in the worst possible taste to take advantage of such knowledge and spread gossip based on it.

Bank and hospital employees in particular are in a position to know intimate facts concerning individuals their institutions serve.

Divulging personal and confidential information about customers can cause irreparable harm to a bank or hospital's reputation. Develop the habit of forgetting anything you learn about the personal business of customers. There are people brash enough to question you. Just pay no attention to them or, if you want to reply, smilingly say that if there are any secrets to be discovered where you work you haven't yet come across them.

Etiquette for Retail Sales Personnel

Is the customer always right? Retail stores certainly work on this theory. It is a good idea for anyone who works with the general public to assume that the average person is honest and will only seek adjustment or redress when compelled to. Naturally, the customer won't always be right, but you should always behave towards him as though he were. Even when the customer is wrong to the point of absurdity, you should refrain from arguing and keep your personal feelings to yourself, even though it is difficult.

Handling the dissatisfied customer. Each and every complaint, whether made in person or by letter or over the telephone, should be carefully investigated. The individual who handles complaints must be solicitous and anxious to correct any error. He must strive to maintain good will even when he feels the complaint is unwarranted or unjustified. When the complaint is a legitimate one, the adjustment should be made in accordance with the customer's request—whether it be for a cash refund, replacement, or credit—unless it is impossible.

High pressure tactics. Pressure persuades some people to purchase things they might otherwise do without. However, if steady customers are what you want, it's best to avoid high pressure selling; people who have been induced to purchase things they don't really want don't often return.

Customers don't like to wait. Even if you are waiting on someone, don't let another customer just stand there. At least say, "I'll be with you in just a moment." Or ask if there is anything you can show her while she is waiting.

One of the most frequently heard complaints from shoppers—both male and female—is that if sales people are talking together when they approach a counter or department they are made to wait until the conversation is brought to a close. It is the height of rudeness not to offer to help a customer immediately. No matter how fascinating the gossip, excuse yourself and give your attention to the customer.

Etiquette for Service Personnel

Good tips are the direct result of good service performed willingly and politely. Of course there are always a few individuals who will accept a great deal in the way of service and callously disregard the fact that the person giving it relies on tips for a living. In general, though, doormen, waiters and waitresses, bellmen, maids—all those who rely on tips—can earn more by greeting the people they serve in a friendly manner, anticipating their needs whenever possible, and being cheerful and respectful. Just put yourself in the customer's place, and you'll understand why.

Etiquette for Hospital Employees

Patient comfort and well-being should be the prime consideration of non-professional hospital employees. The public—patients or visitors—is quick to judge a hospital by the help it employs and to note whether uniforms are neat and clean and the service kind and efficient.

Ethical considerations. Non-professional employees must learn to cooperate with the hospital's professional staff. Critical opinions of doctors and nurses or of medical treatment must never be expressed to patients or fellow workers or to friends outside the hospital.

Never discuss their illnesses with patients and don't tell them how your grandmother used to treat a sickness like theirs, or what you think really ails them, or when you think they'll recover.

Mail and telephone calls. Employees who live in may receive mail at the hospital, but non-resident employees should not receive mail there. Department telephones are for hospital business and emergency calls and should never be used for personal calls.

Using the elevator. Step aside graciously when the elevator is needed for patients or by the medical staff; they have priority.

Tips and gifts. Hospital employees should not accept tips or gifts from patients or from their family and friends.

Personal appearance. Clean uniforms and the practice of personal hygiene as described earlier are mandatory requirements for hospital personnel. Excessive makeup, earrings, gaudy jewelry—poor taste at any time—are totally unacceptable when you wear a uniform.

Duty and behavior. Hospital hours of duty are strictly enforced and no matter what emergency arises your shift of duty must be covered at all times. Loud talking or laughing is out of place where people lie ill. Smoking is prohibited except in specified areas.

Etiquette for Bank Employees

Attitude toward customers. Bank employees who meet the public are in effect doing public relations work on behalf of the bank. The friendlier the greeting and the service, the more good will towards the institution is felt by the customer. Make every effort to call steady customers by name. Never argue when a question of accuracy is raised; have it checked and give the answer as graciously as possible.

Handling requests for information. All requests for information about accounts or records should be referred to officers or department heads. No matter how trivial the question, don't give answers over the telephone if you don't recognize the caller's voice. Unless you are in a position of some authority, it is wiser for you not to answer questions in regard to bank policy. Refer the questioner to an official of the bank.

Personal visitors. Naturally, friends will stop to say hello while they're in the bank on business, but never invite them, or accede to their requests to be invited, behind the scenes.

Your personal life. Anyone who works in a bank will learn to be prudent about certain aspects of his or her personal life. Personal debts are frowned upon, for one thing; speeches and written articles usually must be cleared by a bank official, and permission must be granted to anyone wishing to run for office.

Safety regulations. Smoking at work is forbidden by banks for the simple reason that everyone is working near or handling paper currency, securities, and other valuable papers. One slight accident could cause damage totaling thousands or millions of dollars. Smoking is confined to restricted areas such as lounges.

Rules about locking up or putting things away at closing time also must be strictly adhered to. An attitude of carelessness in a bank is as out of place as a "Please help yourself" sign would be over the cash drawers.

• Part 3 • Traveling on Business

•20• Planning the Business Trip

Courtesy and trip planning. Many American businessmen do a great deal of traveling as part of their job. Others travel only occasionally. In neither case is a business trip a spur-of-the-moment affair; it must be planned if it is to be successful.

The planner may be the businessman or businesswoman who will be the traveler, but very often it is a secretary or traffic manager who handles the details of planning. It is in making arrangements for someone else that courtesy and etiquette come into play. That is why this chapter is written for the person who plans a trip for another. But many of the hints and suggestions given here will be helpful to the person planning his own trip.

Basically, there are two kinds of travelers. One kind travels to see specific people and companies; he makes appointments, then lays out an itinerary that will get him to those appointments. The other kind of traveler, who is apt to spend more time on the road, is the area or territory traveler. He tends to plan his route first, then make appointments according to the route.

When you plan a trip, no matter how long or short, you can save the traveler's time and temper if you get all necessary information before you try to get reservations. Have the traveler tell you the departure time, cities to be visited and when he must arrive there to keep any appointment he might have, length of stay at each place.

Learn the personal likes and dislikes of the traveler in regard to hotels, modes of travel, and so on.

Arranging an Itinerary

It is an absolute "must" that you set up a written itinerary, or trip plan. If you don't you will find that information on train, plane and bus schedules will get lost in the shuffle.

Keeping track of itinerary plans. Set up a work sheet with plenty of room for alternate methods of travel. Include the following columns:

- Date
- Destination
- Method of transportation (make this a wide column)
- Departure time
- Time of arrival

Start by noting the date and destination for the first lap of the trip. If for some reason the traveler does not give you instructions about the method of transportation he wants, get information on both plane and train accommodations. This will take a little more time than if you knew how he planned to travel, but it may save you both aggravation and time later, when you are making final arrangements. Don't forget to get both arrival and departure times in every case.

► **Note.** Also be sure to include which airport or railroad station the plane or train leaves from (and arrives at) in your "method of transportation" column. The traveler will be quite unhappy waiting at East Terminal while his train pulls out of West Station.

Little things mean a lot. Below are some points that may seem elementary but are easy to overlook in the task of getting information together. These are the "little things" that can make a business trip a pleasure instead of a chore.

- Remember that there is a difference in time zones. Be sure that everyone concerned with the trip is talking about the same time.
- Include in your list (if you know it) the amount of time that the traveler will need to get from the airport or railway station to his appointment. It is disconcerting for a traveler to reach his city of destination at 1:50 when he has an appointment on the other side of town for 2:00 o'clock.
- Find out if he can have lunch or dinner en route. If not, allow time for him to eat before his appointment.

A sample itinerary. Now that you have planned the itinerary and made the necessary arrangements, type up the final itinerary in the form shown below:

ITINERARY FOR WARREN WILSON

Feb. 28	Leave New York, Grand Central Sta.	NY Central RR	6:00 pm EST	
Feb. 29	Arrive Chicago, LaSalle St.		9:00 am CST	Allerton Hotel
	Leave Chicago, LaSalle St.	Rock Island RR	10:25 pm	
Mar. 1	Arrive Des Moines, Rock Island Sta.		5:40 am	Franklin Hotel
Mar. 2	Leave Des Moines, Rock Island Sta.	Rock Island RR	8:05 pm	
Mar. 3	Arrive Denver, Union Sta.		8:25 am MST	Cosmopolitan Hotel
Mar. 5	Leave Denver, Union Sta.	Union Pacific RR	6:15 pm	
Mar. 6	Arrive Kansas City, Union Sta.		6:50 am CST	Town House
Mar. 7	Leave Kansas City, Union Sta.	Santa Fe RR	8:30 am	
	Arrive Oklahoma City, Santa Fe Sta. Note: No Pullman accommodation on this train		6:15 pm	Biltmore Hotel
Mar. 8	Leave Oklahoma City, Santa Fe Sta.	Santa Fe RR	6:30 pm	
	Arrive Fort Worth, Union Sta. Note: No Pullman accommodation on this train		10:55 pm	Texas Hotel
Mar. 9	Leave Fort Worth	American Airlines	6:20 am	
	Arrive New York, La Guardia airport Air Coach Flt. 650T		3:58 pm EST	Home

Extra copies of the itinerary should go to the traveler's family and to co-workers who may need to know how to reach him.

Making Reservations

Pointers on flying. If a businessman is pressed for time and cost is not a major factor, he can get aboard a first class jet and arrive swiftly, comfortable and well-fed. If both time and money are a consideration, he can go jet economy class, which is actually cheaper on many commuter runs than propeller first class. If the only consideration is keeping expenses to a minimum, the traveler can fly propeller economy class.

First class jet and economy jet seats can be on the same plane, as can first and economy class propeller accommodations. On first class flights, either by jet or propeller aircraft, excellent meals are served. The meals on economy flights, although usually of fine quality, consist of sandwiches and beverages. Some airlines, however, are inaugurating a "one class" schedule. That is, the traveler will be able to get first class service and meals at prices only slightly higher than those for economy class.

Certain airlines have a service between major cities whereby the traveler can simply go to the airport and get aboard the plane. He pays his fare on the plane, eliminating bothersome reservation procedures.

The traveler is the one who must choose the type of accommodations he will want. You can help him by giving him all the information possible on airline services so that he can make an intelligent choice.

You might find the *Official Airline Guide,* published by American Aviation Publications, Inc., 209 W. Jackson Boulevard, Chicago, Illinois 60606, helpful. The book is an alphabetical listing of the cities in the United States and its possessions, and Canada. It tells of the airlines servicing each city, and gives information on car rental and air taxi services there.

Making a plane reservation. After the traveler decides which airline he will use, you should get that line's timetable. Remember, however, that the timetable is subject to change. You should check all times carefully when making the reservation.

When placing reservations, you phone the reservations desk of the individual airline. Make sure that you get the name of the reservations clerk so that you can make any further arrangements through that person. This will save your traveler time, because it will get his reservations handled much more quickly and efficiently. It also eliminates that "I'm sorry, but I think Miss Jones can help you" problem.

A typical conversation might go something like this:

> "Good Morning. This is Mr. Doe of the Wilson Company. I would like to make reservations for Mr. Paul Houts of this company on American Airlines flight No. 6 from New York to Los Angeles, economy class, at 10:00 a.m. on July 15. Is space available?"
>
> "Yes, Mr. Doe, we have economy class space available on flight 6 on July 15, but that flight leaves at 10:35 a.m."
>
> "That will be satisfactory. When does the plane arrive in Los Angeles?"
>
> "It gets into Los Angeles at 1:30 p.m., Pacific Standard Time. It's a non-stop jet flight."
>
> "Thank you very much. Please book Mr. Houts on that flight. May I have your name in case any question arises?"
>
> "Surely. Just ask for Jon LeCompte at the reservations desk. And now let me take down complete information on Mr. Houts."
>
> "The reservation is for Mr. Paul Houts, the Wilson Company, 666 Fifth Avenue, New York City. The phone number of the company is WA-6-2233, and Mr. Houts's home phone number is HA-7-7019."
>
> "Thank you very much, Mr. Doe. I have Mr. Houts booked on that flight."

It is not always possible to get just the flight you want. This is no reason to be disheartened. Tell the reservations clerk to put your traveler on the waiting list for the flight he wants. Then if reservations become available you will be notified. While you are waiting you can phone any of the other airlines to see if they can accommodate your traveler. If after this you are still unable to get the reservation, consult the reservations clerk, who can, in most cases, suggest a suitable alternative.

► **Note.** As soon as you receive confirmation from one airline, cancel any other arrangements you may have pending for some other flight. This will help you keep the good will of the people you deal with at the airlines. It will also show consideration for other people who may be on the waiting list for that flight. Wouldn't it make you happy if someone would cancel just in time for you to get the seat you want for your traveler?

Unless the traveler has an account with the airline, you or he will have to pay for the tickets when they are picked up. Many airlines have credit plans that make it possible to travel now and be billed later. Check with the airline you decide to use if your traveler wants to do business on a charge basis.

Be sure to confirm reservations. One last word about air travel reservations: It is necessary to re-confirm plane reservations for each lap of the trip, except for the initial point of departure. The traveler should do this in each city on his itinerary. You confirm, or re-confirm, a reservation simply by calling up the airline ticket office and telling them that you would like to confirm a reservation. It is best to ask for the person at the reservations desk that you spoke to when you first made the reservation. Make sure that you give the clerk all information as to flight number, date, destination, and the like.

Reservations must be confirmed at least six hours before flight time on domestic flights. On international flights, reservations must be confirmed twenty-four hours before flight time. You are thoughtful if you remind the traveler of this just before departure.

Pointers on train travel. In order to give the traveler complete information on rail reservations and accommodations, you should know just what is available. The various types of Pullman accommodations are listed below:

· *Upper or lower berth:* A single bed, with a space provided for personal articles. Toilet facilities are located at one end of the car.

· *Roomette:* A private room, usually for one person, with a bed folding into the wall and with a sofa seat for daytime use. Toilet facilities are in the same room.

· *Bedroom:* A private room with a lower and upper berth. The lower serves as a sofa for daytime use. Toilet facilities are in the same room.

· *Compartment:* A private room with lower and upper berth. Toilet facilities are in the same room.

· *Drawing room:* A private room with lower and upper berth, and a sofa that can be converted into an additional lower berth. There is a private toilet adjoining.

Not all overnight trains have all of the above accommodations. Some day commuter trains have none of them. Most of the timetables for the various lines list the accommodations available. If the information you want isn't in the timetable, you can get it either from the reservations desk of the railway or from a travel agency. Find out, too, whether the train has a diner or club car, observation car, and so on. By telling the traveler these facts you smooth his way toward a more pleasurable trip.

Making a train reservation. When you are ready to make the reservation you will find that the procedure is similar to that of making plane reservations. You should have a concrete idea of what you want before you phone. Note that railroads will not make reservations for the entire trip if it is broken by plane travel; airlines, on the other hand, will handle plane reservations all the way through, despite interruptions.

You can find all the schedules and timetables for all railroad and steamship lines in the United States, Canada, Mexico, and Puerto Rico in the *Official Guide of the Railways.* The *Guide* is published by the National Railway Publications Company, New York. Single copies can be purchased and the publication can also be obtained by subscription. Included in this publication is information such as accommodations offered by the different lines, mileage between stations, maps of the roads, and so on.

Another source of information is the individual line itself. You can either telephone or call at the company's offices personally.

When you are ready to make the reservations, it is best if you become acquainted with the "passenger representative" of the railroad. If you do, you will have an advantage in that you can deal with the same person every time you have to call. If you don't know the passenger representative, call the reservations desk.

It is considerate to give the person you are talking to complete and precise information on departure point and destination, time, train number and accommodations desired. If what you want is not available, this enables him to suggest an alternative.

If your traveler wants to do business with the railroad on a charge basis, accounts based on his personal credit rating are available. These accounts work in a manner similar to that of the airline accounts. If the traveler has no account, you or he will have to pay for the tickets when they are picked up.

Whoever picks up the tickets should check them carefully. Check for time, date, destination, train number, railway station, and the like.

Traveling by automobile. If the business trip is fairly short, the traveler may want to go by automobile. Being a member of the American Automobile Association will be a great help if this is the case. Aside from their emergency road service, they will prepare a special "Triptik," which is a detailed, up-to-the-minute strip map of the entire trip. Also provided with this service is a list of recommended hotels, motels and AAA service stations along the route.

The AAA will also help its members obtain advance hotel and resort accommodations.

If your traveler is not a member of the AAA, you can get all the necessary road maps at any local gas station.

The traveler may want to leave his own car at home and rent one for the trip. If this is the case, you can get in touch with a car rental firm in your area. There is a service charge plus a mileage charge ranging from around six to fifteen cents a mile. You can leave the car at any of the branch offices of the firm in any city. The cars are covered by accident insurance, which protects the driver as wall as the renting firm. Car rental is a very convenient service, but it can be expensive.

Making hotel reservations. Never wait until the last minute to make hotel reservations. Begin the job as soon as the travel arrangements are decided. It sometimes takes a long time to get the travel plans just right, but you can begin making hotel reservations as soon as you know the traveler's destination and approximate time of arrival.

Most communities have a local hotel association you can phone for information. The association is usually happy to supply you with the names of reliable hotels.

You can get a wealth of information from the *Hotel Red Book,* issued annually in June and published by the American Hotel Association Directory Corporation, 221 West 57th Street, New York, New York. This book lists hotels by state and city, indicates the number of rooms, rates, and whether the hotel is on the American plan where rates include meals or European plan, where they don't. It also gives the telephone and teletype numbers for each hotel, and tells whether or not the hotel belongs to a chain.

Another source of information is *Leahy's Hotel Guide and Travel Atlas of the United States, Canada, and Mexico,* published by the American Hotel Register Company, in Chicago.

If you don't have access to any of these sources, you might write to the Chamber of Commerce in the city of destination, asking for the names of recommended hotels, but remember that it takes quite a while for correspondence to travel back and forth. You will need a lot of time to write first to a Chamber of Commerce and then, after receiving a reply, to a hotel. Perhaps there is no vacancy at the time the traveler needs a room. You would then have to write to some other hotel. Usually you won't have time enough for this exchange of correspondence.

If the traveler is going by automobile, you can get information on places to stay from *Lodging for a Night,* a book published by Duncan Hines, Inc., New York. This book lists good hotels, inns, motels and overnight guest houses.

How reservations can be made. Below are mentioned some of the ways you can go about making hotel reservations:

1. You can call the hotel directly. Some hotels list their numbers in the directories of distant cities to make it easier for customers to call and make reservations.

2. Some hotels, particularly in large cities, have a service whereby you can phone the hotel in your city and have reservations made for you at the hotel in the city of destination. This service, of course, applies only to hotels in the same chain. If this service is available, you receive your confirmation from the hotel in your own city. You can get the information from the *Hotel Red Book.*

3. You can make the reservation by letter. Naturally, there must be enough time for an exchange of correspondence before the traveler is to leave on his trip.

The letter on the following page asking for a hotel reservation is short and to the point, but gives all necessary information.

March 19, 19__

Sherman Square Hotel
70th Street and Broadway
New York, New York

Gentlemen:

Please reserve a single room with bath for Mr. John Rafferty, beginning Friday night, April 17. Mr. Rafferty plans to leave the afternoon of April 20 and would appreciate knowing your check-out time.

Since Mr. Rafferty will not reach New York until Friday night, please hold the room for late arrival.

Please confirm this reservation as soon as possible.

Yours very truly,
Henry Roe

jb

4. If your firm has a teletype machine and the hotel chosen also uses this service (you can find out from the *Hotel Red Book*), send a teletype message.

5. If you don't have too much time to make reservations, send a night letter to the hotel. You might say something like this:

> Please wire collect confirmation single room with bath for John Rafferty April seventeenth through twentieth. Hold for late arrival. Advise checkout time.

6. You can make reservations through the Hotel Reservation Service of Western Union. Phone your nearest Western Union office and give the Reservation Service the destination, arrival date and time, length of stay, room requirements, and the hotel preferred. They will take it from there. They will handle anything from a single-city trip to a complete travel itinerary, for business or pleasure.

7. The traveler may have to leave on very short notice. When this happens, try Western Union's "Reserve and Hold" service. All arrangements are made while the traveler is en route. When he arrives, he calls the Western Union Reservation Desk to get details of his reservation. There is a charge for this service, but when time is short, the traveler will be grateful indeed if you can get him his reservations quickly.

No matter what method you use to make a reservation:

- Give the traveler's name and address
- Explain the type of accommodation desired
- Give the date of arrival
- Indicate the approximate time of day the traveler will arrive
- Mention the probable departure date
- Ask what the hotel check-out time is (it may conflict with the traveler's appointments)
- If the traveler will arrive in the late evening, mention the fact that the room is to be held for late arrival.

Always get written or wired confirmation of a hotel reservation. If some mistake has occurred at the reservation desk of the hotel (and that is possible even in the best-run hotels) the traveler will not have a leg to stand on without the confirmation. He will at least be able to put up a good argument if you have provided him with the confirming letter or wire. If you have been thoughtful enough to do this, the hotel will be obliged to find a spot for him.

If the traveler is going by car, he may want to make reservations at motels along his route. Various independently owned motels have formed associations that aid you in making reservations. You simply go in person to the association motel nearest you and request reservations at one of the other associated motels. The clerk will then either phone or send a teletype message to the motel and have them reserve rooms. You then pay him the price of the room and he gives you a ticket which the traveler presents to the motel clerk where his rooms are reserved. Once the traveler reaches his first stop, he can have the clerk there phone ahead to make his next reservation. There is usually no charge for this reservation service.

Canceling reservations. In order to save the traveler's time and money there are certain procedures you should follow when it becomes necessary to cancel reservations. Below you will find the correct ways of canceling reservations and also how to get refunds on unused tickets or deposits for the traveler.

Occasionally a traveler may change his plans en route. If he does, he probably will have to handle the cancellations himself. The traveler should always try to give as much advance written notice as possible to the airline or railroad of any cancellation.

Airlines will usually make refunds en route, and the traveler can cash in his unused tickets at the airline office in the city where he happens to be.

If your traveler brings his unused airlines tickets back with him, return them to the airline at the point of purchase, or to the Refund Accounting Department address shown in the *Official Airline Guide,* with a short covering letter. Mention the date, city of departure and destination, ticket number, and the cost.

Your letter might read:

May 6, 19__

Manager, Passenger Refund Accounting
American Airlines, Inc.
910 South Boston
Tulsa, Oklahoma

Dear Sir:

Re: Ticket No. 101-15-464
New York City to Phoenix
Flight No. 507

The above ticket was issued to Mr. John Rafferty of this company for use on April 17.

Unfortunately Mr. Rafferty was forced to cancel his reservation and would now like a refund on the ticket. The fare paid for the ticket was $100.30.

Please make the check payable to John Rafferty. The ticket is enclosed.

Sincerely,
Robert J. Roe

mlh

Encl.

The carbon of this letter will give you a record of all the pertinent information you should need to follow up later if there is some delay or error in the refund. It is important that you remember, however, to expect some delay in refund if the tickets were paid for by check. When payment has been made in cash, an immediate refund can be obtained by presenting the tickets at the ticket office. Or the amount of the refund can be credited to the account of an air travel card holder.

Pullman refunds cannot be obtained en route. For refunds, send the unused tickets to: The Pullman Company, Passenger Department, 79 East Adams Street, Chicago 3, Illinois.

When you wish to cancel a hotel reservation, write the hotel a letter of cancellation if there is time. This is the polite thing to do, especially when you have requested the room be held for late arrival.

When a hotel has requested a deposit in advance, as some of the smaller hotels do, try to have your deposit returned. You may be successful if the cancellation is made in sufficient time before the intended arrival date.

Never cancel a hotel reservation by telegram. Telegrams are expensive and you usually have time to send a letter. Besides, unless you requested that the room be held for late arrival, and the traveler was expected during the day, the hotel will usually automatically cancel the reservation when he doesn't show up.

To cancel motel reservations that have been made in advance, usually it is necessary to notify the motel by 6:00 p.m. on the day of your intended arrival. To obtain your refund you can either go to the motel, or, if this is impossible, give the motel your name and address and have them send you a check. Although 6:00 p.m. is usually the latest time for cancellation, it is considerate to give the motel as much advance notice of cancellation as you possibly can.

Using the services of a travel agency. The easiest method of obtaining reservations, either for domestic or foreign travel, is through the services of a travel agency.

If you have had no previous contact with an agency, obtain a list of qualified travel agents from The American Society of Travel Agents, Inc., 501 Fifth Avenue, New York, New York.

You can make the agent's job simpler by giving him complete information on what you want. Tell him the traveler's name, his business and home phone numbers, and detailed information on dates, times of arrival and departure at each city, and the type of transportation preferred.

As far as expense is concerned, there is no charge for obtaining airline or hotel reservations because the agency receives a commission from the airline or hotel. There *is* a charge for obtaining rail reservations, unless they are part of a "package" deal; that is, a prearranged package tour. The service is excellent and generally everything is planned without a hitch. You owe it to your traveler, however, to make sure that everything is perfect. For this reason you should always follow up with the agency. Call them a few days before the scheduled departure to make sure that all reservations are in order and that everything is ready for a pleasant, well-planned trip.

Arranging Appointments

When making appointments for a traveler keep in mind the pointers below:

1. When arranging the traveler's appointments, make sure that you get all the necessary information from him. This means the name of the person to be visited, the date, location, and time of the visit, the phone number of the firm and any special remarks or reminders about the visit.

2. If an appointment is made quite a while before the actual visit, it is best to confirm the appointment with the secretary of the person to be visited, a few days in advance of the actual visit.

3. Always find out from the traveler if he has made any appointments on his own. If he has, include them in the appointment schedule.

On the next page is an example of a well-planned and well-laid-out appointment schedule.

Once the appointment schedule is set up, make sure that the traveler has at least two copies (one for his wallet and the other for his briefcase) with him.

Things the Traveler Will Need

Anyone planning a trip for a businessman should prepare two things for him to take from the office: information and supplies.

A file of information for the trip. If you are the traveler's secretary or assistant, you can help him by preparing an information folder for each appointment. Each folder should contain:

- A list of the names and positions of the people he plans to see during that particular visit, and his reason for seeing them.
- All correspondence or memos that deal directly with the appointment, plus any papers that might be useful as background or supporting ammunition during his meeting.
- A list of people he might try to see if he has the time, just to keep up old acquaintances.

Arrange these folders in order of appointments, so that he can consult each in turn beforehand. It is best to play safe and include

Schedule of Appointments for Robert Strauss - February 29 to March 18

City	Date	Time	Appointment	Firm	Remarks
Chicago, Ill.	2/29	11:15 am	Mr. Harold Jones Mr. Wilbur Ashton	Carlton Construction Co. 125 Hughes St. WH 6-4523	
	2/29	4:00 pm	Mr. Robert Howard	Brighton Cement Co. Alexander & Burn St. WH 6-6224	
Des Moines, Iowa	3/1	9:00 am	Mr. Charles Roberts	Appleton, Inc. 312 Johnson St. WI 4-7763	
	3/1	11:00 am	Mr. Fred Norris	Norris & Brown, Inc. 418 Brownley Place WI 4-6859	
	3/1	8:00 pm		The Red Wheel 810 Maple Avenue	Testimonial dinner for Mr. Fred Norris

every paper the traveler could possibly want; a record is of no use to him in the files when he is miles away in a customer's office.

Supplies he will need to get things done. There are many little things a busy man needs when he is on a business trip. For example, he may find it a nuisance to correspond with his office unless he has has own supply of stationery and stamps with him. Or if he must prepare reports as he goes, but forgets to take report forms, his work is made more difficult. If you arrange trips, here is where you can provide that "something extra" in considerate planning.

The best way to make sure that none of the essentials will be forgotten is to write up a list and then assemble everything, checking off each item as you get it. An example of a well-prepared check list is given below. Naturally, you will probably add or remove items, depending on your traveler's needs.

☐ Stationery of all kinds	☐ Pens and pencils
☐ Envelopes, airmail & plain	☐ Erasers
☐ Envelopes addressed to the company	☐ Clips
☐ Large manila envelopes	☐ Scissors
☐ Memo paper	☐ Rubber bands
☐ Stenographer's pad	☐ Blotters
☐ Legal pads	☐ Scotch tape
☐ Carbon paper	☐ Calendar
☐ Address book	☐ Mail schedules
☐ Legal folders	☐ Pins
☐ Business cards	☐ Bottle opener
☐ Dictation equipment	☐ Ruler
☐ Mailing folders or boxes for dictation belts or tapes	☐ Band aids
☐ Cash	☐ Aviation guide
☐ Personal checkbook	☐ Timetable
☐ Office account checks	☐ Paste
☐ Expense forms	☐ Stamp pad & stamps
☐ Other office forms	☐ Postage stamps

A business trip can be tiring and discouraging, or it can be comfortable and rewarding. Much depends on the planning and preparation that go into it. You can make a contribution to the success of a business trip if you plan it thoroughly, with the traveler's needs in mind.

•21• When You Are Traveling

The Expense Account

The proper use of a company expense account is less a matter of etiquette than it is one of following the company's rules. Nevertheless, there is a proper way to handle an expense account.

It is never proper to "pad" an expense account in order to get more from the company than it owes you; it is simply dishonest. On the other hand, you have every reason to take full advantage of reimbursements or payments to which you are entitled.

This section discusses common "do's" and "don'ts" for the business man or woman who uses a company expense account.

What the company pays for. Here are examples of what companies will and will not allow as entries on expense accounts.

· *Transportation and related expenses.* A company will usually pay the cost of train, plane, bus or boat fares and car rental fees that are necessary for business traveling. If you use your own car for business travel, the company probably pays you a specified amount per mile to cover the cost of operating and maintaining the car during its business use. Note that you cannot expect your company to reimburse you for the cost of commuting to and from work.

Many companies will pay only for the class of travel they authorize; for example, they will pay only for air coach or Pullman berth accommodations, and not for more luxurious classes.

· *Room and board.* Hotel, motel or club charges incurred by an employee on a business trip are usually paid by the company. Many companies will not pay more than a specified amount for a hotel or motel room. If you stay at a hotel but eat somewhere else, the company may expect you to get an itemized bill for your meals. There is often a specified allowance for each meal in the day.

· *Tips.* Tips count as part of the cost of traveling or of entertaining and are legitimate expense account items. However, tips incurred during personal entertainment activities while on a business trip are not the company's responsibility.

· *Valet services.* The costs of looking presentable during an extended trip—over a week in duration—are often paid by the company, within reason. Getting suits cleaned and pressed, and having laundry done and shoes shined, fit into this category.

· *Secretarial and office services.* A businessman away from his office may need the services of stenographers and typists, or may rent a typewriter or dictating machine. Such costs are usually paid by the company.

· *Business dinners and entertainment.* Within limits, wining, dining, and entertaining customers is a legitimate business expense that is recognized as such even by the Internal Revenue Service. Careful record-keeping is essential; see below, under Reporting and Accounting for Expenses.

· *Phone calls, telegrams and mailing costs.* So long as these are necessary for transacting business, companies generally include these as expense account items.

The company should never be expected to pay any personal expenses of an employee who travels on business. The cost of personal phone calls, or money spent on the employee's own entertainment or for souvenirs, are not the company's responsibility. Such items are not proper expense account entries.

How payment is made. Minor or unexpected expenses are sometimes handled through a petty cash fund. However, major or repeated expenditures are generally handled by the expense account method.

The company usually makes an advance payment to any employee who will be incurring expenses on the company's account. If an employee is on a non-recurring trip or assignment, he may submit an account of his expenses (along with whatever remains of the advanced sum) when the trip or assignment is completed. If he incurs expenses regularly, he will submit an accounting at regular intervals, probably monthly. The company then reimburses whatever he spent during the preceding period, to restore his expense fund to its original level.

For expenditures that are credit transactions, as many business luncheons are, for example, the employee should keep records, even though he may not have the responsibility of handling cash. Without some notation of expenses, it can be difficult to check the bill of the credit concern when it comes.

The importance of keeping records. The company must require an accounting from you of money that you spend on its behalf in the course of business. One obvious reason is that it is entitled to know exactly where its money goes. Just as important, the company can justify business expenses as deductions in computing its tax return *only* if it can prove the business nature of those expenses. It can prove this only if careful and accurate records are kept by employees who do the spending.

How to keep records of expenses. While most companies provide forms on which to report expenses, it is usually the employee's individual responsibility to keep track of expenses as he incurs them. Remember that it can be difficult to obtain receipts or itemized bills after time has passed; you should make getting a receipt an automatic part of every business transaction. For outlays for which receipts are not available—taxi, bus and subway fares are examples—make as accurate a recording as you can at the end of each day.

It is simpler and surer to keep a daily record of expenses than to try to sort through piles of receipts at the end of the month. However, it is more than a matter of convenience; the Internal Revenue Service can refuse to honor the authenticity of records that were not kept currently.

The requirements of the Internal Revenue Service also have a direct bearing on just what information you should be keeping in your records. You should record:

- When the money was spent
- How much money was spent
- What it was spent for
- The business connection, if this is not self-evident.

You can buy standard books or forms designed specifically to help you keep records of expenditures. Or you can easily make up a form that will meet your own needs. For example, if you travel frequently a columnar sheet such as the following may do:

Mo. Day	Description	Fares	Meals	Lodging	Tips	Automobile Expenses	Misc.

In completing your expense account form, keep in mind that yours is only one of many, most likely, and that verifying and handling the accounts of everyone in the company is a tedious and painstaking job. Be neat, and always double check your own figuring. Be sure there is no confusion between expenses you list and the documents that support them. Attach vouchers or receipts in a way that will keep them from getting lost or torn.

Many salesmen and other businessmen who entertain find that the use of credit cards has advantages. For one thing, it does away with the awkward and time-consuming process of bringing out cash, figuring out the bill and paying it, waiting for change, and leaving a tip, all while a customer is waiting and perhaps making persistent offers to do the paying. With a credit card you simply figure the bill, add a tip to it and sign.

At the end of the month you get an itemized bill, usually with copies of sales slips. This makes it much simpler to keep track of expenses.

When You Are the Guest of a Businessman in Another City

How to be a gracious guest. When you travel on business, you may often find yourself enjoying the hospitality of businessmen on whom you are calling. Essentially there is little difference between this situation and a similar one in your own city. Yet there are some factors that you should be aware of.

1. Be punctual. As a traveler, you may have an erratic schedule. Nevertheless, your host will be following his day-to-day schedule, and to force him to interrupt or suspend it unnecessarily is inconsiderate. Make a special effort to be on time for appointments, or to

let the other man know if you will be late. Give yourself extra time for finding your destination, if the city is strange to you.

2. Be adaptable. In a strange city, especially, it is important that you not embarrass (or offend) your host by behavior that is unsuited to local custom. For example, a businessman from a metropolitan Northern city may be accustomed to having a cocktail with lunch; as a visitor to a Southern city he is apt to find that this practice is far less common there. He should accept this graciously and not make his host uncomfortable by loud expressions of disappointment or by dwelling at length on how it is done back home.

3. Be on your best behavior. You may feel less restrained in a distant city or town than you would under similar circumstances in your own. The temptation might be to go out on the town, to do more drinking and nightclubbing than you would at home. This temptation is especially strong when your business host has made it clear that he wants to make your stay a pleasant one.

Remember that indiscreet or ungentlemanly behavior is as unwise and unwelcome in a distant place as it is in a familiar one. You are a representative of your company, and your conduct reflects directly on the company. As for the impression you make on your host, it is quite possible that, although he may have encouraged you to enjoy yourself, he may not be happy with a string of bar bills run up at his expense. Businessmen have also found that the fruits of hours of work spent at a conference table can be undone by things that are said after one drink too many.

4. Express your thanks. Anyone who has extended hospitality to you during a business trip will appreciate a note of thanks. Such a letter is most effective when it is informal, brief, and sincere. The following is an example of such a letter:

> Dear Jim,
>
> Thank you for your exceptional hospitality during my three days in San Francisco. I was pleased with the progress we were able to make in working out specifications for our new building, but you made the trip twice as rewarding by giving me a native's view of the city in the bargain. It took a lot of your time, and I want you to know how much your trouble was appreciated.
>
> Don't forget that when you are in Denver in March I have first claim on your free time—if the schedule you described leaves you any. I look forward to seeing you then.
>
> Sincerely,

When you must refuse hospitality. It can happen that you have a definite, valid reason for declining an invitation from a man on whom you are calling during a business trip. If so, be gracious in turning him down, just as you would if it were a purely social invitation.

More troublesome is an invitation that you feel you should not accept for reasons that would be difficult to explain to the other party; for example, you may feel that the entertainment he offers is far out of proportion to the amount of business you think is possible between you. Or perhaps you feel that to accept would place you under an obligation that would complicate your business dealings with him. In such a situation you might politely suggest an alternative activity, one you could accept with a clear conscience. Or you might accept on condition that you be allowed to pay your share of the costs. If you must decline altogether, try to do so in a way that will not be an obvious rebuff to the other man.

How to Be a Considerate Traveler

During the long hours you spend actually getting from one place to another, it is inevitable that your sense of etiquette will be put to use again and again. This section tells you about particular etiquette problems you are likely to face when you are underway on a business (or personal) trip, and explains how to handle them.

Train etiquette. Train travel places you in close contact with strangers, all of whom must share with you the necessarily limited facilities that a train can provide. Unless you respect your fellow travelers' wishes, and they respect yours, your journey has little chance of being a pleasant one. Below are some ways in which you can show your consideration toward fellow train passengers.

· *Pullman car etiquette.* On the standard Pullman car, where the seats are converted at night into upper and lower berths for sleeping, there are certain specific points of etiquette to be observed.

If you hold a lower berth you are entitled to sit facing forward during the day, but it is polite to invite a fellow passenger from the upper berth to sit beside you if there is room. Should the person in the upper berth be very old or infirm, or otherwise have difficulty negotiating the ladder they must climb to reach their berth, they would be grateful to you if you were to exchange berths.

You must ring for the porter when you want your bed made in the evening, and, if you have an upper berth, whenever you wish to get in or out of it. Since the dressing rooms on a Pullman car cannot accommodate everyone at once, it is best to do as much of your dressing and undressing in your berth as you can manage. In using the dressing room, remember that there are probably others waiting; you should take as little time as possible, and should leave your space in a clean condition for the next user.

· *Roomettes, compartments, bedrooms.* If you occupy the more expensive and comfortable roomettes, compartments or bedrooms, you will not have quite the problems of travelers who have berths. You have a private dressing room. There is no problem of requiring a ladder to get in and out of your berth, and you have much more privacy.

In these larger quarters you may play a radio, entertain friends, and the like, without the fear of disturbing fellow passengers. This would be inconsiderate in a standard berth.

· *The dining car.* When you enter the dining car, you are taken to your seat by the chief steward (equivalent to the headwaiter in a restaurant). You will usually be seated with a person who is a total stranger, unless you have enough people in your party to take up an entire table. Once you are seated, it is entirely proper that you greet the person across the table from you. You should not, however, force a conversation on an unwilling traveler.

When you are finished with your meal, you leave the dining car promptly because there may be others waiting to be seated. Or, if you are among the last to dine, the clean-up crew will want to start their work.

· *The club car.* Proper behavior in a club car aboard a train, where drinks are served, is no different than it would be in a restaurant, bar or tavern elsewhere. However, keep in mind that a boisterous and noisy performance on returning to a Pullman car is very inconsiderate; some fellow travelers may find it difficult to sleep on a train. You should also be aware that you cannot be served a drink during the time a train is passing through a "dry" state. You should accept this as a matter of law, one the bartender must obey.

· *Tipping.* For tipping procedures on a train, see page 192.

When you travel by air. If for some reason you can't make a flight for which you had a reservation, notify the airline at least twenty-four hours in advance. This is necessary because most airlines have stand-by lists. Also, some have a surcharge of as much as twenty percent on reservations that are not canceled within twenty-four hours of flight time.

Limit your luggage to the most essential articles. You are allowed to carry a small amount of hand luggage with you to your seat, so make sure that you put all the things that you may need during the flight in these bags. Airlines have very high charges for overweight luggage. And some lines won't take baggage in excess of a certain amount. Your company may have strict rules about how much baggage they will pay for.

General procedures. When you enter the plane, you return the greeting of the stewardess. Your coat goes in the rack above the seat; if you are carrying a bag, it goes under the seat. Once seated, you fasten your seat belt and wait until the stewardess checks it. During take-off you are not allowed to smoke. Watch the "no smoking" signal that notifies passengers when they may or may not smoke (the sign goes on when smoking is forbidden; when it's out, you may smoke). You will notice a small compartment on the back of the seat in front of you. This compartment contains a small, waterproof bag or canister for use in case of airsickness. You will also find a card marked "occupied" that you can use to reserve your seat at any stop you might make.

If you are in a mood to talk with someone, remember that it is impolite to force conversation on a person who is virtually a captive audience beside you in the plane. Nor should you recount stories of near-accidents you have been through, or the like; there are many people who are very uneasy about flying, and it is unkind to frighten them. Remember, too, that the speed of modern commercial planes forces stewardesses to keep busy if they are to accomplish their job between take-off and landing. Unless you have a problem or an important question, don't try to monopolize a stewardess' time.

When you leave the plane, you say good-bye to the stewardess and thank her for her service (a "no tipping" rule is general in the airline industry, by the way). You then proceed to the baggage counter to pick up your luggage. You must secure and pay for your own transportation to and from the airport. In most cases, however, this is made easy for you by the line of limousines and taxicabs that wait in front of the entrance to the terminal.

• *Seating.* Seats on an airplane are not reserved; seating is on a "first come, first seated" basis. However, on flights where two classes of accommodations are on the same place, naturally you cannot sit in the first-class part of the plane if you bought a tourist ticket.

• *Meals.* On most first-class trips, meals are complimentary. On some transcontinental jets the meals served are like those in an elegant restaurant. Most tourist class ships, however, do not serve meals, with the possible exception of coffee and sandwiches. An interesting etiquette pointer given in the United Airlines booklets aboard its San Francisco-Hawaii bound jets was the advice that it was perfectly proper to tuck the napkin into one's shirt-front or dress collar while dining.

• *Sleeping accommodations.* Some of the major airlines provide sleep service on overnight transcontinental flights. There is an additional charge for these services. The arrangement of berths on an airplane is much the same as that of Pullman accommodations on a train. As on a train, lower berths are preferred. Again, you should do as much of your dressing and undressing in your berth as possible. When you are in the dressing room, and when you leave it, tidiness is the keynote (see the section on Pullman car etiquette on page 186 for further information pertaining to sleeping accommodations).

Correct Tipping Procedures

Tipping is a bothersome custom that is often embarrassing to travelers. Nevertheless, it is the system that prevails throughout most of the world today. And if you want good service, you must know the correct amounts to tip in all the situations that arise in traveling.

The discussion below mentions specific amounts, but these are only meant to serve as a guide. Although these figures are based on commonly accepted practice in many places, tipping procedures change gradually, and they differ in various sectors of the country. The traveler must be alert and make adjustments for these factors.

Tipping in a hotel. In a hotel, as in a restaurant, the tips you give depend on variables such as the size and quality of the hotel, and the service rendered you by its employees.

• *Doormen.* For simply removing your luggage from a taxi or car when you arrive at the hotel, doormen are not tipped. No tip is required if a doorman opens the door of a taxi that is on a waiting line in front of the hotel for you. Doormen are tipped if they give you service that requires some extra effort on their part. If one goes out onto the street to hail a taxi for you, he is given 25¢. If it is raining, you would naturally tip him more (perhaps 50¢) since he has gone through extra trouble and saved you from getting wet. If it is raining and you are in evening clothes, you would tip him $1.00 since he has saved you from getting your good clothes wet. If he watches your car or gets it from the garage for you, 25¢ is sufficient.

· *Bellboys*. Bellboys are tipped 25 to 50¢ for each bag they carry, depending on the size and weight of the bag. These rates also apply to redcaps in railway stations.

· *Pages*. The correct tip for a page who has paged a party for you can vary from 10¢ to 50¢ depending on the size of the hotel and the difficulty the page has had in getting your party for you.

· *Chambermaids*. If your stay in the hotel is only one night, then you leave the chambermaid 25¢ to 50¢, depending on the size and quality of the hotel. If the stay is of a week or more in length, you tip them at the rate of $1.00 for each week. You do not have to seek chambermaids out since it is accepted practice to leave the tip on a dresser in the room. Of course, you tip them more if they perform a service such as sewing.

· *Checkroom attendants*. These people are tipped 25¢ unless there is only an attended coatrack in front of the restaurant. In this case, the tip is 10¢.

· *Elevator starters*. For a weekend or overnight stay, no tip is necessary. Starters *are* tipped, however, between 50¢ and $1.00 for a stay of approximately one week. Individual elevator operators are tipped 50¢ a week. If your stay is a month or more, then the starters are tipped $1.00 each month as are the operators.

· *Room waiters*. Most hotels have a 25¢ to 50¢ charge for room service. The waiters are tipped ten to fifteen percent of the bill in addition to this charge. You can either pay the waiter in cash or make a notation on the bill for the amount that you wish to tip him. Then you sign for the new total. The hotel will pay his tip and add the amount to your bill. Never tip a room waiter, or any other waiter, less than 25¢ if you expect to get good service.

· *Valets*. No tip is necessary since the work is usually done by an outside cleaning establishment. The cost of delivery is part of the valet charge on your bill.

• *Delivery boys.* For making deliveries to the room, delivery boys are usually tipped 25¢.

Tipping in a restaurant or night club. Naturally, any figures that are given here cannot be taken as unyielding law. Much depends on the quality of the restaurant or night club. Variables such as the nature of the service, the number of people being served, how you are dressed, what you order, and so on, must be taken into account when figuring what a fair amount to tip is.

If you were to go to a small, unknown restaurant, you might tip less than you would at the Twenty-One Club in New York. Or if you went to a restaurant in business clothes, you would not be expected to tip as much as if you went to the same restaurant in evening clothes. If you go to a restaurant or night club and stay at your table three or four hours, you will naturally be expected to tip the waiter more than if you stay just to eat.

Aside from these variables, there are certain guidelines that you can use in determining the amounts that you will tip. They are:

• *Maitre d'hotel.* The maitre d'hotel or headwaiter is not tipped if all he does is show you to your table or bring you to the captain who seats you. Of course, if he gives you some exceptional service such as finding you a table "where there were no tables," he is given a tip which should never be less than $1.00. As a rule, when the maitre d'hotel is tipped, the tip should be between $2.00 and $5.00.

• *Captain.* Some restaurants and night clubs have a maitre d'hotel who takes you directly to a captain, who is in charge of a certain section of tables or a certain room. The captain then takes you to your table, seats you, and hands you the menu. If this is the extent of his service, he is not tipped. Again, if he gives you some service that is out of the ordinary, he is tipped. The captain's tip is never less than $1.00, and can be anywhere from $2.00 to $5.00.

• *Waiter.* The waiter receives from 15 to 20 percent of the bill, depending on the service he has given and the quality of the restaurant. If you are in a large group, 15 percent still holds as minimum.

• *Bus boys.* Bus boys are never tipped directly. In most establishments there are agreements between waiters and bus boys as to how bus boys will share in tips. The same is true of roll, relish or jelly servers.

• *Wine steward.* If you are served by a wine steward, he is tipped between twelve and fifteen percent of the wine bill.

• *Hat-check attendant.* The tip here is the same as in a hotel—25¢.

• *Bartender.* If you are drinking at the bar, the bartender should receive ten percent of the bar bill.

Tipping on a train. You generally tip for certain services on a train, as follows:

• *Redcaps.* The tip for a redcap is 25¢ to 50¢ a day and 50¢ for each bag he carries, depending on the size and weight of the bag.

• *Pullman porters.* Twenty-five to 50¢ a day and 50¢ a night is a good tip for a porter. Of course if you occupy a roomette, compartment, or bedroom space, the tip will be larger in proportion to the size of your accommodations. If the porter does some extra service such as getting you ice, cigarettes, papers, and the like, he should be tipped an additional 25¢.

• *Stewards.* In the club car or dining car of a train stewards are tipped 15 percent. For breakfast or lunch service the minimum tip is 25¢.

Tipping on a plane. Most airlines have rules which prohibit their employees from taking tips from passengers.

Tipping aboard ship. In almost all cases, tips are distributed at the end of the voyage. The correct amounts to tip are:

• *Room steward, table steward and headwaiter.* These men are all tipped $7.50 to $10.00.

• *Deck steward.* One dollar is a good tip for the deck steward, unless you have used his services quite frequently. If you have, then you tip him more in proportion to the amount of service that he has given you.

• *Bath steward.* If you have had accommodations without a private bath and have had to use the public bath, you tip the bath steward $1.00.

• *Cabin boys.* You tip cabin boys 25¢ to 50¢ at the time they perform their services. No tip is required or expected at the end of the trip.

• *Bar attendants.* You usually tip these men at the time they give you service, in which case they are given ten percent of the bar bill.

• *Chief steward.* The chief steward is considered one of the officers on most ships and, as such, is never tipped.

Tips in foreign countries. The problem of what to tip in foreign countries is complicated by the need to translate into a different currency, and by differences in customs. Since so many Americans are traveling abroad on business now (and for pleasure), a chart of suggested tips abroad is included here. This chart was compiled by Mary Gordon, travel advisor for Trans World Airlines, and is reproduced with their kind permission. The sums given in U. S. currency are the nearest practical equivalents of European currency. Again, such a chart (on the following page) can only be a guide.

	WAITERS	CHAMBERMAIDS	BELLHOPS & BAGGAGE PORTERS	DOORMAN	CONCIERGE	TAXICAB DRIVER	STATION PORTER	LADIES' ROOM ATTENDANT	HAIRDRESSER	THEATRE USHER
GREAT BRITAIN	10% to 15% of check.	1 shilling (14¢) a day, or 7-10 shillings (98¢-$1.40) a week.	1 shilling (14¢) a bag, but not less than 2 shillings.	1 shilling (14¢) for calling a cab.	3-7 shillings (42¢-98¢) for special service.	Nine pence (11¢) if fare is less than 5 shillings; 1 shilling if more; 15% if fare is over 10 shillings.	1 shilling (14¢) a bag, but not less than 2 shillings.	Sixpence (7¢).	15% to 20% of the bill.	Nothing.
FRANCE	2 francs (41¢) over service charge. If none, tip 12% to 15% of check.	1 franc (20¢) a day, 4-6 (81¢-$1.21) a week.	2-3 francs (41¢-61¢) for a load of luggage, 1 franc (20¢) a bag or a service.	1 franc (20¢) for calling a cab.	1 franc (20¢) a service, 5-6 francs ($1.01-$1.21) a week even if no services are performed.	10% to 15% of the meter.	1 franc (20¢) a bag, 3 francs (61¢) a load of luggage.	½ franc (10¢).	15% to 20% of the bill, if not included.	½ franc (10¢) at a cinema, up to 2 francs (41¢) for orchestra seats at a play or concert.
GERMANY	5% of check over usual service charge.	50 pfennige (12¢) for 1 night's stay, 2 marks (48¢) a week.	50 pfennige (12¢) a bag or a service.	20-50 pfennige (5¢-12¢) for calling a cab.	1-2 marks (24¢-48¢) a special service.	15% of the meter.	10% above regular fee.	10 pfennige (2¢) above fee.	50 pfennige-3 marks (12¢-71¢).	Nothing.
ITALY	5% of check over service charge.	100 lire (16¢) a day, 500 lire (80¢) a week.	50-125 lire (8¢-20¢) a bag or a service.	100 lire (16¢) for calling a cab.	10% of his bill for cables, phone calls, etc.	15% of the meter. Average, 50 to 100 lire.	100 lire (16¢) a bag.	50 lire (8¢).	100-300 lire (16¢-48¢).	50 lire (8¢).
SWITZERLAND	12% to 15% of check. If service charge, leave small change in addition.	Included in hotel service charge. Tip 2 francs (46¢) for a special service.	Not included in hotel service charge. Fr.—.50 per bag or Sw. Fr. 1—minimum.	50 centimes (12¢) for calling a cab.	Sw. Frs. 2-5 (47¢-$1.15) for special service, given on departure.	12% to 15% of the meter.	Local tariff plus 10%.	50 centimes (12¢).	15% of the bill.	Nothing.
SPAIN	5 pesetas minimum (9¢) over 15% service charge; 5% over check.	10 pesetas (17¢) a day, 50 pesetas (83¢) a week.	10 pesetas (18¢) a bag, or a service in room; 5 pesetas to bellhops.	5 pesetas (9¢) for calling a cab.	No tip if not much service; 25 pesetas (42¢) a day or more, depending on service performed, if by hotel.	2-5 pesetas (3¢-9¢).	5-10 pesetas (9¢-18¢) a bag.	2-5 pesetas (3¢-9¢).	5 pesetas (9¢).	2 pesetas (3¢) per person (bullfights, football matches, etc.).
PORTUGAL	5% to 10% of check over service charge.	20 escudos (70¢) a week.	5 escudos (18¢) a bag, 2$50 escudos (9¢) a service.	2$50 escudos (9¢) for calling a cab.	10 escudos (35¢) a service.	15% of the meter.	5 escudos (18¢) a bag.	1$50 escudos (5¢).	5-10 escudos (18¢-35¢).	1$50 escudos (5¢).
GREECE	15% service charge is made; add 5% to 10%.	15 drachmas for a day; 100 drachmas for a week.	5 drachmas (17¢) for a lot of luggage, 10 drachmas.	5 drachmas (17¢) for calling a cab.	50 drachmas for special service.	5 drachmas (17¢).	5 drachmas (16½¢) for a load of luggage.	2 drachmas (7¢).	10 drachmas. (33¢).	2 drachmas (7¢).
EGYPT	5% of check over 10% service charge, or 15%.	35 piastres ($1) per week.	5 piastres (14¢) a bag or a service.	5 piastres (14¢) for calling a cab.	10 piastres (29¢) at end of stay.	10%	5 piastres (14¢) per bag.	2 piastres (6¢).	20% of the bill.	5 piastres 14¢).

·22· When Men and Women Travel Together

When the woman executive travels on business. The female executive who travels with male business associates has fewer restrictions on her behavior than a secretary would have in similar situations. She is accepted as an equal by her male counterparts (she may even outrank them). On the other hand, the added freedom she enjoys is offset by added social responsibilities.

An example of the woman executive's greater freedom in traveling is the fact that she can take a hotel room on the same floor as her male companions. She can—*if* she is invited first—go nightclubbing with the men. She can dine out frequently with her male associates, even though she probably doesn't do so at the home office. Yet to a degree she still enjoys the natural deference a woman expects from men.

On the other side of the coin, her position makes certain demands of her that would not affect the secretary. She is generally expected to take care of her share of the bills for meals and entertainment while in the company of the men. She must handle her own tips and settle her own hotel and travel tabs. In other words, while she shares some of the privileges of a man, she must also assume some of the responsibilities that are normally his. She accepts this gladly, of course, since it is really a tribute to her ability and success.

Why the secretary accompanies her boss. There are many occasions when a secretary may be needed on a business trip. It is not unusual for employers belonging to outside organizations to be required to take turns providing stenographic or secretarial help at important meetings. Sometimes secretarial help is needed at a convention. Or perhaps a traveling executive expects to transact a great volume of business for which he needs secretarial help. Whatever the purpose of the trip, an employer takes his secretary along because she knows his work and can take his dictation easily. He takes her also because it is more efficient than hiring strange help in a strange city.

Making room reservations. (For a discussion of general reservation procedure see "Making Reservations" on page 171.) When the executive and his secretary travel together, the laws of etiquette demand that their hotel accommodations be on different floors. The secretary shouldn't overdo it, however, by going to another hotel. That would make it much too inconvenient to take dictation and might defeat her employer's reason for bringing her along.

The executive may want a suite for himself, but the secretary's accommodations should be a little more modest. A room with bath is adequate. The letter asking for reservations for executive and secretary can be patterned after the following:

January 30, 19__

Hotel Washington
Pine and Jackson Streets
Palisades Park, New Jersey

Gentlemen:

Please reserve a room and bath, together with a large connecting sitting room for Mr. Gerald English beginning Wednesday night, January 25. Mr. English plans to leave early January 30.

Mr. English's secretary will accompany him and would like a single room with bath for the same period.

Inasmuch as their flight does not reach Newark Airport until 9:30 p.m., please hold both reservations for late arrival.

Please send confirmation as soon as possible.

Yours very truly,
Phillip Hudson
Traffic Manager
English Bros., Inc.

As you can see from the letter, it is not necessary to specify that the executive and secretary have rooms on different floors. Hotels automatically reserve rooms on different floors when they receive a reservation for a businessman and his secretary. This may seem to be carrying convention too far, particularly if the man and his secretary have worked closely together for several years in complete trust. However, it is one of the rules of etiquette and both are expected to know the rules as well as they know their business.

Making Pullman reservations. Ordinarily, Pullman reservations are not made for daytime travel, but if the executive is going to be busy, he may want to reserve a drawing room for privacy. The secretary can take a coach seat in the same car so that she can be near the executive should he want her for dictation. Her accommodations can be in the same car of the same train as her employer's. The executive may want a drawing room or compartment (see page 168). His secretary's accommodations should be more modest. A roomette or a bedroom should do.

On an overnight trip, reservations are made in much the same way as plane reservations. Below is a sample conversation requesting overnight Pullman reservations for executive and secretary:

> "Good afternoon. This is Mary Jones of the Lux Corporation. I would like to make Pullman reservations for Mr. James Carlstedt of this company and myself on the Twentieth Century Limited from New York to Chicago at 4:00 p.m. on March 15. Please reserve a drawing room for Mr. Carlstedt and a roomette for me. Are these accommodations available?"
>
> "Yes, Miss Jones, we have those accommodations available on the Twentieth Century for March 15, but the train leaves at 6:00 p.m. each evening."
>
> "That will be satisfactory. What time does the train arrive in Chicago?"
>
> "At 9:00 a.m. Central Standard Time."
>
> "Thank you very much. Please make the reservations for Mr. James Carlstedt, the Lux Corporation, 532 Sylvan Avenue, Englewood Cliffs, New Jersey, and Miss Mary Jones, same address. The phone number of the company is WH-5-1274, and Mr. Carlstedt's home phone number is WI-7-2934."
>
> "Thank you, Miss Jones. You can pick up the tickets at Window 6, Grand Central Terminal, any time after 3:00 p.m. today."

Most railway companies will require that you pick up Pullman tickets two or three days in advance of your departure. This is done so that if you must cancel, some other traveler can get accommodations.

Etiquette Problems En Route and at Your Destination

How to register in a hotel. The executive usually signs the register, but the secretary may do it. Whoever does sign should do so for both. The register should read as below:

John Doe, Lux Corporation, Englewood Cliffs, N.J.
Miss Mary Jones, Secretary to Mr. Doe, Englewood Cliffs, N.J.

The secretary's business relation to her employer should always be included. This insures that the room clerk will give you rooms on separate floors, unless you otherwise specify. Also, the address should be the same for both executive and secretary—the address of your business.

When you are given rooms on the same floor. If the hotel has mistakenly given you rooms on the same floor, there is no reason to become overly upset.

If, however, the hotel should give you adjoining rooms, you are right to voice your objections. Simply tell the clerk in a quiet manner that your accommodations are not what you requested and let him take it from there.

Dictation in the executive's room. The executive who has a sitting room adjoining his room may ask his secretary to take dictation from him there. If he has only one room, the hotel lounge or sitting room might better be used for that purpose. Sometimes, however, it is necessary that the secretary work in her employer's room. But under no circumstances may the secretary's room be used.

If the secretary is to take dictation in her employer's room, the following rules of etiquette should be observed.

1. The room should be made up. If this is not possible, the bed-covers should be pulled up and the bed put in order.
2. The door may be closed but it should not be locked.
3. Both the executive and his secretary should be dressed the way they are always dressed for the home office.

Taking lunch and dinner on the trip. The executive and his secretary may dine together while traveling on a train or in the hotel dining room, if their normal business relationship involved the occasional lunch or dinner together. But since a business trip is merely a continuation of regular business dealings, it would be unnatural to expect an executive and his secretary, who meet only during business hours, to dine together at all times during the trip.

Whenever the executive and his secretary dine together, they should avoid having cocktails or drinks together. Also it is not a good idea for them to have breakfast together in the executive's room.

Your behavior as a traveling secretary. Your behavior while away on a business trip should be more circumspect than it might be at home. At home people most likely know that you are a fine person and any noise or exuberance is weighed against their total knowledge of you. This is not true in strange surroundings. Remember to behave at all times in a manner that will reflect to your employer's credit. Do not discuss business with others after hours. You never know who is listening.

If you will not be needed during the evening, make arrangements for your own amusement. Your employer should not be expected to entertain you, and you shouldn't give him the uncomfortable feeling that he must look after you. Of course, if you are needed in the evening, perhaps when attending a convention or something similar, be on call.

Working in a strange office. You may be asked to do your work in a strange office, perhaps a branch of the company. Be very polite to everyone you meet. Remember that you are an intruder, so don't expect to be given the best typewriter, or the complete freedom of the office. You will undoubtedly need help in getting around the office, or in locating people or supplies, and people are not going to be willing to help you if you have offended them by your manner.

You probably will not be able to go back to the "borrowed" office after hours, so be sure you have all the supplies or information you are likely to need before the office is closed.

Office materials to take with you. In addition to the supplies you ordinarily pack for your employer on a trip, take along materials you will need. Several shorthand books are indispensable. Be sure to have enough letterhead paper and regular typing paper, as well as envelopes, carbon paper, pencils, pads, and anything else you can think of that you might need. Do not rely on the possibility of getting office supplies from some branch office your employer may be visiting. Postage stamps are very important. Hunting for stamps at nine o'clock at night in a strange city can be annoying.

Typing facilities in a strange city. Your typewriter is your most important tool and you will probably need one on a business trip. Settle the question of typing facilities before you leave your home office. Perhaps your office has portable machines it supplies to its salesman or other traveling personnel and you can take one of those. Your employer may be visiting a branch office and you may be expected to use a machine there. Otherwise arrange to rent a machine in the city of destination. Write ahead, giving the approximate period of time you will need the typewriter, so that it will be available on your arrival. It is ordinarily best to either take a portable typewriter or to arrange to rent a machine because you may have typing to do in the evening at your hotel.

• Part 4 • Business and Office Entertaining

•23• Entertaining Customers and Clients

Entertaining clients, customers and business associates is an accepted practice in business life. By far the most common form of business entertainment is the business lunch, where men and women meet to discuss business problems over a meal.

Informal luncheons. The host usually has his secretary telephone his favorite restaurant or club to reserve a table for himself and his guest or guests. This can be done a day in advance or, if necessary, the same day.

Many executives prefer to entertain informally in their own small dining rooms, in which case their secretaries telephone the orders to a caterer and brew coffee in a kitchenette.

Inviting the guests. Invitations for an informal luncheon are usually extended by telephone, either by the host or his secretary. On occasion, a written invitation to an informal lunch may be sent out, as, for example, the following one to an out-of-town business acquaintance:

> Dear Hal:
>
> We look forward with real pleasure to your visit here on April 7. If your plans permit, I would like you to have lunch with Cal Hodges, our new advertising manager, and myself that day.
>
> I'm going to enjoy showing you through our new plant, and am anxious to tell you of some exciting plans for the future.
>
> Cordially,

An invitation of this kind could be answered as follows:

Acceptance

> Dear Jim:
>
> There is nothing I'd enjoy more than having lunch with you and Cal Hodges on April 7. Make whatever arrangements as

to time and place that suit you best. I have heard a great deal of flattering comment on your new advertising manager, and look forward to meeting him.

I should arrive at your office about 9:30 a.m. and after touring the plant would like to work out the details of our new contract. By the way, will you try to have the figures we discussed ready for me on the seventh?

Cordially,

Regrets

Dear Jim:

Having lunch with you and your new advertising manager on April 7 is something I'd very much enjoy, as I've heard some fine reports on Cal Hodges. But I'm already committed to a luncheon meeting with the board of directors of Halsted, Inc. I plan to be at your office about 9:30 a.m. but will have to leave at 11:45.

However, if agreeable to you, I can stay over for another day. I am anxious to hear of your plans for the future, and feel that a talk with Hodges at this time would be to our mutual advantage. Would lunch on the eighth suit you?

Cordially,

Lunching in the company cafeteria. When time is limited, or the host's office is in an isolated surburban area, guests may be entertained at lunch in the company cafeteria. The host should be certain that if there are procedures to be followed, such as obtaining guest tickets, he has it all taken care of beforehand. If the cafeteria affords a separate room, this would be the best place to meet, in which case the host should make a reservation if it's required.

Introducing the business topic. When the guest at lunch is either a client or a customer, the host allows him to introduce the subject of business into the conversation. No matter how anxious the host is to talk about the signing of a contract, or prices, or deliveries, or any other matter, he should wait for his guest to bring it up. When the guest is neither a customer nor a client, the host may bring up at any time the topic of business he wishes to discuss. It is courteous, however, to wait until the main course has been eaten and dessert ordered.

How long should lunch last? It is polite to allow the client or customer to decide how long the lunch is to last. Whether the guest is in a hurry or is willing to stretch the lunch hour to two or three, the host must accommodate himself with good grace.

A formal luncheon in a private room. The purpose of calling together a group of men for a luncheon of this kind is not only to entertain them elegantly but to provide a relaxed, secluded atmosphere in which to discuss matters of business. A private company dining room, a private room at a club, hotel, or restaurant makes a suitable setting for an occasion of this kind. While the luncheon will not take all afternoon, it will be unhurried and free of interruptions, except for the serving of food and drink.

While there is a social element to this type of gathering, that is not the main purpose of the luncheon. Usually cocktails will be served, with tomato juice or soft drinks available for those who don't drink alcoholic beverages. Very often the host will explain during cocktails why the luncheon meeting is being held and what he hopes to accomplish. He may sketch in the background of events leading up to this meeting and describe existing differences of opinion, or courses of action that have been considered.

Should business be discussed during the meal? Conversation during the first part of the meal should be confined to small talk of one kind or another—vacations, trips, news of people and happenings, the theatre, art, whatever you think would interest the people you are lunching with. The host will usually introduce the subject of the meeting after the main course plates are removed and dessert is served.

When you are the host. While a luncheon meeting of this kind is a leisurely affair, bear in mind that your guests have other work to do. Don't permit the cocktail hour to run on. Give everyone the opportunity to get a second drink, and then have the meal served.

How to plan a formal luncheon. Arranging a formal business luncheon is a task that usually falls to the lot of the host's secretary. The following list of things to do in planning the event will prevent overlooking any of the important details.

1. *Reserve a dining room.* Your employer will probably tell you whether he prefers the company private dining room or a room in a hotel, restaurant, or club. Be sure the room is the right size for the number of people who will be present.
2. *Plan the menu.* If your employer has not expressed a preference for a certain dish, discuss with the company cook or chef, or the caterer, banquet manager, or maitre d'hotel the number of courses, whether the main course is to be meat or fish, what kind of salad dressing, and so on. Then submit the menu

you decide on to your executive for his approval. As soon as you get it, call whoever has helped you plan the meal and either give him the changes that have been made in the menu or tell him it's all right as it stands.

3. *Send out the invitations.* Invite the guests at least two weeks in advance of the luncheon date. Keep a list of those invited and check off the acceptances and regrets as they come in. (Type a list of the names and rule off "accepts" and "regrets" columns next to them.) When all the replies are in, let the cook or caterer or whoever will handle it know exactly how many will attend the luncheon. He may give you a deadline for this.
4. *Order flowers.* If the luncheon is to be a small one, order a centerpiece for the table. If there is to be more than one table, order as many arrangements as are necessary.
5. *Plan the seating.* Draw the tables as they will be set up for the luncheon. You will probably have to confer with your employer as to where to seat his guests. Buy place cards (of heavy stock in white or cream). Write, in ink, each guest's last name and title, such as Dr. Johnson, Senator Grant, Mr. McElroy. Either have the caterer's or manager's staff put the cards on the table (you'll have to send the seating plan and cards) or go there yourself before the luncheon and place them.

A last minute check. Someone—the host's secretary, if she has arranged the luncheon—should check the room before the guests arrive, to be sure that everything is as it should be.

Dinner Parties for Business Guests

Inviting business associates and their wives to dinner is a social courtesy that is a popular part of business entertaining. Usually the group goes on to the theatre or the opera or a sporting event after the dinner, winding up the evening with supper afterwards at a nightclub or hotel.

Dining outside the home. Frequently the host takes his guests to dinner in a hotel or restaurant, and when he does he must be as alert to their welfare as though they were in his own home and the waiters part of his household help. This concern must not be allowed to grow into anxious fussing over trifles, as this will detract from the enjoyment of the occasion.

Entering a restaurant. Men check their hats and coats with the hatcheck girl. A woman may wear her coat to the table or leave it with the ladies' room attendant. In some restaurants, her escort may check a lady's coat in the coatroom. The headwaiter leads the women guests to the table, with the men following.

Seating arrangements. When there are two couples and the head waiter pulls out a chair, the hostess defers to the woman guest. When there are more than four people they remain standing until the host or hostess seats them. The men help the ladies nearest them to remove their wraps and fold them over the backs of their chairs.

Just as they would at home, the host and hostess sit opposite each other when the number of guests permits them to do so. When the guests number eight or twelve, then (again as you would do at home) a man sits opposite the host, with the hostess placing herself at the right or left of the man opposite her husband. When two couples are seated at a table with a banquette or wall seat, both the ladies sit against the wall.

When a business man alone is entertaining a client or customer and his wife, the woman should sit between the two men.

Ordering the meal. After the order for cocktails, if any, has been given, dinners may be ordered individually from the menus. The host takes each lady's order and relays it to the waiter. Since a guest with good manners is usually reluctant to order the most expensive choices, the host or hostess should suggest an expensive dish by way of permission to order freely.

The host or hostess may order the meal ahead of time. In this case no menus are handed to the guests; they eat whatever the host or hostess has selected, and the meal is served as it would be at home.

Paying the bill. When the bill is brought, the host should go over it, making sure the figures are correct. This should be done as swiftly as possible. The guests can go on with their conversation. It's as rude for them to sit and stare at the host as he checks the figures as it is for him to mull over them for so long that everyone feels uncomfortable. If the host questions an item on the check he should call the waiter over and quietly question him. If he is charging the meal, he can add the tip to the bill. When he pays in cash, he leaves the tip for the waiter on the salver or plate on which his change is returned. Tips for the wine steward, captain and maitre d'hotel are given to them individually. This is never done ostentatiously—the host slips a folded bill into their hands while still seated at the table or when he rises to leave.

Leaving a restaurant. After the women are helped with their wraps one of the men precedes everyone else in order to open any doors on the way out.

Dining at home. Most business entertaining is done outside the home. Many men prefer to keep separate their business and private lives, and, on the whole, it is generally easier for all concerned if business acquaintances are taken out to dinner and the theatre or some other event. Occasionally, though, business entertaining is done at home, and sometimes in a most formal manner.

The formal invitation. Engraved or handwritten invitations are sent out about two weeks before the date on which the dinner is to be held. Shown below is a partially engraved invitation. Cards of this kind are used by hostesses who do a great deal of entertaining. The names of the invited guests, what they are invited for, the date, and the time are all filled in by hand (italic type in the example). An invitation that includes the business acquaintance's wife is sent to his home. If, for some reason, he is invited alone, the invitation may be sent to his office.

The traditional request for a reply to an invitation (whether formal, semi-formal, or informal) is the abbreviation for the French phrase, Répondez s'il vous plaît (Answer, if you please). The abbreviation may be written in capital letters, R.S.V.P. or with only the first letter capitalized, R.s.v.p.

Mr. and Mrs. Pierre Renaud
request the pleasure of
Mr. and Mrs. Smith's
company *at dinner*
on *Thursday, the fifteenth of April*
at *half past seven* o'clock
550 Park Avenue

R.S.V.P.

Still another type of invitation is the one entirely engraved on the front page of fine quality double-fold letter paper.

Mr. and Mrs. Norton Cooperman
request the pleasure of your company
at dinner
on Friday, March the fifteenth
at eight o'clock
1250 Fifth Avenue

R.S.V.P.

Handwritten invitations. Formal invitations also may be written by hand. The style used is the same as in the engraved invitations. Only the finest quality double-fold writing paper may be used for this purpose.

Black tie or white tie? An engraved invitation calls for a black tie; that is, a dinner jacket. When full evening dress, or white tie, is to be worn, this should be noted on the invitation. On a handwritten invitation the hostess writes in either "Black tie" or "White tie" in the lower right hand corner. If neither appears on the handwritten invitation, a dark suit is acceptable.

Replies to formal invitations. All invitations should be answered promptly, whether or not you can attend. A formal invitation follows a set pattern. It is answered in the third person and should be written in long hand on fine quality white or off-white double-fold stationery. If the invitation comes to the home the wife may answer it or the husband may ask his secretary to do it. If the invitation is to the man only and is sent to his office address, he may reply on his personal business stationery. Follow these pointers in responding to formal invitations:

1. If the invitation names more than one person as a sender, or as intended guests, mention each name in your reply.
2. The only abbreviations allowed are Mr., Mrs., and Dr. The word junior is written out, with no capital—Mr. Robertson, junior.
3. The correct way to write the time, when it is not on the hour is "half past seven o'clock" or "half after seven o'clock." Never use "seven-thirty."
4. Never refer to yourself by a courtesy title, such as Excellency or Honorable, either in issuing or replying to invitations.
5. In an acceptance, specify the day and hour on the invitation,

but mention only the date in a regret. The year is never used, either in the invitation or the reply.

6. In an acceptance, use the words "kind invitation." When you send your regrets, use "very kind invitation" or "kind invitation."
7. It is not necessary to give a reason for not being able to attend—unless, of course, your invitation is from the White House or royalty.

Here is a sample of a formal reply:

Acceptance

Mr. and Mrs. George Franklin Smith
accept with pleasure
the kind invitation of
Mr. and Mrs. Renaud
to dine
on Thursday, the fifteenth of April
at half-past seven o'clock

Also acceptable are these replacements for the third, fourth and fifth lines:

. . . .
. . . .
Mr. and Mrs. Renaud's
kind invitation for dinner
. . . .

Regrets

Unless you are "regretting" an invitation from the White House or the head of state in another country, it is no longer considered necessary to give an excuse. The formal note of regret is written by hand in the third person on fine quality double-fold writing paper.

Mr. and Mrs. David Baxter

regret that they are unable to accept

Mr. and Mrs. Renaud's

very kind invitation for dinner

on Thursday, the fifteenth of April

Most authorities consider it good form to use "*very* kind invitation" when regretting an invitation. Others consider that "kind invitation" is perfectly proper.

Giving an excuse may be old-fashioned, but it is still polite. The formal excuses are standardized and the only ones considered valid are illnesses, a previous engagement, or absence from the city.

Mr. and Mrs. David Baxter

regret that owing to a previous engagement

(. . . . . *to their absence from San Francisco*)

they are unable to accept

Mr. and Mrs. Renaud's

very kind invitation to dinner

on Thursday, the fifteenth of April

Also acceptable are these wordings:

. . . .

regret that a previous engagement

prevents their accepting

. . . .

. . . .

. . . .

. . . .

regret that their absence from San Francisco

will prevent their accepting

. . . .

. . . .

. . . .

Informal invitations. The usual home dinner party is at most semi-formal, and the invitation may be telephoned or sent out on the hostess's calling card (or the host's, if he is a bachelor):

Dinner

Wednesday, June 2, 8 o'clock

Mrs. John Paul Shelton

4 Glenwood Road

R.S.V.P. *Black Tie*

(The guest takes it for granted that street clothes will be worn unless "Black tie" is written on invitations of this type.)

Also used for informal invitations and acceptances are informals, which are fold-over cards on which the individual's name, or a husband and wife's joint names, are engraved or printed. Here is an example of an informal invitation sent out by a couple:

Dinner Friday

Mr. and Mrs. David Minor Root

March 8, 7:30 P.M.

R.s.v.p. *Duck Pond Road*

Or the hostess may write an informal note of invitation, as follows:

> *Dear Mrs. Cory,*
>
> *Will you and Mr. Cory dine with us on Wednesday, the tenth of October, at seven o'clock, and then go on to see "My Fair Lady"?*
>
> *Do hope you can be with us.*
>
> *Sincerely,*

In social notes, either a comma or no punctuation at all is used after the salutation.

Replying to informal invitations. A telephone acceptance or regret is the usual reply to an informal invitation. However, your reply may be sent on a calling card or on an informal.

Accept with pleasure!
Friday at 7:30
Mr. and Mrs. Vincent Carberry

Sorry we can't join you
Friday—it's Opera Night.
Mrs. Charles Lawrence Mendham

A note of acceptance is brief and repeats the date and the time.

> Dear Mrs. Allen
>
> We will be pleased to dine with you on Wednesday the tenth at seven o'clock and then go on to see "My Fair Lady."
>
> Many thanks for thinking of us.
>
> Sincerely,

A note of regret would express thanks for the invitation and state the reason you are unable to accept.

Inviting a business friend home for dinner. Unless you have competent help in your home on a full-time basis, it isn't fair—either to your wife or to the guest—to invite someone home to dinner at the last minute. It might be the night a rib roast is to be served, but then again it might be the time your wife plans to serve scrambled eggs and leftover ham because she's been working hard for some good cause all day.

The diplomatic thing to do is to telephone home first before issuing an invitation. This saves embarrassment all around. The whole point in entertaining business guests is to establish a feeling of good will between them and you. This won't be the case if you put a guest in a situation where he feels awkward and unwanted and is conscious of your wife's discomfiture because she hasn't been given the opportunity to appear at her best.

When a Woman Entertains Business Guests

The woman who does business entertaining has to use tact and diplomacy in order not to intrude on what men assume is their territory. There's a fine balance to be maintained, and it takes a clever woman to buy a man lunch, discuss business and at the same time defer to him in the time-honored ways a woman does to a male escort. Fortunately, it can all be handled smoothly.

Taking a man to lunch. To prevent embarrassment, the woman executive should avoid taking a male guest to lunch at a restaurant where she cannot use a charge account or a credit card. Although the fact that business women have occasion to invite men to lunch is accepted with equanimity in the business world, it is a rare man who can sit by unconcernedly while a woman pays the luncheon check and tips the waiter. A credit card can be handled so unobtrusively that even the people at the next table won't be sure whose it is. And signing a check can also be done swiftly and without fuss. The female executive will give her luncheon order to the man she is with, just as though he were her escort.

The business woman entertains at dinner. The woman who takes business guests out to dinner will find it to her advantage to order dinner ahead of time. Her guests need only order their own cocktails. When this plan is not followed and guests choose from the menu, the hostess should ask one of the male guests to give the order of the women guests to the waiter. He will also order wine, if she has not already done so and wishes it served with the meal. If she has a male escort or a husband, of course he will perform these tasks.

·24· Invitations to Official Dinners and Functions

There are numerous occasions when large groups of business men are entertained. A dinner might be given to honor a retiring officer of a company or a distinguished person; as a means of stimulating interest in a civic or cultural project or a fund-raising campaign; to mark an anniversary; and so on.

Examples of Invitations

The following are examples of invitations and replies to various types of official events.

An invitation to a testimonial dinner

You are cordially invited to attend a

TESTIMONIAL DINNER

in honor of

A. A. KIRKLAND
Official of the Borough of Lakely
for Fifty Years

To Be Held On

April 25, 19__
at seven-thirty o'clock
Twin Brook Country Club

R.S.V.P.
By April 5

$10.00 per plate
Informal Dress

Committee to Honor A. A. Kirkland
C. D. Allen and B. G. Rosen, Co-Chairmen

This invitation to a testimonial dinner is printed on a 4½ x 5½" card.

An invitation of this type usually includes a small printed card on which the recipient indicates how many reservations he wishes.

> Enclosed please find my
> check for $............in payment
> of .... reservations for the
> A. A. Kirkland Testimonial Dinner.
>
> (Signature) ....

A really efficient arrangements committee might then send back the following acknowledgment card on which is printed the guest's ticket numbers and table assignment.

> We acknowledge with thanks
> your reservation for the
>
> A. A. Kirkland Testimonial
>
> Dinner on April 25,
>
> 7:30 p.m. at the Twin
> Brook Country Club.
>
> TICKET NUMBERS: 143-144
>
> TABLE NUMBER: 12
>
> Committee to Honor A. A. Kirkland
> C. D. Allen and B. G. Rosen, Co-Chairmen

This invitation to a reception is engraved on the first page of fine quality double-fold letter paper.

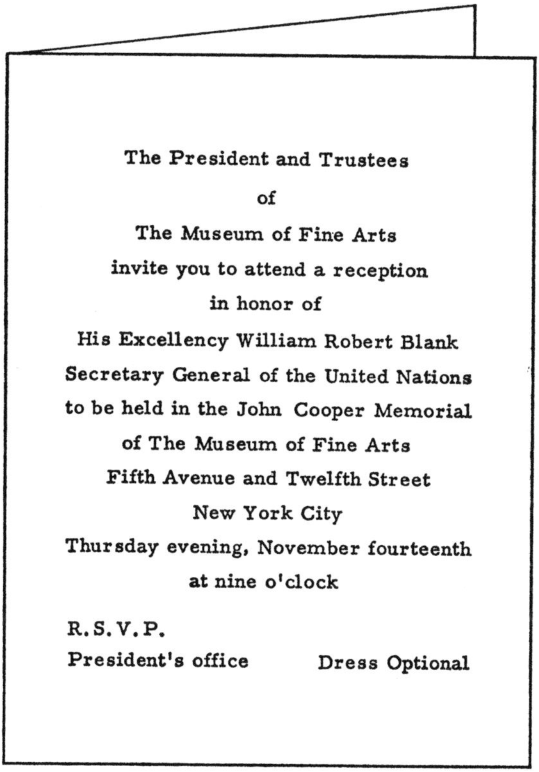

The President and Trustees
of
The Museum of Fine Arts
invite you to attend a reception
in honor of
His Excellency William Robert Blank
Secretary General of the United Nations
to be held in the John Cooper Memorial
of The Museum of Fine Arts
Fifth Avenue and Twelfth Street
New York City
Thursday evening, November fourteenth
at nine o'clock

R.S.V.P.
President's office Dress Optional

Invitations to a cocktail party and reception

The International Construction Company
cordially invites you to attend
a cocktail party and reception
at its new offices in the
Triangle Building
26th floor
442 Jay Street, Troy, New York
Friday, the tenth of April
From four until six o'clock

R.s.v.p.

The officers and directors
of the
Hopkins First National Bank
request the pleasure of your company
at the
Formal Dedication
of their new building
at
Broad Street and Front Avenue
Jonesboro, Pennsylvania
on Saturday the twenty-ninth of March
Nineteen hundred and seventy-nine
at three o'clock

R.s.v.p. Cocktails

An invitation to a motion picture premiere

Darell Zeckendorf

President of

Zenith Film Distributors of America

requests the pleasure of the company of

____

at the American Premiere of

While We Sleep

starring Jonathan Clements

Tuesday, December 16, 1972, at 8:30 p.m.

Baron Theatre

Forty-sixth Street and Collins Avenue

R.s.v.p.
Card enclosed

Black Tie

An invitation to attend a preview of a new theater

You are cordially invited to attend

a press review

of the

new Golden Door Theater

Market at 50th Street

and a preview showing of a Jim Warren production

Tall Tales

starring

May Morton Jeffrey Smith Kenneth Moss Barbara Roe

on Saturday afternoon, March 28th

at 2:30 o'clock

Invitation for two

R.s.v.p.

An invitation to a special dinner

(Here is an example of an invitation to a stag dinner in honor of a distinguished guest. When the address to which the reply is to be sent differs from the location of the scheduled event, it is given below the request for a reply.)

Mr. Henry Latham
requests the pleasure of
Mr. Garner's
company at a dinner
in honor of
William Robert Blank, LL.D., Ph.D.
President, Columbia University
on Friday the twenty-fifth of March
at seven o'clock
Sert Room
Waldorf-Astoria
New York

R.s.v.p.
9 Rockefeller Plaza

Black Tie

Examples of Replies

When a reply is requested on a formal invitation the answer must be equally as formal. (See page 209.) When the invitation is addressed to the man at his office, he answers on his personal stationery. This may be double-fold or single sheet of fine quality with engraved initials or house address.

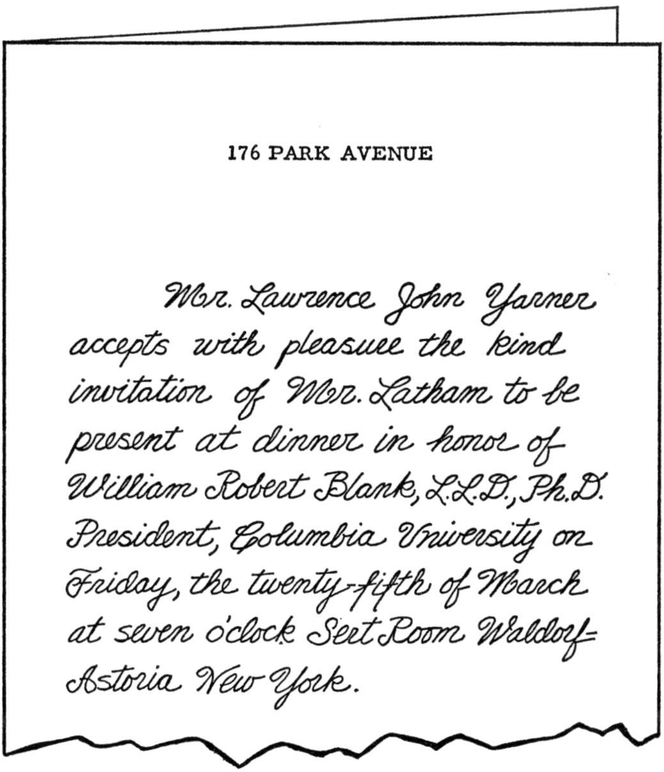
176 PARK AVENUE

Mr. Laurence John Yarner
accepts with pleasure the kind
invitation of Mr. Latham to be
present at dinner in honor of
William Robert Blank, LL.D., Ph.D.
President, Columbia University on
Friday, the twenty-fifth of March
at seven o'clock Sert Room Waldorf-
Astoria New York.

When regretting an invitation, an excuse is not necessary (except to The White House; see page 210). This is the form a man would use to send regrets.

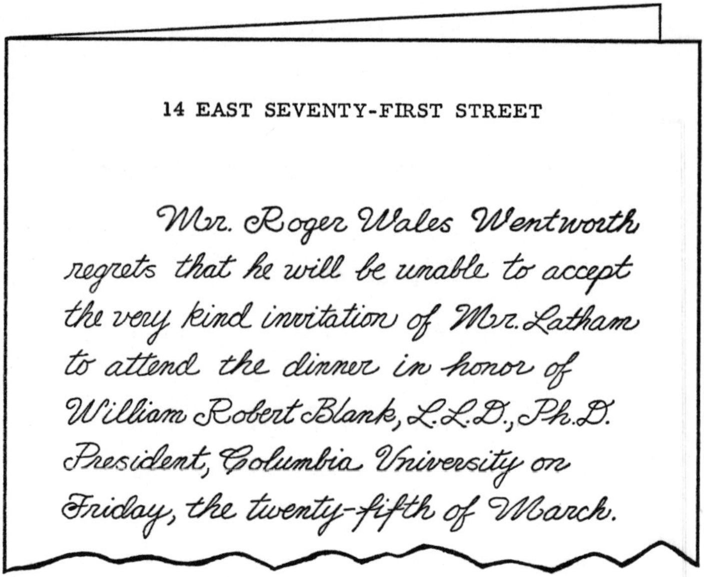

14 EAST SEVENTY-FIRST STREET

Mr. Roger Wales Wentworth
regrets that he will be unable to accept
the very kind invitation of Mr. Latham
to attend the dinner in honor of
William Robert Blank, L.L.D., Ph.D.
President, Columbia University on
Friday, the twenty-fifth of March.

Official dinners are usually preceded by a private reception for the guest of honor, at which a group of the more important guests are given the opportunity to meet and talk with him. A card enclosed with the invitation will give the hours and place of the reception.

Celebrating the Business Anniversary

Arrangements for a dinner are substantially the same as those described on page 205 for a formal business luncheon. For an anniversary dinner it is advisable to plan a souvenir program including important dates in the company's history, names of present and perhaps past officers, the menu, the list of speakers, and the entertainment for the evening. Invitations may be formal or informal.

Formal invitations should be engraved in black on heavy white or off-white stock. No address, monogram or initial is put at the top. A 4″ x 5½″ card may be used, or double-fold notepaper with the engraving on the front page. An example of the latter style follows:

In honor of

the Fiftieth Anniversary of

its founding

The Smith-Dunn Company

requests the pleasure of

your company

at dinner

on Friday, the twenty-first of April

at seven o'clock

Sert Room

Waldorf-Astoria

New York

R. s. v. p.
30 Rockefeller Plaza — Black Tie

Instead of R.s.v.p., a small response card (with return addressed envelope) can be enclosed on which is printed the following:

I will attend ....

I will not attend ....

Signature ....

Another response card:

M______________________________

will________________attend

If the dinner is to be a fairly small one, confined to close friends and business associates, the invitations may be as informal as the following letter:

Dear Mr. Johnson:

On Friday, January 7, Speare and Company will observe its Fiftieth Anniversary with a banquet in the Terrace Room of the Plaza Hotel. Dinner will be at seven o'clock, with cocktails at six.

It is our sincere hope that you will attend as our guest. The long and fruitful association of our two companies makes it particularly appropriate that you share this happy occasion with us.

A brief program of entertainment will follow dinner.

Cordially yours,

Warmth and sincerity should characterize your reply to an invitation of this kind. The following is an example of a reply to an informal invitation to an anniversary dinner:

Dear Mr. Hall:

It is with a real sense of pleasure that I accept your invitation to attend your company's Fiftieth Anniversary Banquet on Friday, January 7. I shall join you in the Terrace Room of the Plaza as soon after six o'clock as I can make it.

Our association through the years has been a mutually gratifying one, and I wish you continued success in the years to come.

I look forward to helping you celebrate this auspicious occasion.

Cordially,

·25· Entertaining at the Office or Plant

There are occasions when a company wishes to entertain on its own premises customers or clients or the public in general. Luncheons, tours, open-houses and cocktail parties are the most widely used means of celebrating special events, or merely having people get to know your plant and the people who work in it.

Basic check list. No matter what form your entertaining takes, these are the essential arrangements:

1. Establish a date.
2. Prepare a guest list.
3. Select employees who will act as guides, hostesses, hosts, speakers, and whatever else your plans call for.
4. Issue invitations.
5. Keep a record of acceptances.
6. Make arrangements with the caterer, if refreshments or a meal will be served.
7. Arrange for transportation facilities.

Establishing a date. Select a date far enough in advance so that the chances are good of invited guests being able to accept. If there is to be a guest of honor, first ask him what date would be most suitable.

Preparing a guest list. Make a list of the people you think should be invited and write their affiliation next to each name. As you do this, make sure in your own mind that each person is important enough to you or your company to warrant an invitation. The list will doubtless need the approval of a company officer. After this is received, copies of the list and a rough outline of the plans should be sent to each company participant. If you wish, the names of the guests can also be typed on individual 3 x 5 cards for filing and future reference.

Selecting employees to assist. Attractive people make a good impression as guides, hosts, and hostesses, but it is even more important that they be articulate, so that if anyone asks a question about the company he won't get a blank stare or a meaningless reply.

Give assistants a preliminary briefing on the event. Assign each a definite job, if possible, and make sure he or she understands the duties involved. Follow up the briefing with a reminder memorandum that spells out the details again.

Issuing invitations. The invitations themselves can be as formal or informal as you wish, but they should be sent out at least four weeks in advance of the event. If all the replies are not in by the week before the occasion, follow-up telephone calls should be made to those not heard from to determine whether they expect to attend. If special buses or cars will be used to transport guests, include on the invitation (or on a small card enclosure) details as to the time they will leave and from where.

Keeping a record of replies. Keep a list (as described on page 206) of replies to invitations.

From the list of acceptances, have identification badges made up with the names and affiliation of each guest. Company employee name badges should be a different color from the ones for guests.

Making arrangements with the caterer. The caterer will need to know the number of people expected and the menu, at least a week before the event. Discuss with him the type of food most suitable to the occasion.

Transporting guests. Hire enough buses or limousines for the number of people who need transportation. Arrange for parking space for those who will arrive in private cars. A section of the company parking area may have to be roped off, or similar precautions taken.

The Reception

Make arrangements according to the list on page 227. At least 15 minutes before the guests are due to arrive, all company people attending the reception should gather for last-minute instructions and a review of the objectives of the affair. The guest of honor, if there is to be one, should be present for this.

Greeting guests. A welcoming committee greets guests, asks them to sign the guest book, and hands out name badges.

Mixing with guests. Hosts and hostesses circulate among the guests, introducing lonely looking guests to others and making sure that neither guests nor employees monopolize the attention of company executives. When executives and employees have been conversing with guests for a while, a host or hostess should bring new people to the group or suggest that the guests might like to meet one of the other executives. Employees should not gather in groups by themselves.

Employees should offer to have guests' glasses or cups refilled whenever they see an empty one. When liquor is served, employees are well advised either to limit the number of drinks they take or to abstain altogether.

Ending the party on time. Quietly closing the bar and clearing the refreshment table at the time the party is supposed to end will prevent the "I never want to go home" type of guest from overstaying his welcome.

The Tour

The general list of arrangements given at the beginning of this chapter serve in setting up a tour of your company's building or buildings. Guests should be met by their host in the reception room and invited to sign the guest book. Limit the number of guests on a tour to about eight, but if you cannot avoid having a larger group, break it down into several smaller units with individual guides.

Timing the tour. Don't rush tours through, even if a limit must be set on the areas covered by the tour. Describe in as interesting a fashion as possible the work of various departments, and provide an opportunity for guests to ask questions and have them answered, and to talk with executives and department heads.

It is a good idea to have members of large and important tours meet together at the conclusion of the tour for a brief wind-up talk by an executive of the company and a question and answer period.

Serving refreshments. When refreshments are to be served, this can be done at the conclusion of the tour or of the follow-up session. Depending on the hour of the day, tiny sandwiches, cakes and cookies, and tea, coffee or punch (non-alcoholic) may be served.

A follow-up letter. Although not necessary, it is a gracious gesture to send each tour guest a letter thanking him or her for the visit. The following is an example of a letter of this type:

> Dear Mr. Jones:
>
> It is always a pleasure to have our friends and neighbors—particularly those who are members of local governing bodies—visit us and acquaint themselves with our methods of operation and our products.
>
> We enjoyed having you as our guest on ______(date)______, and hope you will come again.
>
> Sincerely,
> John J. Blank
> President

The Luncheon

Follow the list of planning procedures at the beginning of this section (page 227).

After all the acceptances have been received, work out a seating plan and make out place cards.

When an executive of the company is to be guest speaker, the host (president or chairman of the board) should send him a detailed outline of topics he would like to have covered. This should be done as soon as the invitations are sent out so that he will have time to work on his speech.

The Open House

There are two types of open house—the general open house, a large affair to which employees and their families, members of the community, and dignitaries from surrounding towns are invited, and the special (and smaller) open house for specific groups such as librarians, educators, the press, high school seniors, and so on.

Here is an example of an open house invitation that one company used. It was printed on a folded card.

50 YEARS 1913 – 1963

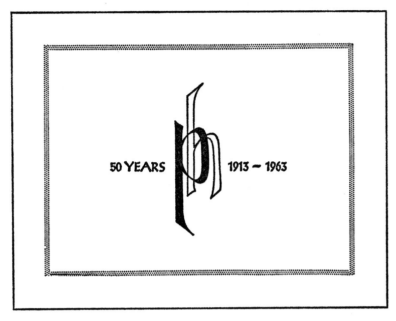

cover

YOU AND THE MEMBERS OF YOUR FAMILY

ARE CORDIALLY INVITED TO ATTEND

THE OPEN HOUSE AND RECEPTION

OBSERVING THE

FIFTIETH ANNIVERSARY OF

PRENTICE-HALL, INC.

ADMINISTRATIVE OFFICES
ENGLEWOOD CLIFFS
NEW JERSEY

SUNDAY
OCTOBER THIRTEENTH
1:00 TO 5:00 P.M.

message

Extra planning for an open house. In addition to the regular list of planning procedures on page 227, the following points must be considered:

1. Begin planning for an open house early—several weeks before the invitations go out. If residents of nearby communities are to be invited, check the town calendars to make sure the date you select doesn't conflict with some previously scheduled event. (Sundays are good days for a general open house.)
2. Mail tickets of admission with the invitations.
3. Ask the help of the local Police Department if the traffic is expected to be heavy.
4. Arrange for department heads to institute clean-up campaigns in preparation for the event.
5. Train additional guides.
6. Arrange to have the First Aid Room open and the company nurse on duty.
7. If you have no public relations or publicity department, either hire someone on a free-lance basis or appoint a staff member to see that news of the event reaches all the newspapers that cover your area. Be sure he invites the newspapers to send a reporter and photographer (or either one) the day of the open house. When time permits he should also plan a folder of informative material about the company, and possibly a souvenir of the occasion, to be given to each guest.
8. Plan with the caterer the amount of food that will be required.
9. Order whatever flowers are necessary for the tables or as decorative accents.
10. The day before the general open house, have a committee inspect the grounds and the individual departments. Make sure directional signs and displays are adequate and informative.

Receiving the guests. Guests are received as they would be for a tour; that is, a committee welcomes them in the reception room and invites them to sign the guest book. Have a host or hostess accompany guests when they join the party and stay with them for a few minutes until they feel at home. Identification badges are not necessary at a large open house. Souvenirs may be handed to guests as they leave; perhaps a folder of descriptive and informative material.

Follow-up letters should go to all who sign the guest book. Individual (not form) letters should be sent to dignitaries among the guests.

·26· Entertaining Employees

The company that doesn't have an occasional party for its employees is a dull, lifeless place indeed. It boosts morale for management to sponsor an annual gala at which everyone from the president on down can enjoy himself.

Service club luncheons or dinners, Christmas parties for employees and their families, and summer outings are a few of the ways in which the officers of a company show appreciation to the people who work for them. While management sponsors and pays for these events, arrangements are usually turned over to employee committees.

How to Plan a Large Company Party

Meticulous attention to detail is essential to the success of a large party. Only exact planning of every detail will permit everyone attending to relax and have a good time—which is, after all, the main purpose of a party.

The following is a checklist you can use in arranging a large company luncheon, or dinner, or banquet.

1. Set the date.
2. Reserve the room.
3. Prepare and mail invitations.
4. Plan program.
5. Decide on menu.
6. Print program.
7. Select souvenirs.
8. Order flowers.
9. Plan seating.

Setting the date. When the affair is to be a large one, it is advisable to get a choice of dates from two or three hotels so that the committee can make a choice. This should be done well in advance of the event—a year ahead isn't too long in many cities. Talk to the banquet managers in person about the availability of dates and rooms.

Deciding where to hold the party. If space in the company cafeteria permits, a company luncheon or dinner may be held there. But it usually adds to the festivity of the occasion to hold it somewhere else. As soon as the committee makes its decision as to where to hold the party, confirm the date in writing with the hotel or restaurant decided on.

Preparing and mailing invitations. A stiff white or ivory card about 3½ x 5 inches in size is proper for invitations. When the affair is an annual one, the invitations can be engraved or printed in quantity, with space left for filling in the date and time. The following sample invitation is issued by one company for its annual service club dinner:

Your Presence Is Requested at

The Annual Dinner of

The Quarter-Century Club

of

PARSONS-HILBERT

On
At
R.S.V.P.

Another type of invitation—this one to a service club luncheon—shown on page 237. This is double-fold style on quality paper.

50 WEST FIFTIETH STREET
NEW YORK 20, N.Y.

You are cordially invited to attend
the 1975 Service Award Luncheon
honoring members of the
Blank Organization
with Ten or More Years of Service
at the Hotel Waldorf-Astoria
on Thursday, December seventeenth

Cocktails in the East Foyer at Noon
Luncheon in the Grand Ballroom at
twelve-thirty

There will be no seating reservations
except for those guests who this year
are celebrating
Ten or Twenty-five Years of Service

R.S.V.P.

Use the inter-office mail to send invitations to employees, and send them out at least three weeks in advance of the event.

Planning the program. When the occasion is a service luncheon, awards to those being inducted into a service club can form an important part of the program. They should be presented at the finish of the meal. Personal recognition is given at the time of the presentation. An answering speech is not necessary, but the employee should be informed that if he cares to he may respond to the recognition with either a few words or a brief speech.

For a dinner party, a pianist, organist, or an accordionist may be hired to play during cocktails and while the meal is being eaten. However, a large group of people eating and talking tends to make noise enough to drown out the most determined musician. For this reason, it is usually better to confine the musical periods to before and after the meal.

Invite the company choral group or glee club to present a few songs and if you know of a talented group of employees that writes and performs skits, by all means have them put on a few. When the budget allows, professional talent can be hired—perhaps a monologist or a humorist or a singer—through a talent agent or bureau.

The entire tone of the proceedings is set by the master of ceremonies. Choose as experienced a person as you possibly can for this task. He should have, if possible, a good voice, a ready wit, and a wide acquaintanceship among the employees.

Deciding on the menu. Always plan the menu with the aid of the caterer or banquet manager. Try not to make the meal an ordinary, creamed-chicken-and-peas-in-a-patty-shell kind of thing, but don't choose something too exotic either. In general, it is wise to have a choice of fish or meat for the main course. Specify the cocktails or wine to be served.

Printing the program. The program should be attractive, whether it is a detailed one or merely a listing of the menu. If the program is for a service club luncheon or dinner, all the members can be listed in it or only those joining on this occasion. If there is entertainment, include it in the program so that guests will know what they're watching and what comes next.

Selecting souvenirs. For a large affair, the program makes an excellent souvenir and should be designed with this in mind—that is, on fine quality paper with an attractive, commemorative cover. It can include information pertinent to the event, as well as the menu, committees, and so on. Otherwise, a small item appropriate to the occasion can be given as a souvenir.

Ordering the flowers. Flowers for the head table and leaves or ferns for the other tables should be ordered from your usual florist about a week ahead of the party. He will deliver and arrange them the day of the affair.

If boutonnieres and corsages are purchased for the guests at the head table, they can either be presented to them during cocktails or put at their places at the table.

Indicating seating arrangements. At many large affairs, place cards are used only at the head table. Even then, if the head table is a large one, a diagram of the seating arrangement helps people find their places more readily than if they have to walk up and down reading each card. If guests are assigned to certain tables, post at the entrance to the banquet room an alphabetical list of the guests with the number of the table next to each. Also helpful is a numerical list of tables, opposite each of which is a list of the names of the guests who are to sit at it.

When a buffet is served, guests serve themselves and take seats where they please at small tables. This is informal, and gives executives the chance to mingle with the employees.

Identifying who's who. Name badges for everyone attending help people get to know each other; in a large company this is especially important. An identification badge will give everyone a chance to link names with faces that look familiar. It's a memory aid, too, because the chances are you won't easily forget a name you've seen as well as heard. The badges can be laid out alphabetically on a table at the entrance.

The tipping problem. If tips for the waiters were included in the overall cost—and they should be—a small "stand up" card should be placed on each table with the information printed on it that gratuities have been taken care of by the Committee on Arrangements. If tips have not been arranged for, the waiter will pass a small plate (or one man can ask him for one) into which each guest should put a tip.

Behavior at the Office Party

Discretion and moderation are the foundation of proper behavior at an office party. Remember, you'll be back on the job when the party's over.

How to conduct yourself. Whenever possible, introduce people to one another, taking special notice of the wallflowers who stand silently in corners. But don't try to be the life of the party; you'll only make a nuisance of yourself.

Younger employees should be alert to the needs of older ones and can politely serve hors d'oeuvres and offer to replenish drinks. But these thoughtful efforts shouldn't be carried to the point where senior employees are made to feel ancient and decrepit.

Should a fellow employee behave badly, or say something in poor taste, it's best to just smile pleasantly and say nothing.

Keep your manner friendly and pleasant and be prepared to enjoy yourself. Executives of a company should move freely among the employees, who must refrain from monopolizing their time or making use of what should be a festive occasion to bring up grievances or argue about company policy. At an occasion of this kind everyone should forget about work and its problems and make every effort to have a good time himself and see that others have a good time.

The drinking problem. Unfortunately, drinking at office parties can become a serious problem. There are always those who drink too much for their own good (and everybody else's), then return to work with the uncomfortable feeling that they made fools of themselves.

Anyone who knows he is inclined to drink immoderately would be well advised to stay away from a party of this kind. If you drink at all at an office party, do so in moderation. Laxity in this respect is no more excusable at an office party than at a social event.

• Part 5 • Etiquette in Business Meetings

•27• Formal and Informal Meetings

Formal Meetings

The courtesies and protocol that smooth the progress of meetings are determined mainly by the size and kind of meeting that is held. For example, parliamentary procedure, or some form of it, is traditionally followed at corporate or stockholders' meetings. At less formal meetings the chairman will indicate the procedure to be followed.

Conduct of a formal meeting. Etiquette is the base on which rest the rules governing the conduct of formal meetings, whether it be a club meeting or a corporate meeting. These rules are embodied in a system known as parliamentary procedure, under which participants in a formal meeting discuss and vote on the business at hand in a courteous, democratic, yet efficient way.

The basics of parliamentary law govern:

1. Presentation of motions from the floor
2. Recognition of members by the president
3. Debate or discussion of motions
4. Taking of the vote.

NOTE: For more details on parliamentary procedure, see the special section beginning at page 287.

The Stockholders' Meeting

Meetings of stockholders are held by all business corporations. Preparations for such a meeting include the following:

1. Sending notice of the meeting, and proxies, to stockholders
2. Handling proxies as they are returned by stockholders
3. Deciding who shall be nominated as directors
4. Preparing ballots
5. Compiling list of stockholders
6. Scheduling the order of business
7. Deciding who shall be nominated as inspectors of election
8. Preparing a tentative draft of the minutes of the meeting and of any resolutions to be presented at the meeting.

The purpose of a stockholders' meeting. The purpose of convening investors and management is so that stockholders may hear a report on the financial condition of the company and also exercise their rights in regard to corporate action. The general management of a corporation is handled by the board of directors, but certain rights (which vary in different jurisdictions) are reserved to the stockholders as the owners of the corporation.

Calling a stockholders' meeting. The call for a meeting is the exercise by the proper person or persons of the power to bring the meeting into being. Usually the call consists of a written direction to the secretary or other officer authorized to notify the stockholders. In some instances a copy of the call must be posted on a bulletin board in the main office of the corporation.

Sending notice to the stockholders. The notice of a meeting tells the stockholders when a meeting is to be held, and where, and at what time. In the case of special meetings, the notice may also state the matters to be discussed and the business to be transacted.

The notice may be sent out on a postcard or in a sealed envelope. Stockholders generally prefer the latter method, feeling that the use of cards exposes their private affairs to the eyes of the curious. Proxy forms accompany the notice of the meeting.

What to do with a proxy form. A stockholder who does not plan to attend the meeting signs the proxy and returns it to the corporation. A proxy is authorization for someone—usually a director—to vote at the meeting in place of the absent stockholder. The need for proxies is based on the fact that meetings generally cannot be held unless a quorum (a certain portion) of the stock is represented.

Stockholder's proxy for annual meeting

............Company

Stockholder's Proxy

No. ....

Number of Shares

Preferred ....

Common ....

KNOW ALL MEN BY THESE PRESENTS, that the undersigned hereby constitutes and appoints .... and .... and each of them, Attorneys and Agents with power of substitution to vote at the Annual Meeting of the Stockholders of .... Company, to be held at the office of the Company, ... Street, ... City, on the ...... day of ...., 19 ...... at twelve o'clock noon, and at any adjournment(s) thereof, according to the number of votes that the undersigned would be entitled to vote if then personally present.

WITNESS the hand of the undersigned this .... day of .... one thousand nine hundred and ....

(Sign here).....................

Follow-up for proxies. In order to assure a quorum at the annual meeting of stockholders, many corporations follow up the original notice of a meeting and proxy request by sending letters to those stockholders who have not mailed in their proxies. Proxies become particularly important when a proxy campaign is being conducted by a group of stockholders opposed to the management. A follow-up must not violate the regulations of the Securities and Exchange Act. Here is an illustration of a follow-up used by one corporation:

Proxy follow-up

.... 19 ......

Dear Sir:

The proxy form sent to you with the annual report has not been received by us. A quorum at our annual meeting depends upon proxy returns. The vast number of our shareholders, numbering close to .... reside at points so remote from .... that they cannot attend in person. Consequently, the timely receipt of proxies has an importance which it is the purpose of this notice to emphasize.

We hope you will attend this year's meeting. If, however, you do not expect to do so, please sign and mail the proxy. In the event that you have mislaid the previous copy, a duplicate proxy is enclosed.

We will be very appreciative of your help.

Yours very truly,

....

President

Receipt of proxies is frequently acknowledged with a courteous letter, although this is not required by law.

A common error. Frequently the call and the notice of a meeting are combined over the signature of the secretary. There is no indication that the meeting was called by the individual or group empowered to do so. Care should be taken to avoid this irregularity. Properly, the notice of the meeting should end with a paragraph reading "By order of," followed by the title of the officer who has the power to call the meeting and the signature of the secretary, indicating he is issuing the notice pursuant to a call by the authorized officer.

Here are examples of a call and a notice of a stockholders' meeting:

Call of regular annual meeting of stockholders by president

To ...., Secretary:

Under power given to me by the By-laws of the .... Corporation, as President of the .... Corporation,

I hereby call the regular annual meeting of the stockholders of the ...., to be held on (day of week), ... 19 ..... at .... A.M., at the principal office of the Corporation, No. .... Street, City of ...., State of ...., for the following purposes: (1) to elect a board of .... directors for the ensuing year; (2) to consider and vote upon the approval and ratification of all contracts, acts, proceedings, elections, and appointments which shall have been theretofore made or taken by the Board of Directors, as set forth in the minutes of the meetings of the Board of Directors; and (3) to transact such other business as may properly come before the meeting or any adjournments thereof.

You are directed, as Secretary of the .... Corporation, to give notice of the meeting in the manner prescribed in the By-laws.

Dated at ...., this .... day of ...., 19 ....

....

President

Notice of annual meeting of stockholders

.... 19 ......

The annual meeting of the stockholders of the .... Company, for the election of Directors and the transaction of such other business as may properly come before the meeting, will be held at the office of the Company on (day of week), ... 19 ......, at ...... A.M.

If you cannot be present at the meeting, please sign and return the accompanying proxy in the enclosed envelope.

....

Secretary

Where and when the meetings are held. Meetings of the stockholders must be held at the place designated in the by-laws or the charter. They must start promptly at the hour set. Generally the corporation serves a meal—usually a catered box lunch—to the stockholders present.

At one time corporations went out of their way to hold annual meetings in such remote and inaccessible places that stockholders were hard put to reach them. In recent years, due in large part to the efforts of a few articulate stockholders, there has been a trend away from this practice. In fact, corporations are now so anxious to keep investors informed that many of them follow up their regular annual meeting with regional meetings in major cities or wherever there is a large concentration of holdings. Usually, the ballroom of a good hotel is hired for these regional meetings, with either luncheon or dinner provided by the corporation. A further step is to have closed-circuit telecasts of annual meetings for the benefit of stockholders in large cities throughout the country. In this way the proceedings of the annual meetings become accessible to a maximum number of stockholders simultaneously.

Special features of stockholders' meetings. In line with courteous treatment of stockholders and the wish to keep them informed, motion pictures or slide films on some aspect of the business of a corporation are frequently shown at stockholders' meetings. Promotion literature is distributed, as are product samples, when the product is something that can be carried home. Also, stockholders are exhorted to visit home offices, plants, and branch offices as guests of the management.

Arriving at a meeting. Stockholders are permitted to sit where they please, but ushers are usually present to help the old or the lame find a comfortable spot. First, though, a clerk asks each person his name and address and whether he is a stockholder or has been appointed proxy for a stockholder. This information is checked against a list the clerk has. If the stockholder has not signed a proxy, he may be asked whether he wishes to do so. Or, if he has filed a proxy, the clerk may inquire whether the stockholder wishes to revoke it or let it stand. Some corporations discard the proxy if the stockholder is present in person at the meeting.

Order of business. A corporation's by-laws usually prescribe the order of business. Although it is not mandatory that this order be followed, it is the proper (and wise) thing to do. A logical order of business, such as the following, expedites the conduct of a meeting of stockholders:

1. Call to order
2. Election of a chairman and, if necessary, the appointment of a temporary secretary
3. Presentation of proofs of the due calling of the meeting
4. Presentation of list of stockholders
5. Presentation and examination of proxies
6. Announcement of a quorum
7. Reading and settlement of the minutes of the previous meeting
8. Reports of officers and committees
9. Appointment of inspectors of election
10. Opening of polls
11. Election of directors
12. Closing of polls
13. Report of inspectors
14. Declaration of election of directors
15. Ratification of directors' and executive committee's acts
16. New business
17. Adjournment.

Who presides at the meeting? The by-laws usually provide who shall call the meeting to order and who shall preside. Usually the president or some other officer is given the power to preside at all stockholders' meetings. Occasionally the provision appears in the corporate charter. If there is no provision, or if the proper officer is not present, any person entitled to participate in the meeting may call it to order and the meeting may choose its own chairman by a per capita vote. If there is any dissent, it is wiser to take the vote by shares. It is advisable to have some executive officer attend a meeting of the stockholders, although officers and directors of a company are not required to attend. A large corporation has its general counsel attend also, as adviser to the chairman.

Behavior of a chairman. Chairing a meeting requires patience, tact, and a sense of fairness. If the by-laws provide that the meeting shall be conducted according to the rules prescribed by a manual on parliamentary procedure, the requirement must be enforced. While a stockholders' meeting is not so formal that the rules of parliamentary law *must* be observed, ordinary parliamentary usages apply to it. The chairman recognizes members who are entitled to address the meeting, states the questions and puts them to a vote, calls for nominations in elections, announces the results of all votes, preserves order, and has the right to refuse to put a motion to a vote if the matter proposed by the motion is not within the legal powers of the meeting. As he must insist on ruling on matters of procedure and points of order, the chairman should have beside him copies of his corporation's charter and by-laws, as well as a copy of one of the well-known manuals on parliamentary procedure.

The chair is also responsible for declaring the meeting closed and vouching for the correctness of minutes by putting his signature to them.

Behavior of the stockholder. Those who attend a stockholders' meeting are expected to abide by ordinary parliamentary usages. The chair is addressed as "Mr. Chairman" or "Sir." When a woman presides, it is permissible to address her as "Mr. Chairman" but more courteous to say "Madam Chairman" or "Madam."

A stockholder wishing to speak doesn't just get up and start talking. He must rise and address the chair. When two or more persons rise to speak, the chairman calls upon the one who first rose in his place. Each person who rises to speak must direct his speech to the motion under discussion, to a motion or amendment to be proposed by himself, or to a question of order. No one may speak twice on a question except in explanation or reply, and he may not interrupt in order to do so.

When a stockholder wants to present a new idea he should work out a systematic plan of presentation and express it with confidence. Speakers should keep their remarks impersonal and as brief as possible. Screaming and yelling are to be heard at some annual meetings, much to the disgust of those who must sit and listen. Needless to say, such behavior is rude and uncalled for, as are contemptuous references to the remarks of others and a display of anger towards anyone who argues from the opposite point of view. Chatting with a neighbor when someone else has the floor also is a breach of etiquette.

For further pointers on behavior, see the "Guide to Parliamentary Procedure" in the back of this book.

Directors' Meetings

Meetings of boards of directors may be either regular or special, the time and place of the former usually being provided for in the by-laws or in the statutes.

Calling a directors' meeting. The by-laws or statutes usually indicate who has the authority to call a meeting of the board of directors. In general, the chairman of the board has this power, or, in his absence, the president.

Quorum requirements. The presence of a quorum at a directors' meeting is necessary. The presence and vote of directors owning a majority of the stock is not a substitute for quorum requirements. When there is no provision in the statutes, charter or by-laws, a majority of the required number of directors is the minimum for a quorum.

Voting. Unless the statutes, charter or by-laws provide otherwise, a majority vote of the directors present (not the full board) is sufficient. Directors cannot vote by proxy.

Who presides. The chairman of the board, usually the senior officer of the corporation, presides at meetings of the board of directors.

Directors' fees. Frequently fees are paid only to those directors who do not receive a salary as officers of the corporation. Some corporations pay no directors' fees even when all or a number of the directors are not salaried officers of the company. The usual fee is $50 or $100 a meeting, with some of the larger companies paying $500 a meeting. A growing number of corporations are placing their directors on a retainer basis. A quaint custom followed by many corporations is the paying of directors' fees in bank notes. It is also the custom to distribute the amount appropriated for directors' fees among those present at the meeting, so that the greater the number of absentees, the larger is the share for each director who attends.

Preparing an agenda. Several days before the day of the meeting, the secretary of the corporation prepares a list of the things which should be put before the board of directors. This is called the agenda, and when it is printed, matters of a confidential nature are usually omitted.

Agenda form

DATE: PLACE: TIME:

ORGANIZATION:

CHAIRMEN:

SECRETARY'S READING OF MINUTES:

OFFICERS' REPORTS:

COMMITTEE REPORTS:

OLD BUSINESS:

NEW BUSINESS:

ADJOURNMENT:

The secretary also prepares whatever resolutions he deems necessary to carry out the business of the meeting, consulting with whatever legal or technical advisers are necessary. A copy of each resolution and report, as well as a copy of the order of business and a program of the meeting, are placed on the table at each director's place on the day of the meeting.

Sending out notices to the board. Below are samples of the types of notices used to convene boards of directors. Directors may be notified by telephone of a special meeting called in haste.

Notice of regular meeting of directors

A regular meeting of the Board of Directors of The .... Corporation will be held on ...., 19 ..... at .... (Street) .... (City) .... (State).

Business: ....

....

Secretary

Call of regular meeting of directors by president

. . . . 19 . . . . . .

To the Directors of . . . . Corporation:

The undersigned, President of the . . . . Corporation, hereby calls the regular meeting of the Board of Directors of said Corporation, to be held at the office of the Corporation, ... (Street) . . . . (City) . . . . (State), on the . . . . day of . . . . 19 . . . . . ., at . . . . o'clock in the . . . . noon.

. . . .

President

Preparing the board room. When corporate directors meet, they are entitled to clean, quiet, comfortable accommodations. The meeting room must be well aired and tidy and dusted. At each place there should be scratch pads, pencils, and pens. Large ashtrays should be placed on the table so that they are within easy reach of everyone. A water carafe and glasses or paper cups may be placed on a nearby table, or one at each end of the conference table.

Seating the board of directors. Meetings of boards of directors are usually conducted in a formal manner. The chairman sits at the head of the directors' table. Usually the secretary of the corporation sits to his left so that they may consult on the order of business and the secretary may hand the chairman any papers he might need in the course of the meeting. The corporation president sits to the right of the chairman of the board. If a company has no board chairman, then the president presides at board meetings.

What a director does. A member of a board of directors must consider conscientiously every question involving the interests of the company. He is expected to act in good faith and with reasonable care and prudence. Each director exercises his independent judgment concerning matters that come before the board, but it is expected that he will take into consideration the views and arguments advanced by the other board members.

Directors occupy positions of trust and confidence and are considered by the courts as standing in a fiduciary relationship to the stockholders and as being trustees for them. They are expected to represent fully the interests of the corporation and may not use their positions of trust and confidence to further their private interests.

While a director need not attend every meeting of the board of which he is a member, he is expected to be present as often as circumstances permit.

Handling messages during a board meeting. Directors may agree that there shall be no interruptions, in which case the telephone operator or the president's or board chairman's private secretary takes telephone messages while the meeting is in progress. Of course, when the board is made up of working members of an organization, their own secretaries take their telephone calls as usual.

There may be a telephone in the board room, but only vitally important calls are put through.

In some instances arrangements are made for telephone messages to be brought to the secretary during meetings and he, at his discretion, gives them to the board members involved. Unless they are urgent, he may hold them until the meeting is over.

Bringing messages to a board room. When a message or requested papers are delivered to a board room, it is not necessary for the messenger to knock on the door before entering, unless he has been told not to enter. Usually the messenger goes right in, delivers the note or papers to the secretary, and leaves immediately.

Recording the minutes of the meeting. At corporate meetings, the secretary of the corporation usually takes notes. On occasion a stenographer records the entire meeting. If the person keeping such records doesn't hear something that is said, he or she should speak up immediately and ask to have it repeated. This is considered perfectly proper at a formal business meeting; it is important that the minutes be accurate.

Informal Meetings

No parliamentary rules govern informal meetings. Yet, despite the informality—or rather because of it—each participant must observe basic rules of courtesy in order to prevent chaos at such a meeting.

Prompt arrival at meetings and conferences. There are few valid excuses for being late to a meeting or conference. Besides showing a lack of consideration for others, latecomers risk missing out on important decisions and the discussion leading up to them.

Taking notes of the meeting. At an informal meeting of department heads, or at a staff meeting, it usually isn't necessary to have someone take notes of the proceedings. If minutes of the meeting are required, one of the company's secretaries or stenographers can sit in on the meeting. When the meeting is taking place out of the office, a public stenographer can be hired to take notes. Only in an extreme emergency should this task be allotted to one of the participants in the meeting.

Responsibility of the chairman to keep order. Even though parliamentary rules are not in use, the chairman must exercise control over the meeting. Rapping with the gavel is one way of doing this, but there are various other methods by which a chairman can guide and control the behavior of the group.

Keeping calm. No matter how provoked a chairman becomes, he is well advised not to lose his temper. Argument, contradiction, sarcasm, shouting may be momentarily soul-satsifying but they will diminish you in the eyes of others and only serve to further antagonize your opponents. The chairman of a meeting must know a number of courteous ways to circumvent irritating and annoying individuals.

Putting a stop to private conversations. At informal meetings, participants are apt to become involved in discussions among themselves, even though someone else is addressing the meeting. When the chairman decides private conversations are getting out of hand, he may interrupt the person who has the floor, saying, "Just a minute, Ken," and then looking pointedly at the talkers until they cease. Another way of doing this is to look at the men who are talking and say, "I'll call on you gentlemen as soon as I can. Mr. Blank has the floor now." The chairman may be forced to interrupt the speaker and point out that private conversations only hamper the proceedings. Usually, though, catching the eye of one of the men will suffice as a warning and will bring the conversation to an end.

Coping with the monopolizer. When a meeting is not being held under parliamentary rules, there may be one participant who tends to monopolize a discussion. The chairman of the meeting is well advised not to treat the monopolizer discourteously, for such a person frequently has a great deal to offer. His enthusiasm and knowledge can be put to use in many cases, and the meeting speeded up, by appointing him chairman of a committee to study the problem at hand, or by asking him to bring in a detailed report.

If the monopolizer becomes annoying, the chairman may politely but firmly tell him that his views have been heard at length and that he would like to hear what others have to say on the subject. The chairman should then ask a direct question of someone he knows has an opinion and can express it well.

Handling the speaker who wanders. Some speakers, although well-intentioned, just can't address themselves to the topic at hand for any length of time; they soon get off on a tangent. When this happens the chairman should at the first opportunity say something like this: "You've given us a very complete picture, John. With this in mind, let's see where we stand at the moment in relation to the problem under discussion." He can then bring the discussion back to the original topic.

Handling the man who wants to run things. The chairman with a quick temper has a difficult time with this type of person who makes it plain that he thinks he can do everything better than anyone else. One way to meet this challenge is to turn to another member of the group and say, "Don, how would you handle this problem (or proposal) in your department?" Be ready with another question either to the same person or another one, as soon as you get an answer. Be sure the questions are specific and not just general ones.

Handling the crank. The chairman should avoid arguing with this type of person, particularly when it is the chairman's ideas he opposes. When the chairman knows such a person is present at the meeting he can arrange to call on him last for his opinion. If the chairman lays down the following ground rules they will help to control the crank:

- Everyone who wishes to speak will be heard from at least once.
- No one is to object to what is said ahead of him on the first time around.
- No one is to speak twice until all are heard from.

Handling the fellow who has an ax to grind. When someone harps on one particular thing, give it added emphasis whenever possible. If there's a blackboard write it down, underline it at the next mention, and put a check mark next to it for each repeated mention. After a while the fellow with the one-track mind is bound to feel the problem has received the attention he thinks it merits and will keep quiet.

Handling an argument. Only the chairman can effectively handle a situation of this kind. He should stand and remain standing, in order to attract attention. But if he is standing up when the argument breaks out, he should walk to the main trouble spot as though interested, but then ask a direct question of someone a good distance away. A more direct method of ending the argument is to simply request the offenders to end the argument so the meeting can continue.

Handling the silent type. If the discussion doesn't actually affect the silent man or his department, his silence can be overlooked. However, if his department is involved, and you think his ideas should be heard, ask him specific questions in order to bring out his views.

Luncheon and Dinner Meetings

A considerable number of service organizations and business groups hold meetings in conjunction with either lunch or dinner. The chairman of such a meeting must make every effort to see that careful planning and certain small courtesies are observed. It is discourteous to ask people to attend a luncheon or dinner meeting that neither starts nor ends on time; where the atmosphere is noisy, the food poor, and the speeches, reports and announcements too lengthy.

Preparing for the meeting. The chairman should prepare an agenda of all the business, announcements, reports, speeches, and so on that are to be taken up at the meeting. Then if he times everything, adds on approximately 45 minutes for the serving and eating of the meal, he will know how long the meeting will last. Each speaker should be told how many minutes he has and advised that he will be clocked.

Starting on time. Don't put on the invitations a time that you know is merely a guess. If time is being allowed for cocktails before the meal, invite people a half-hour earlier. For instance, the invitation could have on it:

Cocktails	12:30
Lunch	1:00

This would enable the non-drinkers to arrive in time for lunch and not have to waste time waiting for the others.

Organizing the head table. Nothing detracts more from a luncheon or dinner meeting than a head table set for more people than are seated at it. The head table should be filled, even if the dining room captain has to set up a smaller table than had been planned.

Another unwise procedure is to try and seat everyone of some degree of importance at the head table. This can result in a head table so long that it looks ridiculous. When the occasion demands that you have a large number of people at the head table, set up more than one table. As many tables as you need may be placed one in front of the other at different levels. Even a single head table should be raised above the rest of the tables in the room whenever possible.

Invitations to sit at the head table. Let the people you want at the head table know ahead of time. It's bad manners to wait until just before the meal and then go around inviting people to sit at the head table. It's usually a good idea to have all the head table guests enter and take their places as a group.

Head table guests certainly ought to include the speakers for the evening, the master of ceremonies, officials of the sponsoring organization, government officials, ministers, priests, and rabbis, and the heads of important local organizations.

If you have to arrange a head table for a series of luncheons or dinners, try varying the group that sits at it. It gets a little dull for everyone to have to look at the same people time after time. As a variation, senior employees or members could be honored in this fashion one day, or the newest ones, or division heads, and so on.

Seating at the head table. The chairman sits in the center at the head table, with the guest speaker to his right. If there are several speakers, then the second sits to his left, the third next to the first, the fourth next to the second, and so on. When there is a toastmaster, he sits to the right of the chairman and the main speaker to the right of the toastmaster.

If there are women at the head table, alternate them with men, regardless of other seating protocol.

Usually anyone who has a report to give is seated at the head table, but if you have a full table of speakers and distinguished guests, then have reports read from the front of the room and let the people who make them sit elsewhere. When there are no special guests, the principal officers of the organization or club sit at the head table.

When to start the program. The program or business should start as soon as the group has finished eating. If time is limited, announcements and introductions of guests can be made during the meal. But the tables should be cleared of main course dishes before the program or serious business is started.

When noise is a problem. Delegate someone with a sense of diplomacy to handle kitchen noises, outside disturbances, and talking after the program begins. If drinking causes someone to become thoroughly obnoxious, have him escorted outside as quietly and unobtrusively as possible.

When the chairman wants to attract attention. The chairman should stand quietly for a few seconds and tap lightly with his gavel. He can then begin talking in a normal voice to the first few tables. Those sitting at the back tables will become curious and start listening.

Actions at the head table. Anyone who sits at the head table is bound to attract a certain amount of attention. Little mannerisms of which the individual isn't aware can be irritating to the members of the audience. Common examples are squirming in a chair or tilting it back, scratching, tugging, and (the unpardonable rudeness) yawning. Also to be avoided are note taking and obvious glances at a watch or clock. The only acceptable behavior for guests at the head table is to sit quietly and listen attentively to the speakers.

How the chairman should look. The appearance of the person who conducts a meeting is of the utmost importance. The audience will notice hair that needs combing, clothes that are unpressed, shoes that need to be shined, and, in the case of women, hems that are uneven. Men are advised to wear a neat, well-pressed, conservative suit, an immaculate shirt, an unobtrusive tie and socks of a matching hue, and polished shoes on which the heels are not run down. For women the recommended attire is a well cut suit or plain dress in solid colors. Extreme designs and bold patterns are taboo.

No need for comedy. The person conducting a luncheon or dinner meeting needn't feel called on to be a comedian. If an amusing and relevant story occurs to him, it's all right to tell it, but forced jokes and off-color stories are unacceptable.

Thoughtful acts. It's a polite gesture for the person presiding at the meeting to recognize the individual in charge of arrangements and, when the food and service merit it, the chef and head waiter. He may mention them by name, thank them, and ask them to take a bow. Another thoughtful gesture is to send flowers used as table decorations to ill members of the group, or to a hospital or institution.

The Care of Guest Speakers

Guest speakers are a feature of all but the most formal corporate meetings. The professional speaker has to put up with numerous inconveniences and annoyances as he travels around filling engagements. A little thoughtfulness on the part of the program chairman can make life that much more enjoyable for those who travel the speakers' circuit.

Meeting the speaker. Arrange to have someone meet the speaker at the railroad station, bus stop or airport and bring him to the meeting place. If he is arriving by car, appoint someone to be on the lookout for him.

If he is staying over, be sure a room (a good one) is ready for him, and, if possible, allow him time to rest and work on his speech. If his wife is along and there are wives at your convention, appoint one as hostess to the speaker's wife.

Finding out his needs. Don't wait until the last minute to find out what props, such as an easel or blackboard or projector and screen the speaker needs, and what lighting he prefers. All of these details should be checked out before the start of the meeting.

Treatment of speakers. A person who is being paid by an organization to address it feels a certain obligation to be polite to those who have hired him. Be careful not to take advantage of this politeness by scheduling receptions and cocktail parties in his honor—one combined reception-cocktail party is enough. The sights of the city he is in may be enchanting, but unless he seems genuinely interested, don't insist he go on a sightseeing tour.

At the opposite extreme from lionizing the speaker is ignoring him, and of the two the latter is by far the more discourteous. Don't let him wander about alone before the meeting starts. Introduce him to the others who will sit at the head table or on the platform, give him a copy of the agenda, and tell him how much time he is allotted for his talk. Don't just forget the speaker after the meeting is over. Find out if he has a train or plane to catch and whether he needs help to make it. If you are paying him a fee or honorarium, have the check ready.

Feeding the guest speaker. Some speakers don't care to eat a complete meal—particularly a banquet dinner—before "going on." Perhaps a salad or a sandwich or coffee and dessert is more to their liking. Inquire as to the speaker's wish in this matter, and place the order (making sure later that it is carried out) with the head waiter.

What's expected of the speaker. Naturally, a good speech is hoped for but the speaker's appearance is important. He or she should be as well groomed as it is possible to be. A man should have a fresh shave before appearing on a speaker's platform; his shoes should be shined and his suit pressed.

Women must be particularly careful in their choice of clothes, especially if appearing before an audience of women. Smart, attractive, daytime clothes are suitable for most occasions, but if evening dress is called for, deep decolletage and bouffant skirts are to be avoided. Gloves are never worn on the platform.

It is polite for the guest speaker to arrive promptly at the appointed time, or, better yet, about 15 minutes early. This saves the program chairman the agony of worrying whether the speaker is lost, or sick, or has forgotten the date.

Introducing the guest speaker. Perform the introduction of the speaker to the audience with enthusiasm. Give the audience enough background material to interest it but not so much as to be boring. Don't try to tell the audience everything that's printed in the speaker's publicity material, and don't list every school he attended from kindergarten on up. Give a brief but pertinent account of who the speaker is, what he has done, and why he has been invited to speak.

Timing the speaker. Most speakers keep track of the time as they make their speeches. But if one runs over his allotted time, it is permissible to send up a note reminding him that he is over his limit.

Leaving during a speech. It is the height of rudeness to get up and walk out of the room during a speech. Anyone who knows he will have to leave early should make his apologies to the speaker and the chairman of the meeting and depart before the speech starts.

When the speech is over. The program chairman should express sincere thanks on behalf of himself and his organization. He must never try to sum up the speech, or what he considers to be the point the speaker made, and under no circumstances should he make light of the topic or of something the speaker said. Someone should send the speaker copies of press clippings and other publicity. It is courteous to send a copy of a letter of thanks to the speaker, to his employer (if he has one) or booking agent. It is always courteous for members of the audience to express appreciation to the speaker (or speakers) when the meeting is over.

• 28 • Conventions

Etiquette in Convention Planning

Conventions serve the purpose of gathering together members of a particular industry for discussion of problems common to all. They also give those who attend a chance to meet socially and to get to know each other as individuals instead of solely as company representatives.

Hotels that cater to conventions have both booklets and staff members to aid you in the planning of details. There are small points of etiquette, however, that may prove helpful to the individual who is planning a convention for the first time.

Selecting the site. While some conventions are held annually in the same place, others meet in various locations at different times of the year. Usually the Board of Trustees of the association holding the convention decides where it is to be held. But should the opportunity arise, it is a gracious gesture on the part of the chairman of arrangements for a convention to consult the membership as to where it would like to convene. Make a questionnaire, listing several of the places investigated and give what information is available as to climate, rates, accommodations for exhibits and meetings, facilities for recreation, and the various means of transportation available. Let the choice be whatever the majority prefers.

Asking for program suggestions. A questionnaire may also be used to solicit suggestions for the convention program. From such a query may come fresh ideas for panel discussions, speakers, meeting topics, and so on.

Attention to detail. Thoughtfulness for the comfort of others—the basis of good manners—means painstaking attention to the details that make a convention run pleasantly and smoothly. Mentally, run through the entire program, down to the last detail. Wherever possible, add that last little touch that leads to perfection. For instance, avoid scheduling meetings at too early an hour in the morning; give everyone a chance for a good rest and leisurely breakfast. Equally to be avoided is a meeting hour so late in the day that when it is over the men have little or no chance to relax and unwind before dinner.

Entertaining the wives. Every effort should be made to please the wives and make their visit as delightful as possible. It's as important to gain their good will as their husbands'. Special attention to the niceties of life, the little courtesies that are so important to women, will go far in winning their favor. Be sure to include in the invitation to the convention complete details as to the wardrobe a woman will need at the place selected. When planning a program of activities for wives, remember that fashion shows and luncheons at a leading store are popular with women, as are side trips to nearby points of historic interest; also beach parties, afternoon bridge parties, boat and motor trips.

Invitations to a convention. Invitations to attend a convention should be as complete as possible; all the facts that prospective attendants could possibly need should be included. A letter of invitation might read like that on the following page:

IMPORTANT

August 19, 196__

Dear Member:

Subject: 30th Anniversary Fall Meeting
Cleveland, Ohio
October 23-26, 196__

The Annual Fall Meeting of the Metal Industry Institute this year will be held at the Sheraton-Cleveland Hotel, Public Square, Cleveland, Ohio, from Wednesday, October 23 through Saturday, October 26.

The Fall Meeting this year marks the 30th Anniversary of the founding of the Metal Industry Institute, and we are hoping for a record attendance of member companies and individual members with their wives at our celebration. Here are the highlights:

1. Eleven member companies of the newly-organized MII Great Lakes Chapter are sponsoring the MII Exhibit Booth #6250 at the Cleveland Metals/Materials Show.
2. On Thursday morning, October 24, MII members will present a panel on "Practical Solutions to Some Industrial Problems."
3. Chartered bus trip for visit to members' plants.
4. Special Ladies' Program for Thursday morning and Friday afternoon.
5. Anniversary Banquet and Dance, Hotel Sheraton-Cleveland, Friday evening.

A hotel reservation card is attached to send directly to the hotel, and a registration form to be returned to this office. THE HOTEL SITUATION IS EXPECTED TO BE BAD IN CLEVELAND, SO PLEASE SEND THIS CARD TO THE HOTEL *NOW*. If there is any correspondence with the hotel, mention that you are an MII member or you probably will not get a room. (*Note to MII Exhibitors:* Some rooms have been set aside for your early arrival prior to October 23.)

Send in all the cards and registration forms early, and here's to seeing you in Cleveland.

Sincerely yours,

METAL INDUSTRY INSTITUTE

John B. Doe
Executive Secretary

Here is an example of a registration form to accompany the letter of invitation:

METAL INDUSTRY INSTITUTE

Box 448 New York, New York

PLEASE RETURN AS SOON AS POSSIBLE

Mr. John B. Doe:

The following people, including wives, will attend the 1963 MII Fall Meeting in Cleveland. (Please use *given names* such as Mary, John, etc.)

____

____

____

____

____

____

There will be (number) _____ attending the Thursday Group Lunch.

There will be (number) _____ attending the Friday Group Lunch.

There will be (number) _____ attending the Annual Banquet and Dinner Dance on Friday evening.

The following guests have been invited to join my party at the Annual Banquet, and please reserve a table for (number) _____ people.

____

____

____

Signed ____________________

Company ____________________

Supplying program information. Most people who plan to attend a convention like to have an idea of the events that will take place each day. Enclose with the invitation a copy of the convention program and the time schedule for each day.

Arranging tour transportation. When a tour of member plants in the area of the convention has been arranged, it probably will be necessary to charter buses for transportation to and from the plants. Therefore, send a plant tour reservation slip along with the invitation so that members may reserve seats on the buses. Here is an example:

METAL INDUSTRY INSTITUTE
Box 448 New York, New York

PLANT VISITATION RESERVATIONS

Arrangements have been made for visits to member plants scattered throughout the Cleveland area.

Chartered buses will leave from the Sheraton-Cleveland Hotel at 2:00 p.m. Friday afternoon, October 25. The buses will return to the hotel by 5:30 p.m.

So that we may know how many buses to engage and tickets to issue, please tear off the reservation slip below and return it to me along with your registration form.

Please reserve __________ seat(s) on the buses for the plant tour on Friday, October 25.

Signed ______________________________

Company ____________________________

Preparing name badges. The first names of both conventioneers and their wives should be on the name badges prepared for them. There's something friendlier—as well as easier to remember—about "John Smith" and "Peggy Smith" rather than "Mr. Smith, The Duncan Co." and "Mrs. John Smith." (Note that given names are asked for on the registration form shown on p. 266.)

Including on the badge the name of the State the person is from is a good idea; it serves as a conversation starter.

Starting events on time. Chairman should start meetings, conferences and programs on time. The schedules planned for conventions include lengthy all-day affairs involving hotel facilities, guest speakers, banquets, and so on. If the times set forth on the daily schedules are not maintained, the result is chaos and inconvenience for those attending the convention as well as for the hotel staff.

Etiquette for the Planners Following a Convention

While a convention chairman may feel utterly exhausted and relieved when the whole thing is over, letters of thanks to the various people who helped make the occasion a success should be sent out as promptly as possible. It is polite and thoughtful also for a guest or delegate to the convention (even though he had no role in the arrangements) to write letters of thanks if he wishes to.

These need not be lengthy letters—just brief but sincere expressions of gratitude.

Thanking the hotel staff. Perhaps first on the list of "thank you" notes should be one to the management of the hotel where the convention was held. The hotel's convention staff (as well as the regular staff) contribute much time and effort to the success of a convention. It is a courteous gesture on the part of the chairman to write to the manager and tell him of his gratitude for the contribution of the employees to success of the event.

When you have a complaint to make. A convention chairman may have reason to complain to the hotel management, or to the sales representative who handled the booking, about some lack in the handling of things that disturbed him. By all means send a letter setting forth the incident (or series of incidents) and telling why you believe it had an adverse affect on the delegates. But try to avoid writing an angry letter. Instead, make it clear that your complaint is being made in a spirit of helpfulness. Mention in the same letter some of the things that were well handled.

Here are examples of the kinds of letters that might be written after a convention:

Letter to the hotel manager from the general chairman of the convention

Dear Mr. Renaud:

The convention of the Dairy Products Association at your hotel last week was one of the most successful within recent memory.

While the outstanding service and facilities had a great deal to do with our pleasure and satisfaction, the personal attention you gave to the numerous details that made everything run so smoothly was much appreciated by our entire membership.

The recreational facilities at the Monterey are exceptional and proved immensely popular with the wives who accompanied their husbands. The children's activity program, so capably run by Miss Sally Curtis, contributed greatly to the enjoyment of families at our convention.

The meeting rooms were attractive, also well lighted and ventilated. Comments on the food—particularly Thursday night's banquet—have been most favorable.

May I also congratulate you on a splendid staff of courteous well-trained people. Their efforts to please were most gratifying.

To sum up, our convention at The Monterey was so successful, and so much was done to make our stay a success, that we would like to reserve the same dates—April 16, 17, and 18—for our 78th annual convention next year. Will you send me a confirmation as soon as possible?

Cordially,

H. A. Plummer

Letter to a speaker

Dear Mr. Unsworth:

The Society for Advancement of Management is most grateful to you for the compelling speech you made before our group last week. I have heard nothing but praise for your analysis of our present economic situation and its relationship to world events.

It was very definitely one of the outstanding events of a highly successful convention, and as chairman I am grateful for the opportunity our membership had of listening to your penetrating remarks.

Cordially,

H. A. Plummer

Follow-up by the general chairman. The convention chairman may find it a wise investment to send out a questionnaire to those who attended his convention asking such questions as the following:

- Were the hotel accommodations satisfactory?
- Was the food good and attractively served?
- Did the guest speakers command attention?
- Were the programs too long?
- Did committee reports and meetings run on too long?
- What improvements would you like to see?
- What committee would you like to serve on at the next convention?

The convention chairman can put the answers to these questions to good use in planning for the next convention, or he can turn the results of the questionnaire over to the incoming chairman.

Etiquette for the Delegate

An attitude of friendliness is high on the list of behavioral rules. A convention brings together dealers, suppliers, customers—representatives of all the associated enterprises surrounding an industry. Make a point of meeting as many new people as possible; don't just stick with the same old crowd. In other words, make the most of meeting people in related businesses.

Attendance at meetings. Don't be shy about taking a front row seat. People tend to fill up a meeting room from the back, but this only results in the speaker or chairman having to ask his audience to come up front. No one likes to talk to rows of empty seats beyond which sits an aloof audience.

The man who consents to attend a convention and then avoids all the business sessions because he'd rather fish or play golf is being inconsiderate. Allowance is generally made for leisure time activities, and delegates are expected to attend the meetings and conferences that have been arranged.

Entertaining at a convention. Before leaving for a convention, many businessmen call some of the people they think will be there and invite them for a drink or dinner—or both—while the convention is in session. Others entertain more formally or on a larger scale.

Hospitality suites. Some companies hold "open house" throughout a convention in a hospitality suite or room set aside as an oasis for the tired conventioneer. Here he can rest, be served free refreshments, and visit with other convention delegates, as well as officers and employees of the host company.

Other companies entertain once during a convention, inviting people to their suites at certain hours on a specific day.

The hospitality suite may be in the hotel where the convention is being held, but occasionally a firm with offices in the convention city will entertain in a hospitality suite in its own building.

At an association convention, attended only by members, the "hospitality suite" is actually a members' lounge where everyone can meet. Here, though, refreshments are not free and the members pay for drinks purchased.

Sending out invitations. Invitations to visit hospitality suites are sent in advance to those who plan to attend the convention. The invitation may be in the form of a letter or a printed card like the samples below:

The Linfield Lithograph Company
cordially invites you
to visit its Hospitality Suite
Room 1712
The Merrick Building
1112 Pensacola Boulevard
while you are attending the Metal Show

Hours 2-4
7-9 Buffet

The Chalfont Publishing Company
invites you
to its Hospitality Suite
Room 1010
Hotel Ultimate

Hours 7-9

The above invitations serve to notify conventioneers that the company's hospitality suite will be open each day of the convention. If a party is planned for just one day of the convention the invitation could read as follows:

The Blank Realty Company
cordially invites you
to its Hospitality Suite
on Friday, June eleventh
Suite 1501
Hotel Grand Marnier
Cocktails and Buffet 5-8

Making arrangements. The hotel's banquet department will gladly work out details for entertaining on a formal or informal scale. Members of the company should be in the suite during the hours it is open in order to greet guests. Wives are frequently pressed into service as hostesses, and sometimes professional models are hired to act as hostesses and receptionists. At a large affair these assistants should be assigned to various jobs. There should be at least two at the door to greet guests and take them to the bar for a drink and then on to sign a guest book. At that point, another assistant should bring the guest to the host, introducing him if necessary. Assistant hosts and hostesses should circulate freely to see that drinks are replenished and to make introductions. Name badges at this type of a party are in poor taste, so everyone serving as host or hostess must make a special effort to remember names.

Giving a private dinner party. For a company to hold a private dinner during a convention is rare, but not unheard of. A most successful party of this kind is given annually by the president of a large packaging company, most of whose customers are distributors of Italian grocery products. At the yearly trade convention he gives a small dinner party in his suite for his customers, serving a delicious spaghetti dinner, complete with wine.

The food served at such a party need not be elaborate, but it should be something different from the usual hotel fare.

Invitations to an affair of this kind should be sent out before the convention. A sample invitation is shown below:

The Blackton, Walker Company

requests the pleasure of your company

at dinner

on Friday, April twenty-first

at seven o'clock

Suite 1107

Hotel Grande-Excelsior

R.s.v.p.
1708 Madison Avenue
New York City

Writing letters of appreciation as a guest. A convention guest should never hesitate to write and thank the general chairman, or the chairman of the program committee, or any other convention official he feels merits commendation.

A guest may wish to let the management know how delighted he was with the service, or the food, or even the decor of the room he had.

Letters of this type are thoughtful gestures, because everyone likes to be told when his efforts to please have been successful.

Here are examples of the type of letters that might be written by a conventioneer.

Letter to the hotel manager from a delegate

Dear Mr. Renaud:

As guests at the recent Dairy Products Association convention, my wife and I were impressed by the quality of the service we found at your hotel. I know that handling such a large group of people puts a strain on the staff and the facilities of even the largest hotel, but for the entire period of our convention the helpfulness and courtesy of your staff never faltered. The meals were unusually good, and this fact added immeasurably to the success of our banquet.

My wife was particularly impressed by the way in which Miss Curtis of your convention staff handled the children's program, in which our youngsters were happy participants.

Our thanks to you and to your excellently trained staff for making our visit so delightful.

Sincerely,
William J. Kelly

Letter to a program chairman

Dear Jeff:

The recent American Merchants convention in Miami was one of the finest I have ever attended. Your efforts as program chairman were in no small measure responsible for the general feeling that our meetings were unusually worthwhile and rewarding.

My wife tells me she has never had a better time while attending a convention and that the side trips and entertainment you arranged for the ladies were fascinating.

It was good to see you. I hope you will keep your promise to telephone me when you next visit Akron.

Cordially,
John MacDonald

Etiquette for the Salesman-Exhibitor

The salesman's role. High-pressure selling is taboo at a convention. Salesmen who use their attendance at an industry convention as a means of promoting themselves and their product can be so annoying that they will end up being snubbed by the very people they are trying to impress. Getting to know people, building up good will by being an amiable companion and a good host, are all a salesman need do unless specifically asked questions about his product.

Exhibit booth manners. Your display booth at a trade show exhibit is part of your company's over-all sales promotion effort. For this reason, do not permit it to become a gathering place for conventioneers who want merely to sit and chat with each other.

Arrange to have the people who man the booth on duty for only an hour at a time, and ask them to stand while they are at work in the booth. Request them not to chew gum or smoke while on duty, and not to leave the booth unmanned, even for a few moments. The clothes your staff wears, especially women members, should be conservative.

The manner is which your staff conducts itself will reflect on your company and its products. Make sure the people you hire or bring with you from your home office are friendly, but not to the point where they lack dignity.

Have visitors sign a guest book, and when the convention is over send a note of thanks to all who signed.

• Part 6 • White House Etiquette

•29• Calling at The White House

Businessmen are frequently among the guests at The White House, either making calls related to business or as guests at dinners, receptions, and other social events. Each President sets his own tone of formality, so that the details of what is proper may differ slightly from one administration to the next. Fundamental rules, however, remain largely unchanged. The section below is a useful guide to correct procedure when you have the honor to attend a White House function, or must reply to an invitation.

Making a business call at The White House. Arrive for your appointment a few minutes early. Go directly to The White House executive office.

A man wears a conservative business suit for such a call. A woman wears a simple dress or suit, such as she would wear to the office, and a hat and gloves.

Do not smoke until you are invited to.

Making a social call at The White House. While the ways of entertaining vary with each administration, there are certain things the invited guest should remember to do when attending any social event at The White House.

- Give your name to the guard at the gate, and wait while he checks it against a list of expected guests.
- Arrive at least ten minutes before the time on the invitation. An invited guest must be ready and waiting for the President to make his entrance at the time specified.
- Never take a seat as long as either the President or the First Lady is standing.
- Never leave a room before the President does.
- Address the President as "Mr. President," and the First Lady by the title of "Mrs." ("Mrs. Washington," for example).
- Men bow slightly as they shake hands with either the President or his wife; women incline their heads as they shake hands. Say,

"How do you do, Mr. President" (or "Mrs. Washington"), or "Good afternoon" or "Good evening," whatever is appropriate.

Attending a White House reception. An early arrival is especially important if you have been invited to a White House reception, for they are usually large, crowded affairs and the chances of encountering delays are great.

On a reception line, men precede the ladies they are escorting. An aide presents the guests, who are greeted first by the President and then by the First Lady.

Guests on a reception line are not expected to say anything more than whatever greeting fits the time of day, unless the President or his wife engages them in conversation. This is so the line won't be delayed by talkative people.

Women need not remove their gloves to shake hands (but after you've been through the reception line remember to remove short gloves or turn long ones back at the wrist when you smoke or partake of refreshments).

After leaving the reception line, guests are free to mingle and chat with each other. Being under one roof constitutes an introduction; you may speak to anyone who seems agreeable.

The President sometimes leaves after receiving all the guests. But the First Lady or the acting hostess remains with the guests.

Attending a White House dinner. When you enter The White House the butler will tell you where to leave your wraps. For a large dinner party, cards bearing each guest's name and the number of the table at which he is to sit in the dining room will be on a table at the entrance. Give your name to the social aide or usher and he will find your card. He will also tell you in which room you are to wait for the President and his wife.

When the President and First Lady arrive, they may make a tour of the reception room, shaking hands with each guest. Women need not remove their gloves to shake hands (but must be sure to remove them at the dinner table). Should the dinner be in honor of a visiting foreign dignitary, the President and First Lady and honored visitors will form a receiving line to greet the guests.

When it is time to go in to dinner, guests find the table bearing the number on the card they were handed when they arrived. There will be place cards on the table. Guests remain standing until the

President, escorting the highest-ranking woman guest, and the First Lady, with the highest-ranking man guest, enter and take their seats.

Even when cigarettes are on the table, guests should never construe this to mean they may smoke between courses. It is proper to wait until the dessert course is reached before lighting a cigarette.

After dinner, if there is to be entertainment, the President and First Lady and the guests of honor will lead the way into the room where the program is to be presented.

If no entertainment has been planned, they will lead the way to an adjoining reception room where they will mingle and chat with the guests for a while before bidding them goodnight.

Dressing for a social event at The White House. When in doubt as to what to wear to a social event, most people are guided by the degree of formality of the invitation. But this wouldn't work in the case of White House invitations, as all but the most personal ones are formal and engraved. Therefore a small card stating what to wear—for instance, "White tie" or "Black tie"—is usually attached to White House invitations. If no card is attached, a man wears a business suit and a woman a simple dress or suit.

Women should wear their most elegant long gowns to a "White tie" dinner. Either a short or long dinner dress may be worn when the occasion is "Black tie." A formal afternoon reception calls for a cutaway or black sack coat and striped trousers for a man and a smart afternoon frock for a woman. For a luncheon women wear a silk or thin wool dress or a dressmaker suit. Gloves are removed before you enter the dining room for lunch. Whether or not to wear a hat is a question that perturbs many women in these somewhat informal times. While hats are no longer considered essential items of attire for women, unless one's hair is elaborately coiffed a head covering adds a finishing touch to all but the most informal outfits. A tiny, smart cocktail hat or veil may be worn with late afternoon clothes, and a becoming hat with luncheon apparel.

Leaving Cards at The White House

The rules of etiquette governing visits and visiting cards were at one time both intricate and time-consuming. Modern life, however, provides less leisure time in which to carry out the prescribed ritual.

Even official government and diplomatic circles are more informal than ever before.

"After the party" calls. At one time it was considered the height of ill manners in social circles not to leave a calling card upon one's hostess within three days after being entertained in her home. It was from these cards that many hostesses made up their future invitation lists. However, "party calls" are no longer made, and it is not necessary to leave cards at The White House after you have been entertained there.

Social season calls. During the social season in Washington, which starts in October and lasts until the beginning of Lent, cards may be left upon the President and his wife. However, observance of even this formality is less common now than in the past. Should you wish to leave calling cards, deliver them yourself (do not send them by hired messenger or a servant) to the sentry box at the gate. The caller is not received by either the President or First Lady, nor do they return these calls, but the cards are turned over to the social secretary and used in making up invitation lists for various large social events at The White House. For this reason, your home address should be written on the cards you leave.

A married woman leaves a "Mr. and Mrs." calling card or two of her husband's calling cards and one of her own. A single woman leaves one card; a single man, two cards. Two of a man's cards are left because he leaves one upon each gentleman and lady in the household upon which the call is being made; but a woman leaves her own card only for the ladies in the household, as she does not make a call upon a man. Only personal visiting cards are left, never business cards.

It is correct also to leave the cards of grown sons and daughters living at home. If some other member of your family is in permanent residence with you, his or her personal card should be left (with the address written on it and his or her relationship to you, such as, "Sister of Mrs. Amory Jones").

Answering Invitations from The White House

When a reply to a White House invitation is requested, the wording of the proper form of acceptance differs slightly from the usual formal reply. Instead of "accept with pleasure," the phrases, "have the honour of accepting" or "have the honour to accept" are used.

Replying to a formal invitation. Here is an example of an acceptance of a formal invitation to dine at The White House.

Mr. and Mrs. John Charles Forbes have the honour of accepting the kind invitation of The President and Mrs. Washington to dine on Friday, the first of March at eight o'clock

Fancy forms of acceptance in which the writer presents his "compliments to the President and the First Lady" and states that he is "most happy to accept the courteous invitation for dinner," are not considered good form.

The reply should be handwritten (never typed) on the finest quality, double-fold, white stationery. It is not correct to use business stationery.

Invitations to very large receptions do not as a rule require an answer. However, when seating arrangements are to be made for such an event, the invitation will request a reply.

When you have a conflicting appointment. While there is nothing mandatory about a White House invitation, it is only natural that you would give one the highest priority. An informal social engagement is easily broken or postponed by telephoning the hostess to say you are invited to The White House on the same date. If you are expected at a formal event on the same date as the White House invitation, the following regret should be sent promptly to the hostess:

Mr. and Mrs. Paul John Shilling
regret exceedingly
that an invitation to
The White House
prevents their keeping
their engagement to dine
on Thursday, the seventh of March

Informal invitations from The White House. Usually, informal invitations to lunch or dinner from the President and his wife, or from the First Lady alone, are handled by a social secretary. Nowadays, informal notes of invitation are usually typewritten, or the invitation may be extended by telephone or telegram. Here are examples of written informal invitations:

Dear Mrs. Jones,

Mrs. Washington has asked me to invite you to have lunch with her at The White House on Tuesday, the ninth of November. Luncheon will be at one o'clock.

Yours truly,

Patricia Turner
Secretary to Mrs. Washington

Dear Mrs. MacLean,
The President and Mrs. Washington have asked me to invite you and Mr. MacLean to dine at The White House on Wednesday, the first of October, at eight o'clock, black tie.

Yours truly,

Patricia Turner
Secretary to Mrs. Washington

A reply to an informal invitation is sent to the secretary in the same form in which it was received; that is, by letter, telephone or telegram. A written reply would follow these styles:

Dear Miss Turner,
Will you please tell Mrs. Washington that I shall be delighted to lunch with her at The White House on Tuesday, the ninth of November. Thank you very much.

Sincerely,

Marcia Jones

Dear Miss Turner,
My husband and I shall be delighted to accept the very kind invitation of the President and Mrs. Washington to dine at The White House on Wednesday, October first, at eight o'clock. With many thanks.

Sincerely,
Jean MacLean

A Guide to Parliamentary Procedure

The information given here covers the elements of parliamentary law and is sufficient to carry on most meetings. More specific information needed to cover unusual circumstances or settle minor questions can be found in *Robert's Rules of Order,* the bible of parliamentary procedure. The presiding officer at any meeting should have a copy of *Robert's Rules of Order* and a copy of the bylaws of the organization close at hand to settle any questions of procedure.

Basic Agenda

New and complete agenda should be prepared for each meeting. Following is the order in which business is usually conducted, although all of the steps on the list may not be used in all meetings. The order of business may be set aside or changed by a two-thirds vote or by general consent. "By general consent" means that the Chair states, "If there is no objection, we will, etc."

1. The Chairman calls the meeting to order.
2. Prayer or invocation, if customary.
3. Pledge of Allegiance, if customary.
4. Quorum check. A roll call is not necessary unless it is specified in the bylaws. For a large group a door check may be made, and a silent count can be made of a small group. The bylaws should specify the number necessary for a quorum.
5. Minutes read by the Recording Secretary. The Chair asks "Are there any corrections?" Then, if no corrections, the Chair says "The minutes are approved." If corrections are made, the Chair says "The minutes are approved as corrected."
6. Correspondence by the Corresponding Secretary. (In groups

where there is no Corresponding Secretary the Secretary presents the correspondence at this point.) Motions arising out of correspondence can be handled at this time, or they can be repeated under new business.

7. Treasurer's report.

8. Report of the Board of Directors, or Executive Board. (This report is not the minutes of the meetings of the Board, which are the property of the Board.) Action on the recommendations of the Board can be taken here or can be brought up under new business.

9. Reports of any other officers.

10. Reports of standing committees. The bylaws give the order of sequence of the various standing committees.

11. Reports of special committees. These report in sequence as they were created.

12. Special orders.

13. Unfinished business.

14. New business.

15. Program (speakers or the like). (It is not correct for the Chair to "turn the program over" to anyone. The presiding officer is in the chair throughout the meeting.)

16. Announcements. The Chair announces the time and place of the next meeting.

17. Chair addresses some brief closing remarks to the members.

18. Adjournment. The Chair may adjourn the meeting without asking for a motion to adjourn if there is no further business.

Mechanics of Presenting a Motion

A motion is a means of offering a proposal for consideration and action by the membership of the organization. Once a motion is seconded it becomes an item of business on which the membership must act. The following steps are involved in presenting a motion.

1. The member secures the floor by rising, addressing the Chair and giving his name. For example, "Mr. Chairman (or Mr. President, Mr. Moderator), Albert Jones."

2. The Chair recognizes the member by repeating the member's name and nodding to him.

3. The member makes the motion by saying, "I move that . . ."

4. The motion is seconded by some member other than the one who presented it. The person seconding the motion merely rises and says, "Mr. Chairman, I second the motion," without waiting for recognition. If no second is received for a motion that requires one (not all motions require a second), the motion is lost. (See the following section for a detailed explanation of the various motions.) The Chair so indicates by stating, "The motion is lost for want of a second," or "For want of a second the motion is not before the assembly."

5. The Chair states the motion to the meeting. He may also state whether the motion is debatable or amendable and the vote required. A question is not before the meeting until the Chair has formally stated it. Once he states the question, it belongs to the organization; the member who made the motion in the first place no longer controls it. Such a question is a *pending question.* If a motion is superseded by one of higher rank, the motion stated last is the *immediately pending question.*

6. The motion is debated, or discussed. Any member who obtains the floor may offer his comments. Only the question under consideration may be discussed. Should any speaker deviate from the question, his remarks are out of order.

> *Comment:* Never use the phrase, "You are out of order." It is not the person who is out of order, but his remarks or introduction of business.

7. The Chair asks, "Is there any further discussion?" This remark does not close the debate but merely ensures that all who wish to speak may be heard. A completed vote does close the debate.

8. The question is voted upon. This is called "putting the question." Methods of voting are described on page 298. After the voting is complete, the chairman states, "The ayes have it and the motion is carried," or, "The noes have it and the motion is lost."

Precedence of Motions

Under the rules of parliamentary procedure, motions are ranked in order of importance. Precedence rules are applied to various types of motions to facilitate business at the meeting.

The two fundamental rules of precedence are:

1. When there is a pending question before the organization, a motion with higher precedence may be proposed, but one of lower precedence may not.

2. When several motions are before the organization, those most recently proposed (therefore those of the highest precedence) must be considered and voted upon first.

A chart showing a summary of motions is given at the end of this section.

Main motion: A main motion states an item of business in such a manner that the organization can act upon it.

A main motion

a) has the lowest rank of precedence (if a member makes any other type of motion while a main motion is pending, the main motion must yield to the other motion);
b) must be seconded before it can be considered;
c) is subject to debate and amendment;
d) is subject to reconsideration;
e) may have a subsidiary motion; and
f) needs a majority vote to be carried.

Subsidiary motions: Subsidiary motions are assisting motions which modify or dispose of the main motion. A subsidiary motion can be applied to any main motion and it then supersedes the main motion. All subsidiary motions must be decided before the main motion can be acted upon. Subsidiary motions have a rank of importance within themselves. They are given below, in order, with the most important first.

1. *Lay on the table.* To lay an item of business on the table temporarily delays its consideration. Such action may be necessary to permit further consideration of a question before a decision is reached, or it may be necessary to allow the membership to act on more urgent business. All action on a tabled motion is taken from the table. Any tabled motion that is not taken from the table at the same meeting at which it was tabled or at the next succeeding meeting is automatically killed.

A motion to lay on the table

a) may be applied to a main motion, an appeal that does not

adhere to the main question, or to the motion to reconsider then immediately pending;

b) requires a second;

c) can be neither debated nor amended;

d) cannot be reconsidered;

e) cannot have a subsidiary motion applied to it; and

f) needs a majority vote.

2. *Previous question.* The previous question is a motion to stop debate on the motion under consideration and take an immediate vote. It may be qualified to include "everything before the organization," or it may refer only to the question immediately pending if it is not qualified in any way.

The previous question

a) requires a second;

b) can be neither debated nor amended;

c) can be reconsidered, but only before any vote has been taken under it;

d) takes precedence over all subsidiary motions except the motion to lay on the table, but it yields to privileged and incidental motions; and

e) needs a two-thirds vote.

3. *Motion to refer to committee.* The main reasons for referring a motion to a committee are (1) to obtain more detailed information, (2) to ensure privacy on a delicate matter, (3) to obtain the recommendation of a group smaller than the entire assembly, and (4) to consider the motion in an informal atmosphere.

A motion to refer to committee

a) may specify whether it is to be referred to a special or standing committee (if a special committee is formed, the proposer may specify the size of the committee, how members are to be selected, who is to be chairman, and may also formulate instructions for the committee);

b) requires a second;

c) may be amended or reconsidered, and can be applied to a main motion;

d) limits debate to the question of the propriety of referring the motion to a committee;

e) cannot be laid on the table, nor be postponed except in connection with the main motion; and

f) needs a majority vote.

Observation: If a motion referred to a committee has amendments pending, those amendments are carried with it to the committee. At any time that the organization wishes to dispose of a question which has been referred to a committee, it can withdraw the question from the committee by one of two methods: (1) if the committee has not yet taken up the question, the vote to refer the matter to committee can be reconsidered, and (2) if the committee has taken up the question, the committee can be discharged.

4. *Motion to amend.* Amendments are used to change the form of motions or resolutions before the assembly. An amendment that applies to an original motion is of the first rank, whereas one that applies to an amendment is of the second rank. Only one motion of each rank may be under consideration at any given time. Once an amendment is either adopted or defeated, another of the same rank may be proposed.

An amendment

a) must be related to the subject of the motion it intends to change (an amendment of the first rank must relate to the original motion, while one of the second rank must relate to the first rank amendment);

b) requires a second;

c) can be debated if the original motion can be debated;

d) can be amended if it is first rank; cannot be amended if it is second rank;

e) can be moved before, during, or following debate;

f) may have applied to it motions to limit or extend the limits of debate;

g) can be reconsidered; and

h) can be passed by a majority vote, even though the motion to which it applies requires a two-thirds vote.

5. *Motion to postpone indefinitely.* This motion is an attempt to suppress a question without bringing the matter to a vote. If this motion is carried it suppresses the main motion for the duration of the meeting. A motion which has been indefinitely postponed can

be brought up at a later meeting only if it is proposed as a new motion.

A motion to postpone indefinitely

a) requires a second;
b) opens the main question to debate for those members who have exhausted their right to debate (*see Basic rules of debate,* page 296);
c) takes precedence only over a main motion and can be applied only to a main motion;
d) can have motions to withdraw and to vote immediately applied to it;
e) can be reconsidered only in the case of an affirmative vote;
f) can be debated, but not amended; and
g) needs a majority vote.

Incidental motions: Incidental motions are those that arise from a pending question. They may come up at any time and must be decided before the question to which they are incidental is decided. They have no rank of order among themselves, but they yield to privileged motions. Some of the commonest incidental motions are explained below:

1. *Point of order.* A point of order calls attention to a violation of rules or to a mistake in procedure which may have escaped the presider's attention. The member does not need the recognition of the Chair. He simply rises and says:

"Mr. Chairman, I rise to a point of order."

The chairman asks the member to state his point of order, and then makes a decision on it.

A point of order requires neither a second nor a vote. It takes precedence over the pending question out of which it arises. No debate is allowed on a point of order, unless the chairman refers it to the assembly. It cannot be amended, nor can it be brought up later (after business has been transacted following the mistake), except in cases of error involving violations of the constitution or bylaws. The individual rising to a point of order may interrupt a speaker who has the floor, because a point of order must be raised immediately after the violation or mistake.

2. *Appeal from the decision of the Chair.* The purpose is to se-

cure a reversal of the Chair decision and can only be applied to *decisions* made by the Chair, not to announcements of a vote or to a motion. The motion to appeal from the decision of the Chair requires a second and is carried by a majority vote. It must be made immediately after the decision to which it refers and the vote must be taken at once. It can be debated if the motion preceding it is debatable. A member need not wait for recognition to appeal the decision of the Chair.

3. *Suspension of the rules.* The purpose is to set aside rules which conflict with attention to new business but do not conflict with the bylaws. Rules of order, order of business, adoption of the program can all be suspended, but the bylaws cannot be. A motion to suspend the rules must be seconded and requires a two-thirds vote. It cannot be debated or amended.

4. *Division of the assembly.* The purpose is to verify the accuracy of a vote. Any member may ask for a division of the assembly by merely calling "Division" or "I doubt the result of the vote and ask for a division." The vote is then retaken by a show of hands or a standing vote and the votes carefully counted.

5. *Nominations and elections.* The purpose of a nomination is to name a candidate for an office which must be filled. Nominations can be made from the floor or by a nominating committee. A nomination does not require a second. Members named in a nominating committee's report are considered as though they had been nominated from the floor. Once the report is given, the Chair asks if there are additional nominations. He does this separately for each office. Additional nominations are added to the committee's list as they are made.

A motion to close nominations requires a second and can be carried by a two-thirds majority. It cannot be debated or reconsidered, nor can it have subsidiary motions applied to it. It can be amended as to time alone. It yields to privileged motions.

Once nominations are closed, if the voting has not begun they can be reopened by a motion to this effect. The motion must be seconded and it requires a majority vote. It cannot be debated and can be amended as to time only. It yields to privileged motions, and, if the vote was negative, can be reconsidered.

6. *Parliamentary inquiry.* A parliamentary inquiry can be made by any member to secure information on a parliamentary point. He

merely states, "I rise for parliamentary information." A member who makes a parliamentary inquiry may interrupt a speaker to do so. The chairman asks the member to state his question and then answers it.

7. *Leave to withdraw a motion.* Before a motion has been stated to the assembly, the member who proposed it may modify it or withdraw it at his pleasure. However, once the motion is stated, it belongs to the group. It cannot be withdrawn without the consent of the membership.

This motion can be applied to any motion, and if it receives a negative vote, it can be reconsidered. It takes precedence over all but privileged motions, and it requires a majority vote to carry it.

Privileged motions: Privileged motions are those that affect the convenience of the assembly or one of its members. They have the highest rank of precedence. A privileged motion does not relate to the pending question; it is one of privilege only if it is presented when other business is before the assembly. The most common privileged motions are (1) motion to adjourn and (2) question of privilege.

1. *Adjourn.* A member may move for adjournment when he wishes to formally close a meeting. This motion may or may not be a privileged motion. If made in a group that meets regularly during the year, and if it is unqualified, it is a privileged motion. If it is qualified in any way it becomes a main motion and is subject to subsidiary motions, is debatable, and may be amended.

The unqualified motion to adjourn requires a second and a majority vote. It has the highest precedence of any motion except to fix the time of adjournment.

2. *Question of privilege.* The purpose is to request rights or privileges concerning the rights and comfort of the organization or to request rights pertaining to an individual member. Questions of privilege of the assembly pertain to the membership as a whole and outrank individual rights.

The procedure is for the member to state, "Mr. Chairman, I rise to a question of privilege affecting the assembly," or, when the question affects an individual member, "I rise to a question of privilege."

Privileges affecting the assembly might relate to such things as ventilation, heating, lighting, conduct of officers or control of noise.

An example of a privilege affecting the individual is a request for a list or paper which has been distributed to some of the members and which the member making the motion does not have.

Unclassified motions: Some motions cannot be conveniently classified as main, subsidiary, incidental, or privileged. Two of the commonest of these motions are (1) take from the table, and (2) reconsider.

1. *Take from the table.* To permit further consideration of a tabled motion, a member may move that it be taken from the table. Once a motion has been tabled, the motion to remove it from the table is not in order until some other business has been transacted.

If the motion to take from the table is passed, the original motion comes before the assembly exactly as it was placed on the table. A motion can only be taken from the table at the meeting during which it was tabled or at the next regular meeting.

This motion requires a second and a majority vote; it cannot be debated or amended or reconsidered, nor can it have subsidiary motions applied to it.

2. *Reconsider.* The assembly actually reconsiders the vote, not the motion. It is used to prevent action being taken on a motion already carried. The member who makes this motion must originally have voted on the prevailing side. However, any member may second it. The motion must be made on the day the vote was taken or on the next calendar day.

This motion requires a second and can be carried by a majority vote. It can be debated if the question to be reconsidered is debatable, but it cannot be amended. The motion to reconsider may be applied to the final vote on a main motion, an amendment, a referral to committee, or an appeal if, as a result of the vote, nothing has been done which cannot be undone.

Basic Rules of Debate

There are some basic procedures and rules to follow when a motion is debated. The principal rules are:

1. The member making the motion has the privilege of opening and closing the debate.
2. The chairman must remain neutral. If he wishes to take part

SUMMARY OF MOTIONS

(In order of rank)

Kind of Motion	Recognition of chair required	In order if another has the floor	Second required	Requires immediate decision	Debatable	Debate may extend to main question	Amendable	Vote required	May be reconsidered
Privileged Motions									
Adjourn (when unqualified)	Yes	No	Yes	No	No	...	No	Majority	No
Question of privilege	No	Yes [1]	No	Yes	No	...	No	None	No
Incidental Motions									
Point of order	No	Yes	No	Yes	No	...	No	None	No
Appeal	No	No	Yes	No	Yes [2]	No	No	Majority	Yes
Suspend the rules	Yes	No	Yes	Yes	No	...	No	Two-thirds	No
Division	No	No	No	Yes	No	...	No	None	No
Nominations, to close	Yes	No	Yes	No	No	...	Yes [6]	Two-thirds	No
Nominations, to reopen	Yes	No	Yes	No	No	...	Yes [6]	Majority	Yes [8]
Parliamentary inquiry	No	Yes [1]	No	Yes	No	...	No	None	No
Withdraw a motion, leave to	Yes	No	No	Yes	No	...	No	Majority	Yes [8]
Subsidiary Motions									
Lay on the table	Yes	No	Yes	Yes	No	...	No	Majority	No
Previous question	Yes	No	Yes	No	No	...	No	Two-thirds	Yes [9]
Refer to committee	Yes	No	Yes	No	Yes [3]	No	Yes	Majority	Yes
Amend	Yes	No	Yes	No	Yes [4]	No	Yes [7]	Majority	Yes
Postpone indefinitely	Yes	No	Yes	No	Yes	Yes	No	Majority	Yes [10]
Main Motions									
Main motion	Yes	No	Yes	No	Yes	No	Yes	Majority	Yes
Unclassified Motions									
Take from the table	Yes	No	Yes	Yes	No	...	No	Majority	No
Reconsider	Yes	Yes	Yes	No	Yes [5]	Yes	No	Majority	No

1. Depends upon circumstance or necessity.
2. No if it relates to indecorum, etc.
3. Only as to propriety of committing.
4. If applied to a debatable question.
5. If the motion to be reconsidered is debatable.
6. Time only.
7. Only first degree amendment.
8. Only the negative vote.
9. Before the affirmative vote has been taken.
10. Affirmative vote only.

The above table summarizes the rules of parliamentary procedure which apply to the most common types of motions used at meetings.

in the debate he must call the vice president or next officer to take his place in the chair. The chairman does not return to the chair until the pending question has been voted on.

3. Each member is entitled to speak at least once on a question. He may sometimes speak twice or more often if there is no objection.

4. All inquiries must be made through the Chair.

5. Members should stick to the subject and not make personal remarks concerning other members.

Basic Rules of Voting

The types of votes possible are:

1. Majority—a number greater than half the votes cast.
2. Plurality—the most votes cast regardless of majority.
3. Two-thirds vote—two-thirds of the votes cast.
4. Tie vote—same number for and against, in which case the motion is considered lost.

The basic methods of voting are as follows:

1. By general consent—the Chair states, "If there is no objection we will," etc. This method is used for routine decisions.
2. By voice vote—members vote "aye" or "no" by voice for a majority vote.
3. By a show of hands—members raise hands to "affirmative" or "negative." This method is usually used in small groups.
4. Rising vote—members stand to "affirmative" or "negative" for a two-thirds vote.
5. By roll call—each member's name is called and he votes. This method provides a check on attendance as well as a careful vote.
6. By ballot—this method assures secrecy for the voter.
7. By mail or proxy—this method can be used only if the bylaws so specify.

> *Observation:* Members may waive their right to vote by abstaining. The bylaws of the organization should specify the vote required for legal action. Majority vote is the basic rule, but the bylaws should define "majority." A majority could mean a majority of those present and voting, majority of legal votes cast, majority of members, or the like.

Flag Etiquette

There will be times when your company will want to display the flag, and it is well to remember that there are both laws (Federal) and customs which govern the ways in which the American flag can be displayed.

Raising and lowering the flag. The flag should be raised and lowered by hand. Do not raise the flag while it is furled. Unfurl it, then hoist it quickly to the top of the staff. It should be lowered slowly and with dignity.

Hours of display. The flag should be displayed only from sunrise to sunset or between such hours as may be designated by proper authority.

Days of display. The flag can be displayed on all days when the weather permits (never in rainy or stormy weather) and should be displayed especially on these days:

New Year's Day, January 1
Inauguration Day, January 20
Lincoln's Birthday, February 12
Washington's Birthday, February 22
Easter Sunday
Mother's Day, second Sunday in May
Armed Forces Day, third Saturday in May
Memorial Day, May 30
Flag Day, June 14
Independence Day, July 4
Labor Day, first Monday in September
Constitution and Citizenship Day, September 17
Columbus Day, October 12
Veterans Day, November 11
Thanksgiving Day, fourth Thursday in November

Christmas Day, December 25
Birthdays of states (dates of admission)
State holidays
Days proclaimed by the President

Displaying the flag by itself. When displayed over the middle of the street, the flag should be suspended vertically with the union (blue field) to the north in an east and west street, or to the east in a north and south street.

When the flag is suspended over a sidewalk from a rope extending from house to pole at the edge of the sidewalk, the flag should be hoisted out from the building, toward the pole, union first.

When the flag is displayed from a staff projecting horizontally or at any angle from the window sill, balcony, or front of a building, the union of the flag should go to the peak of the staff (unless, of course, the flag is to be displayed at half-mast).

When the flag is displayed in a manner other than by being flown from a staff, it should be displayed flat, whether indoors or out. When displayed either horizontally or vertically against a wall, the union should be uppermost and to the flag's own right, that is, to the observer's left. When displayed in a window it should be displayed in the same way.

Using the flag as a covering or drapery. Never use the flag as covering for a speaker's table or the edge of a platform, or to cover a statue or other object at an unveiling. When drapings are desired, or festoons or rosettes, bunting of blue, white and red (with the stripes in that color order) can be used, but never the flag. When the flag is used to cover a casket, the union goes at the head and over the left shoulder. The flag should not be lowered into the grave or allowed to touch the ground during burial.

Using the flag as a trademark. A Federal law provides that a trademark cannot be registered which consists of or includes the flag of the United States or any simulation thereof.

Touching the ground. The flag should not be allowed to fall to the ground or floor, nor should it be allowed to brush against things. Every precaution must be taken to prevent it from becoming soiled.

Use as a decoration or costume. Do not use the flag as a portion of a costume or athletic uniform. Do not embroider it upon cushions or handkerchiefs or print it on paper napkins or boxes. The flag may not be used in display advertising, except for Federal government purposes.

Flying the flag upside down. This is a signal of dire distress; it should never be done for any other reason.

Touching water. The flag must never be allowed to trail in or touch water.

Dipping the flag. The flag should not be dipped to any person or thing, with this exception: Navy vessels, upon receiving a salute of this type from a vessel registered by a nation formally recognized by the United States, must return the compliment.

Carrying the flag. It should always be carried aloft and free, never flat or horizontal.

Use as a receptable. Do not use the flag as a receptacle for receiving, holding, carrying, or delivering anything.

Marking the flag. Never place upon the flag or attach to it any mark, insignia, letter, word, figure, design, picture or drawing of any nature.

Flying the flag at half-mast. This means placing the flag at a point roughly mid-way on the flag pole as a sign of mourning. Even when it is to be flown at half-mast, the flag should be hoisted to the peak for an instant and then lowered to the half-mast position. Before lowering the flag for the day it should again be raised to the peak. On Memorial Day the flag is flown at half staff until noon, then hoisted to the top of the staff.

Displaying the flag in church. When displayed in the chancel or on a platform in a church, the flag should be placed on a staff at the clergyman's right; other flags go at his left. If displayed in the body of the church, the flag should be at the congregation's right as they face the clergyman.

With other flags. No other flag may be flown above the Stars and Stripes, except: (1) the United Nations flag at U. N. Headquarters; (2) the church pennant, a dark blue cross on a white background, during church services conducted by naval chaplains at sea.

When displayed with another flag from crossed staffs, the flag of the United States of America should be on the right (the flag's own right) and its staff should be in front of the staff of the other flag.

When flags of states or cities or pennants of societies are flown on the same halyard with the flag of the United States of America, the latter should always be at the peak. When flown from adjacent staffs the Stars and Stripes should be hoisted first and lowered last.

When carried in a procession with another flag or flags, the Stars and Stripes should be either on the marching right, or when there is a line of other flags, in front of the center of that line.

When a number of flags of states or cities or pennants of societies are grouped and displayed from staffs with the National flag, the latter should be at the center or at the highest point of the group.

When the flags of two or more nations are displayed they should be flown from separate staffs of the same height, and the flags should be of approximately equal size. International usage forbids the display of the flag of one nation above that of another nation in time of peace.

Saluting the flag. During the ceremony of hoisting or lowering the flag, or when the flag is passing in a parade or in a review, those present in uniform should render the right-hand salute. When not in uniform, men should remove their headgear with the right hand and hold it at their left shoulder with their hand over the heart; women place the right hand over the heart.

The pledge to the flag. The pledge to the flag, also known as the pledge of allegiance, was first used in the public schools in celebration of Columbus Day, October 12, 1892. The pledge received official recognition by Congress in an Act of June 22, 1942. The phrase "under God" was added to the pledge by a Congressional Act of June 14, 1954.

Here is the pledge of allegiance to the flag:

> "I pledge allegiance to the flag of the United States of America, and to the Republic for which it stands, one Nation under God, indivisible, with liberty and justice for all."

When the flag becomes old and worn. When the flag is in such a condition, through wear or damage, that it is no longer a fitting emblem for display, it should be destroyed in a dignified way, preferably by burning.

Obtaining a flag for use at a funeral. A flag to cover the coffin of any honorably discharged veteran is furnished by the Veterans Administration, Washington, D. C. It may be obtained by filling in Veterans Administration Form 2008 at the nearest post office. The applicant must state his kinship to the deceased. The flag must be presented to the next of kin at the proper time during the burial service. If there is no relative, or one cannot be located, the flag must be returned to the Veterans Administration in the franked (postage free) container for that purpose. Postmasters require proof of honorable discharge before issuing the flag, but it is issued promptly upon proper evidence.

Storing the flag. The flag must be carefully stored, so that it is protected from damage and possible disrespect. For instance, it should not be rolled up and stored on an attic or cellar floor, where it might become dirty or torn or be stepped on.

Notes: An illustrated booklet—"Our Flag"—which tells the story of the flag of the United States of America, is available from your United States Senator or Representative.

All the armed services have precise regulations regarding the display of the flag, which may vary somewhat from the rules and customs described above.

Correct Forms of Address

UNITED STATES GOVERNMENT OFFICIALS

Personage	Envelope and Inside Address	Formal Salutation	Informal Salutation	Formal Close	Informal Close	1. Spoken Address 2. Informal Introduction or Reference
The President	The President The White House Washington, D. C.	Mr. President:	Dear Mr. President:	Respectfully yours,	Very respectfully yours,	1. Mr. President 2. Not introduced (The President)
Former President of the United States [1]	The Honorable William R. Blank (local address)	Sir:	Dear Mr. Blank:	Respectfully yours,	Very truly yours, *or* Sincerely yours,	1. Mr. Blank 2. Former President Blank *or* Mr. Blank
The Vice President of the United States	The Vice President of the United States United States Senate Washington 25, D. C.	Sir:	Dear Mr. Vice President:	Respectfully,	Very truly yours, *or* Sincerely yours,	1. Mr. Vice President *or* Mr. Blank 2. The Vice President
The Chief Justice of the United States Supreme Court	The Chief Justice of the United States The Supreme Court of the United States Washington 25, D. C.	Sir:	Dear Mr. Chief Justice:	Respectfully,	Very truly yours, *or* Sincerely yours,	1. Mr. Chief Justice 2. The Chief Justice
Associate Justice of the United States Supreme Court	Mr. Justice Blank The Supreme Court of the United States Washington 25, D. C.	Sir: *or* Mr. Justice:	Dear Mr. Justice:	Very truly yours,	Sincerely yours,	1. Mr. Justice Blank *or* Justice Blank 2. Mr. Justice Blank

Retired Justice of the United States Supreme Court	The Honorable William R. Blank (local address)	Sir:	Dear Justice Blank:	Very truly yours,	Sincerely yours,	1. Mr. Justice Blank *or* Justice Blank 2. Mr. Justice Blank
The Speaker of the House of Representatives	The Honorable the Speaker of the House of Representatives Washington 25, D. C. *or* The Honorable William R. Blank Speaker of the House of Representatives Washington 25, D. C.	Sir:	Dear Mr. Speaker: *or* Dear Mr. Blank:	Very truly yours,	Sincerely yours,	1. Mr. Speaker *or* Mr. Blank 2. The Speaker, Mr. Blank (The Speaker *or* Mr. Blank)
Former Speaker of the House of Representatives	The Honorable William R. Blank (local address)	Sir:	Dear Mr. Blank:	Very truly yours,	Sincerely yours,	1. Mr. Blank 2. Mr. Blank
Cabinet Officers addressed as "Secretary" [2] *(man)*	The Honorable the Secretary of State Washington 25, D. C. (formal) The Honorable William R. Blank Secretary of State Washington 25, D. C. (informal) The Honorable William R. Blank Secretary of State of the United States of America Washington 25, D. C. (if written from abroad)	Sir:	Dear Mr. Secretary:	Very truly yours,	Sincerely yours,	1. Mr. Secretary *or* Secretary Blank *or* Mr. Blank 2. The Secretary of State, Mr. Blank (Mr. Blank *or* The Secretary)

[1] If a former president has a title, address him by it. For example, General of the Army Dwight D. Eisenhower.

[2] Titles for cabinet secretaries are Secretary of State; Secretary of the Treasury; Secretary of Defense; Secretary of the Interior; Secretary of Agriculture; Secretary of Commerce; Secretary of Labor; and Secretary of Health, Education. and Welfare.

UNITED STATES GOVERNMENT OFFICIALS *continued*

Personage	Envelope and Inside Address	Formal Salutation	Informal Salutation	Formal Close	Informal Close	1. Spoken Address 2. Informal Introduction or Reference
Cabinet Officer (woman)[3]	Same as for a man	Madam:	Dear Madam Secretary:	Very truly yours,	Sincerely yours,	1. Madam Secretary *or* Mrs. (Miss) Blank 2. The Secretary of the Treasury, Mrs. (Miss) Blank (The Secretary *or* Mrs. (Miss) Blank)
Postmaster General	The Honorable William R. Blank The Postmaster General Washington 25, D. C.	Sir:	Dear Mr. Postmaster General:	Very truly yours,	Sincerely yours,	1. Mr. Postmaster General *or* Postmaster General Blank *or* Mr. Blank 2. The Postmaster General, Mr. Blank (Mr. Blank *or* The Postmaster General)
The Attorney General	The Honorable William R. Blank The Attorney General Washington 25, D. C.	Sir:	Dear Mr. Attorney General:	Very truly yours,	Sincerely yours,	1. Mr. Attorney General *or* Attorney General Blank 2. The Attorney General, Mr. Blank (Mr. Blank *or* The Attorney General)
Former Cabinet Officer	The Honorable William R. Blank (local address)	Dear Sir:	Dear Mr. Blank:	Very truly yours,	Sincerely yours,	1. Mr. Blank 2. Mr. Blank

Under Secretary of a Department	The Honorable William R. Blank Under Secretary of Labor Washington 25, D. C.	Dear Mr. Blank:	**Dear Mr. Blank:**	**Very truly yours,**	**Sincerely yours,**	**1. Mr. Blank** **2. Mr. Blank**
United States Senator (man)	The Honorable William R. Blank United States Senate Washington 25, D. C.	Dear Senator Blank:	**Dear Senator Blank:**	**Very truly yours,**	**Sincerely yours,**	**1. Senator Blank** *or* **Senator** **2. Senator Blank**
United States Senator (woman) [3]	The Honorable Louise L. Blank United States Senate Washington 25, D. C.	Dear Senator Blank:	**Dear Senator Blank:** *or* **Dear Mrs. (Miss) Blank:**	**Very truly yours.**	**Sincerely yours,**	**1. Senator Blank** *or* **Mrs. (Miss) Blank** **2. Senator Blank**
Former Senator	The Honorable William R. Blank (local address)	Dear Senator Blank: *or* Dear Sir:	**Dear Senator Blank:**	**Very truly yours,**	**Sincerely yours,**	**1. Senator Blank** *or* **Senator** **2. Senator Blank**
Senator—elect	Honorable William R. Blank Senator—elect United States Senate Washington 25, D. C.	Dear Mr. Blank: *or* Dear Sir:	**Dear Mr. Blank:**	**Very truly yours,**	**Sincerely yours,**	**1. Mr. Blank** **2. Senator-elect Blank** *or* **Mr. Blank**
Committee Chairman—United States Senate	The Honorable William R. Blank, Chairman Committee on Foreign Affairs United States Senate Washington 25, D. C.	Dear Mr. Chairman:	**Dear Mr. Chairman:** *or* **Dear Senator Blank:**	**Very truly yours,**	**Sincerely yours,**	**1. Mr. Chairman** *or* **Senator Blank** *or* **Senator** **2. The Chairman** *or* **Senator Blank**

[3] In addressing a woman official and her husband, the customary form of addressing a husband and his wife applies.

UNITED STATES GOVERNMENT OFFICIALS *continued*

Personage	Envelope and Inside Address	Formal Salutation	Informal Salutation	Formal Close	Informal Close	1. Spoken Address 2. Informal Introduction or Reference
Subcommittee Chairman—United States Senate	The Honorable William R. Blank, Chairman, Subcommittee on Foreign Affairs United States Senate Washington 25, D. C.	Dear Senator Blank:	Dear Senator Blank:	Very truly yours,	Sincerely yours,	1. Senator Blank *or* Senator 2. Senator Blank
United States Representative (man)	The Honorable William R. Blank House of Representatives Washington 25, D. C. (Washington, D. C. Office) The Honorable William R. Blank Representative in Congress (local address) (when away from Washington, D. C.)	Dear Sir:	Dear Mr. Blank:	Very truly yours,	Sincerely yours,	1. Mr. Blank 2. Mr. Blank, Congressman from New York *or* Mr. Blank
United States Representative (woman)	The Honorable Louise Blank[3] House of Representatives Washington 25, D. C.	Dear Madam: *or* Dear Representative Blank:	Dear Mrs. (Miss) Blank:	Very truly yours,	Sincerely yours,	1. Mrs. (Miss) Blank 2. Mrs. (Miss) Blank *or* Mrs. (Miss) Blank, Representative from New York
Representative at Large	The Honorable William R. Blank House of Representatives Washington 25, D. C.	Dear Sir: *or* Dear Mr. Blank:	Dear Mr. Blank:	Very truly yours,	Sincerely yours,	1. Mr. Blank 2. Mr. Blank

[3] In addressing a woman official and her husband, the customary form of addressing a husband and his wife applies.

Former Representative	The Honorable William R. Blank (local address)	Dear Sir: *or* Dear Mr. Blank:	Dear Mr. Blank:	Very truly yours,	Sincerely yours,	1. Mr. Blank 2. Mr. Blank
Territorial Delegate	The Honorable William R. Blank Delegate of Puerto Rico House of Representatives Washington 25, D. C.	Dear Sir: *or* Dear Mr. Blank:	Dear Mr. Blank:	Very truly yours,	Sincerely yours,	1. Mr. Blank 2. Mr. Blank
Resident Commissioner	The Honorable William R. Blank Resident Commissioner of (Territory) House of Representatives Washington 25, D. C.	Dear Sir: *or* Dear Mr. Blank:	Dear Mr. Blank:	Very truly yours,	Sincerely yours,	1. Mr. Blank 2. Mr. Blank
Directors or Heads of Independent Federal Offices, Agencies, Commissions, Organizations etc.	The Honorable William R. Blank Director, Mutual Security Agency Washington 25, D. C.	Dear Mr. Director (Commissioner, etc.):	Dear Mr. Blank:	Very truly yours,	Sincerely yours,	1. Mr. Blank 2. Mr. Blank
Librarian of Congress	The Honorable William R. Blank Librarian of Congress Washington 25, D. C.	Dear Sir: *or* Dear Mr. Blank:	Dear Mr. Blank:	Very truly yours,	Sincerely yours,	1. Mr. Blank 2. Mr. Blank
Other High Officials of the United States, in general: Public Printer, Comptroller General	The Honorable William R. Blank Public Printer Washington 25, D. C. The Honorable William R. Blank Comptroller General of the United States Washington 25, D. C.	Dear Sir: *or* Dear Mr. Blank:	Dear Mr. Blank:	Very truly yours,	Sincerely yours,	1. Mr. Blank 2. Mr. Blank

UNITED STATES GOVERNMENT OFFICIALS *continued*

Personage	Envelope and Inside Address	Formal Salutation	Informal Salutation	Formal Close	Informal Close	1. Spoken Address 2. Informal Introduction or Reference
Secretary to the President	The Honorable William R. Blank Secretary to the President The White House Washington 25, D. C.	Dear Sir: *or* Dear Mr. Blank:	Dear Mr. Blank:	Very truly yours,	Sincerely yours,	1. Mr. Blank 2. Mr. Blank
Secretary to the President with military rank	Major General William R. Blank Secretary to the President The White House Washington 25, D. C.	Dear Sir: *or* Dear General Blank:	Dear General Blank:	Very truly yours,	Sincerely yours,	1. General Blank 2. General Blank
Assistant Secretary to the President	The Honorable William R. Blank Assistant Secretary to the President The White House Washington 25, D. C.	Dear Sir: *or* Dear Mr. Blank:	Dear Mr. Blank:	Very truly yours,	Sincerely yours,	1. Mr. Blank 2. Mr. Blank
Press Secretary to the President	Mr. William R. Blank Press Secretary to the President The White House Washington 25, D. C.	Dear Sir: *or* Dear Mr. Blank:	Dear Mr. Blank:	Very truly yours,	Sincerely yours,	1. Mr. Blank 2. Mr. Blank

STATE AND LOCAL GOVERNMENT OFFICIALS

Personage	Envelope and Inside Address	Formal Salutation	Informal Salutation	Formal Close	Informal Close	1. Spoken Address 2. Informal Introduction or Reference
Governor of a State or Territory[1]	*Formal* The Honorable the Governor of New York Albany, New York *Informal* The Honorable William R. Blank Governor of New York Albany, New York	Sir:	Dear Governor Blank:	Respectfully yours,	Very sincerely yours,	1. Governor Blank *or* Governor 2. a) Governor Blank b) The Governor c) The Governor of New York (used only outside his own state)
Acting Governor of a State or Territory	The Honorable William R. Blank Acting Governor of Connecticut Hartford, Connecticut	Sir:	Dear Mr. Blank:	Respectfully yours,	Very sincerely yours,	1. Mr. Blank 2. Mr. Blank

[1] The form of addressing Governors varies in the different states. The form given here is the one used in most states. In Massachusetts by law and in some other states by courtesy, the form is *His Excellency, the Governor of Massachusetts.*

STATE AND LOCAL GOVERNMENT OFFICIALS *continued*

Personage	Envelopes and Inside Address	Formal Salutation	Informal Salutation	Formal Close	Informal Close	1. Spoken Address 2. Informal Introduction or Reference
Lieutenant Governor	*Formal* The Honorable the Lieutenant Governor of Iowa Des Moines, Iowa *Informal* The Honorable William R. Blank Lieutenant Governor of Iowa Des Moines, Iowa	Sir:	Dear Mr. Blank:	Respectfully yours, *or* Very truly yours,	Sincerely yours,	1. Mr. Blank 2. The Lieutenant Governor of Iowa, Mr. Blank *or* The Lieutenant Governor
Secretary of State	*Formal* The Honorable the Secretary of State of New York Albany, New York *Informal* The Honorable William R. Blank Secretary of State of New York Albany, New York	Sir:	Dear Mr. Secretary:	Very truly yours,	Sincerely yours,	1. Mr. Blank 2. Mr. Blank
Attorney General	The Honorable William R. Blank Attorney General of Massachusetts Boston, Massachusetts	Sir:	Dear Mr. Attorney General:	Very truly yours,	Sincerely yours,	1. Mr. Blank 2. Mr. Blank

President of the Senate of a State	The Honorable William R. Blank President of the Senate of the State of Virginia Richmond, Virginia	Sir:	Dear Mr. Blank:	Very truly yours,	Sincerely yours,	1. Mr. Blank 2. Mr. Blank
Speaker of the Assembly of The House of Representatives[a]	The Honorable William R. Blank Speaker of the Assembly of the State of New York Albany, New York	Sir:	Dear Mr. Blank:	Very truly yours,	Sincerely yours,	1. Mr. Blank 2. Mr. Blank
Treasurer, Auditor, or Comptroller of a State	The Honorable William R. Blank Treasurer of the State of Tennessee Nashville, Tennessee	Dear Sir:	Dear Mr. Blank:	Very truly yours,	Sincerely yours,	1. Mr. Blank 2. Mr. Blank
State Senator	The Honorable William R. Blank The State Senate Trenton, New Jersey	Dear Sir:	Dear Senator Blank:	Very truly yours,	Sincerely yours,	1. Senator Blank *or* Senator 2. Senator Blank
State Representative, Assemblyman, or Delegate	The Honorable William R. Blank House of Delegates Baltimore, Maryland	Dear Sir:	Dear Mr. Blank:	Very truly yours,	Sincerely yours,	1. Mr. Blank 2. Mr. Blank *or* Delegate Blank
District Attorney	The Honorable William R. Blank District Attorney, Albany County County Courthouse Albany, New York	Dear Sir:	Dear Mr. Blank:	Very truly yours,	Sincerely yours,	1. Mr. Blank 2. Mr. Blank
Mayor of a city	The Honorable William R. Blank Mayor of Detroit Detroit, Michigan	Dear Sir:	Dear Mayor Blank:	Very truly yours.	Sincerely yours,	1. Mayor Blank *or* Mr. Mayor 2. Mayor Blank

[a] In most states the lower branch of the legislature is the House of Representatives. The exceptions to this are: New York, California, Wisconsin and Nevada, where it is known as the Assembly; Maryland, Virginia, and West Virginia—the House of Delegates; New Jersey—the House of General Assembly.

STATE AND LOCAL GOVERNMENT OFFICIALS *continued*

Personage	Envelopes and Inside Address	Formal Salutation	Informal Salutation	Formal Close	Informal Close	1. Spoken Address 2. Informal Introduction or Reference
President of a Board of Commissioners	The Honorable William R. Blank, President Board of Commissioners of the City of Buffalo Buffalo, New York	Dear Sir:	Dear Mr. Blank:	Very truly yours,	Sincerely yours,	1. Mr. Blank 2. Mr. Blank
City Attorney, City Counsel, Corporation Counsel	The Honorable William R. Blank, City Attorney (City Counsel, Corporation Counsel) San Francisco, California	Dear Sir:	Dear Mr. Blank:	Very truly yours,	Sincerely yours,	1. Mr. Blank 2. Mr. Blank
Alderman	Alderman William R. Blank City Hall Denver, Colorado	Dear Sir:	Dear Mr. Blank:	Very truly yours,	Sincerely yours,	1. Mr. Blank 2. Mr. Blank

COURT OFFICIALS

Personage	Envelope and Inside Address	Formal Salutation	Informal Salutation	Formal Close	Informal Close	1. Spoken Address 2. Informal Introduction or Reference
Chief Justice[1] *of a State Supreme Court*	The Honorable William R. Blank Chief Justice of the Supreme Court of Minnesota[2] Minneapolis, Minnesota	Sir:	Dear Mr. Chief Justice:	Very truly yours,	Sincerely yours,	1. Mr. Chief Justice *or* Judge Blank 2. Mr. Chief Justice Blank *or* Judge Blank
Associate Justice of a Supreme Court of a State	The Honorable William R. Blank Associate Justice of the Supreme Court of Minnesota Minneapolis, Minnesota	Sir:	Dear Justice Blank:	Very truly yours,	Sincerely yours,	1. Mr. Justice Blank 2. Mr. Justice Blank
Presiding Justice	The Honorable William R. Blank Presiding Justice, Appellate Division Supreme Court of New York New York, New York	Sir:	Dear Justice Blank:	Very truly yours,	Sincerely yours,	1. Mr. Justice (*or* Judge) Blank 2. Mr. Justice (*or* Judge Blank)

[1] If his official title is *Chief Judge* substitute *Chief Judge* for *Chief Justice*, but never use *Mr.* with *Chief Judge* or *Judge*.
[2] Substitute here the appropriate name of the court. For example, the highest court in New York State is called the Court of Appeals.

COURT OFFICIALS *continued*

Personage	Envelope and Inside Address	Formal Salutation	Informal Salutation	Formal Close	Informal Close	1. Spoken Address 2. Informal Introduction or Reference
Judge of a Court[a]	The Honorable William R. Blank Judge of the United States District Court for the Southern District of California Los Angeles, California	Sir:	Dear Judge Blank:	Very truly yours,	Sincerely yours,	1. Judge Blank 2. Judge Blank
Clerk of a Court	William R. Blank, Esquire Clerk of the Superior Court of Massachusetts Boston, Massachusetts	Dear Sir:	Dear Mr. Blank:	Very truly yours,	Sincerely yours,	1. Mr. Blank 2. Mr. Blank

[a] Not applicable to judges of United States Supreme Court.

UNITED STATES DIPLOMATIC REPRESENTATIVES

Personage	Envelope and Inside Address	Formal Salutation	Informal Salutation	Formal Close	Informal Close	1. Spoken Address 2. Informal Introduction or Reference
American Ambassador (man)	The Honorable William R. Blank American Ambassador[1] London, England	Sir:	Dear Mr. Ambassador:	Very truly yours,	Sincerely yours,	1. Mr. Ambassador *or* Mr. Blank 2. The American Ambassador[2] (The Ambassador or Mr. Blank)
American Ambassador[3] (woman)	The Honorable Louise Blank American Ambassador London, England	Madam:	Dear Madam Ambassador:	Very truly yours,	Sincerely yours,	1. Madam Ambassador *or* Mrs. (Miss) Blank 2. The American Ambassador (The American Ambassador or Mrs. (Miss) Blank)

[1] When an ambassador or minister is not at his post, the name of the country to which he is accredited must be added to the address. For example: "The American Ambassador to Great Britain." If he holds military rank, the diplomatic complimentary title "The Honorable" should be omitted, thus "General William R. Blank, American Ambassador (or Minister)."

[2] With reference to ambassadors and ministers to Central or South America countries, substitute *The Ambassador of the United States* for *American Ambassador* or *American Minister.*

[3] In addressing a woman ambassador or minister, the customary form of addressing a husband and his wife applies.

UNITED STATES DIPLOMATIC REPRESENTATIVES *continued*

Personage	Envelope and Inside Address	Formal Salutation	Informal Salutation	Formal Close	Informal Close	1. Spoken Address 2. Informal Introduction or Reference
American Minister (man)	The Honorable William R. Blank American Minister Bucharest, Rumania	Sir:	Dear Mr. Minister:	Very truly yours,	Sincerely yours,	1. Mr. Minister *or* Mr. Blank 2. The American Minister, Mr. Blank (The Minister *or* Mr. Blank)
American Minister (woman)	The Honorable Louise Blank American Minister Bucharest, Rumania	Madam:	Dear Mrs. (Miss) Blank: *or* Dear Madam Minister:	Very truly yours,	Sincerely yours,	1. Madam Minister *or* Mrs. (Miss) Blank 2. The American Minister, Mrs. (Miss) Blank (The Minister *or* Mrs. (Miss) Blank)
American Chargé d'Affaires ad interim (man)	William R. Blank, Esquire American Chargé d'Affaires ad interim (City, State)	Sir:	Dear Mr. Blank:	Very truly yours,	Sincerely yours,	1. Mr. Blank 2. Mr. Blank
American Chargé d'Affaires ad interim (woman)	Mrs. (Miss) Louise Blank American Chargé d'Affaires ad interim (City, State)	Madam:	Dear Mrs. (Miss) Blank:	Very truly yours,	Sincerely yours,	1. Mrs. (Miss) Blank 2. Mrs. (Miss) Blank
American Consul General, Consul, or Vice Consul	William R. Blank, Esquire American Consul General (Consul or Vice Consul) Warsaw	Sir:	Dear Mr. Blank:	Very truly yours,	Sincerely yours,	1. Mr. Blank 2. Mr. Blank
High Commissioner	**The Honorable William R. Blank United States High Commissioner to Argentina Buenos Aires**	Sir:	Dear Mr. Blank:	Very truly yours,	Sincerely yours,	**1. Commissioner Blank *or* Mr. Blank 2. Commissioner Blank *or* Mr. Blank**

FOREIGN OFFICIALS AND REPRESENTATIVES

Personage	Envelope and Inside Address	Formal Salutation	Informal Salutation	Formal Close	Informal Close	1. Spoken Address 2. Informal Introduction or Reference
Foreign Ambassador[1] in the United States	His Excellency,[2] Erik Rolf Blankson Ambassador of Norway Washington, D.C.	Excellency:	Dear Mr. Ambassador:	Respectfully yours,	Sincerely yours,	1. Mr. Ambassador *or* Mr. Blank 2. The Ambassador of Norway (The Ambassador *or* Mr. Blank)
Foreign Minister[1] in the United States	The Honorable George Macovescu Minister of Rumania Washington, D.C.	Sir:	Dear Mr. Minister:	Respectfully yours,	Sincerely yours,	1. Mr. Minister *or* Mr. Blank 2. The Minister of Rumania (The Minister *or* Mr. Blank)
Foreign Diplomatic Representative with a Personal Title[3]	His Excellency,[4] Count Allesandro de Bianco Ambassador of Italy Washington, D.C.	Excellency:	Dear Mr. Ambassador:	Respectfully yours,	Sincerely yours,	1. Mr. Ambassador *or* Count Bianco 2. The Ambassador of Italy (The Ambassador *or* Count Bianco)

[1] The correct title of all ambassadors and ministers of foreign countries is "Ambassador (Minister) of ...." (name of country) with the exception of Great Britain. The adjective form is used with reference to representatives from Great Britain—*British Ambassador, British Minister. See* "British Forms—Government Officials," page 46

[2] When the representative is British or a member of the British Commonwealth, it is customary to use "The Right Honorable" and "The Honorable" in addition to "His Excellency," wherever appropriate.

[3] If the personal title is a royal title, such as "His Highness," "Prince," etc., the diplomatic title "His Excellency" or "The Honorable" is omitted.

[4] Dr., Señor Don, and other titles of special courtesy in Spanish-speaking countries may be used with the diplomatic title "His Excellency" or "The Honorable."

FOREIGN OFFICIALS AND REPRESENTATIVES *continued*

Personage	Envelope and Inside Address	Formal Salutation	Informal Salutation	Formal Close	Informal Close	1. Spoken Address 2. Informal Introduction or Reference
Prime Minister	His Excellency, Christian Jawaharal Blank Prime Minister of India New Delhi, India	Excellency:	Dear Mr. Prime Minister:	Respectfully yours,	Sincerely yours,	1. Mr. Blank 2. Mr. Blank *or* The Prime Minister
British Prime Minister	The Right Honorable Godfrey Blank, K.G., M.C., M.P. Prime Minister London, England	Sir:	Dear Mr. Prime Minister: *or* Dear Mr. Blank:	Respectfully yours,	Sincerely yours,	1. Mr. Blank 2. Mr. Blank *or* The Prime Minister
Canadian Prime Minister	The Right Honorable Claude Louis St. Blanc, C.M.G. Prime Minister of Canada Ottawa, Canada	Sir:	Dear Mr. Prime Minister: *or* Dear Mr. Blanc:	Respectfully yours,	Sincerely yours,	1. Mr. Blanc 2. Mr. Blanc *or* The Prime Minister
President of a Republic	His Excellency, Juan Cuidad Blanco President of the Dominican Republic	Excellency:	Dear Mr. President:	I remain with respect, Very truly yours, (formal general usage) Sincerely yours, (less formal)	Sincerely yours,	1. Your Excellency 2. Not introduced (President Blanco *or* the President)
Premier	His Excellency, Charles Yves de Blanc Premier of the French Republic Paris	Excellency:	Dear Mr. Premier:	Respectfully yours,	Sincerely yours,	1. Mr. Blanc 2. Mr. Blanc *or* The Premier
Foreign Chargé d'Affaires (de missi)[5] *in the United States*	Mr. Jan Gustaf Blanc Chargé d'Affaires of Sweden Washington, D.C.	Sir:	Dear Mr. Blanc:	Respectfully yours,	Sincerely yours,	1. Mr. Blanc 2. Mr. Blanc
Foreign Chargé d'Affaires ad interim in the United States	Mr. Edmund Blank Chargé d'Affaires ad interim[6] of Ireland Washington, D.C.	Sir:	Dear Mr. Blank:	Respectfully yours,	Sincerely yours,	1. Mr. Blank 2. Mr. Blank

[5] The full title is usually shortened to chargé d'affaires.
[6] The words "ad interim" should not be omitted in the address.

THE ARMED FORCES / THE ARMY

Personage	Envelope and Inside Address	Formal Salutation	Informal Salutation	Formal Close	Informal Close	1. Spoken Address 2. Informal Introduction or Reference
General of the Army[1]	General of the Army William R. Blank, U.S.A. Department of the Army Washington, D.C.	Sir:	Dear General Blank:	Very truly yours,	Sincerely yours,	1. General Blank 2. General Blank
General, Lieutenant General, Major General, Brigadier General	General (Lieutenant General, Major General, or Brigadier General) William R. Blank, U.S.A.[2] Fort Leavenworth, Kansas	Sir:	Dear General Blank:	Very truly yours,	Sincerely yours,	1. General Blank 2. General Blank
Colonel, Lieutenant Colonel	Colonel (Lieutenant Colonel) William R. Blank, U.S.A. Fort Dix, New Jersey	Dear Colonel Blank:	Dear Colonel Blank:	Very truly yours,	Sincerely yours,	1. Colonel Blank 2. Colonel Blank
Major	Major William R. Blank, U.S.A. Fort Sam Houston, Texas	Dear Major Blank:	Dear Major Blank:	Very truly yours,	Sincerely yours,	1. Major Blank 2. Major Blank
Captain	Captain William R. Blank, U.S.A. Fort Shelby, Mississippi	Dear Captain Blank:	Dear Captain Blank:	Very truly yours,	Sincerely yours,	1. Captain Blank 2. Captain Blank

[1] At present there is no General of the Army in active service.
[2] *U.S.A.* indicates regular service. *A.U.S.* (Army of the United States) signifies the Reserve.

THE ARMED FORCES / THE ARMY *continued*

Personage	Envelope and Inside Address	Formal Salutation	Informal Salutation	Formal Close	Informal Close	1. Spoken Address 2. Informal Introduction or Reference
First Lieutenant, Second Lieutenant[3]	Lieutenant William R. Blank, U.S.A. Fort Schuyler, New York	Dear Lieutenant Blank:	Dear Lieutenant Blank:	Very truly yours,	Sincerely yours,	1. Lieutenant Blank 2. Lieutenant Blank
Chief Warrant Officer, Warrant Officer	Mr. William R. Blank, U.S.A. Fort Dix, New Jersey	Dear Mr. Blank:	Dear Mr. Blank:	Very truly yours,	Sincerely yours,	1. Mr. Blank 2. Mr. Blank
Chaplain in the U.S. Army[4]	Chaplain William R. Blank, Captain U.S.A. Fort Sill, Oklahoma	Dear Chaplain Blank:	Dear Chaplain Blank:	Very truly yours,	Sincerely yours,	1. Chaplain Blank 2. Captain Blank (Chaplain Blank)

[3] In all *official* correspondence the full rank should be included in both the envelope address and the inside address, but not in the salutation.
[4] Roman Catholic chaplains and certain Anglican priests are introduced as *"Chaplain Blank"* but are spoken to and referred to as *"Father Blank."*

THE ARMED FORCES / THE NAVY

Fleet Admiral	Fleet Admiral William R. Blank, U. S. N. Chief of Naval Operations Department of the Navy Washington, D. C.	Sir:	Dear Admiral Blank:	Very truly yours,	Sincerely yours,	1. Admiral Blank 2. Admiral Blank

Admiral, Vice Admiral, Rear Admiral	Admiral (Vice Admiral or Rear Admiral) William R. Blank, U. S. N. United States Naval Academy[1] Annapolis, Maryland	Sir:	Dear Admiral Blank:	Very truly yours;	Sincerely yours,	1. Admiral Blank 2. Admiral Blank
Commodore, Captain, Commander, Lieutenant Commander	Commodore (Captain, Commander, Lieutenant Commander) William R. Blank, U. S. N. U. S. S. Mississippi San Diego, California	Dear Commodore (Captain, Commander) Blank:	Dear Commodore (Captain, Commander) Blank:,	Very truly yours,	Sincerely yours,	1. Commodore (Captain, Commander) Blank 2. Commodore (Captain, Commander) Blank
Junior Officers: Lieutenant, Lieutenant Junior Grade, Ensign	(Lieutenant, etc.) William R. Blank, U. S. N. U.S.S. Wyoming Norfolk, Virginia	Dear Mr. Blank:	Dear Mr. Blank:	Very truly yours,	Sincerely yours,	1. Mr. Blank[2] 2. Lieutenant, etc., Blank (Mr. Blank)
Chief Warrant Officer, Warrant Officer	Mr. William R. Blank, U.S.N. U.S.S. Texas San Diego, California	Dear Mr. Blank:	Dear Mr. Blank:	Very truly yours,	Sincerely yours,	1. Mr. Blank 2. Mr. Blank
Chaplain	Chaplain William R. Blank Captain, U.S.N. Department of the Navy Washington, D. C.	Dear Chaplain Blank:	Dear Chaplain Blank:	Very truly yours,	Sincerely yours,	1. Chaplain Blank 2. Captain Blank (Chaplain Blank)

[1] U.S.N. signifies regular service; U.S.N.R. indicates the Reserve.

[2] Junior officers in the medical or dental corps are spoken to and referred to as "Dr." but are introduced by their rank.

THE ARMED FORCES — AIR FORCE

Air Force titles are the same as those in the Army, *U.S.A.F.* is used instead of *U.S.A.*, and *A.F.U.S.* is used to indicate the Reserve.

THE ARMED FORCES — MARINE CORPS

Marine Corps titles are the same as those in the Army, except that the top rank is *Commandant of the Marine Corps. U.S.M.C.* indicates regular service, *U.S.M.R.* indicates the Reserve.

THE ARMED FORCES — COAST GUARD

Coast Guard titles are the same as those in the Navy, except that the top rank is Admiral. *U.S.C.G.* indicates regular service, *U.S.G.C.R.* indicates the Reserve.

CHURCH DIGNITARIES / CATHOLIC FAITH

Personage	Envelope and Inside Address	Formal Salutation	Informal Salutation	Formal Close	Informal Close	1. Spoken Address 2. Informal Introduction or Reference
The Pope	His Holiness The Pope *or* His Holiness Pope John XXIII Vatican City	Your Holiness:	*Always Formal*	Respectfully,	*Always Formal*	1. Your Holiness 2. Not introduced (His Holiness *or* The Pope)
Apostolic Delegate	His Excellency, The Most Reverend William R. Blank Archbishop of ———, The Apostolic Delegate Washington, D. C.	Your Excellency:	My dear Archbishop:	Respectfully yours,	Respectfully,	1. Your Excellency 2. Not introduced (The Apostolic Delegate)
Cardinal in the United States	His Eminence, William Cardinal Blank Archbishop of New York New York, New York	Your Eminence:	*Always Formal*	Respectfully yours,	Respectfully, *or* Sincerely yours,	1. Your Eminence *or less formally* Cardinal Blank 2. Not introduced (His Eminence *or* Cardinal Blank)
Archbishop in the United States	The Most Reverend William R. Blank, D.D. Archbishop of Baltimore Baltimore, Maryland	Your Excellency:	Dear Archbishop Blank:	Respectfully yours,	Respectfully, *or* Sincerely yours,	1. Archbishop Blank 2. Archbishop Blank

CHURCH DIGNITARIES / CATHOLIC FAITH *continued*

Personage	Envelope and Inside Address	Formal Salutation	Informal Salutation	Formal Close	Informal Close	1. Spoken Address 2. Informal Introduction or Reference
Bishop in the United States	The Most Reverend William R. Blank, D.D. Bishop of Boston Boston, Massachusetts	Your Excellency:	Dear Bishop Blank:	Respectfully yours,	Sincerely yours,	1. Bishop Blank 2. Bishop Blank
Bishop in England	The Right Reverend William R. Blank Bishop of Sussex (local address)	Right Reverend Sir:	Dear Bishop:	Respectfully yours,	Respectfully,	1. Bishop Blank 2. Bishop Blank
Abbot	The Right Reverend William R. Blank Abbot of Westmoreland Abbey Washington, D. C.	Dear Father Abbot:	Dear Father Blank:	Respectfully yours,	Sincerely yours,	1. Father Abbot 2. Father Blank
Canon	The Reverend William R. Blank, D.D. Canon of St. Patrick's Cathedral New York, New York	Dear Canon Blank:	Dear Canon Blank:	Respectfully yours,	Sincerely yours,	1. Canon Blank 2. Canon Blank
Monsignor	The Right (or Very)[1] Reverend Msgr. William R. Blank Boston, Massachusetts	Right Reverend and Dear Monsignor Blank: *or* Very Reverend and Dear Monsignor Blank:	Dear Monsignor Blank:	Respectfully yours,	Sincerely yours,	1. Monsignor Blank 2. Monsignor Blank

[1] Dependent upon rank. See the *Official* (Roman) *Catholic Directory.*

Brother	Brother John Francis 932 Maple Avenue San Francisco, California	Dear Brother Francis:	Dear Brother Francis:	Respectfully yours,	Sincerely yours,	1. Brother Francis 2. Brother Francis
Superior of a Brotherhood and Priest[2]	The Very Reverend William R. Blank, M.M. Director Birchknoll, New York	Dear Father Superior:	Dear Father Superior:	Respectfully yours,	Sincerely yours,	1. Father Blank 2. Father Blank
Priest	*With Scholastic Degree* The Reverend William R. Blank, Ph.D. Georgetown University Washington, D. C.	Dear Dr. Blank:	Dear Dr. Blank:	Respectfully,	Sincerely yours,	1. Doctor Blank 2. Doctor Blank
	Without Scholastic Degree The Reverend William R. Blank St. Vincent's Church Lynchburg, Virginia	Dear Father Blank:	Dear Father Blank:	Respectfully,	Sincerely yours,	1. Father Blank 2. Father Blank
Sister Superior	The Reverend Sister Superior (order, if used)[3] Convent of the Sacred Heart Sacramento, California	Dear Sister Superior:	Dear Sister Superior:	Respectfully,	Respectfully,	1. Sister Blank *or* Sister St. Teresa 2. The Sister Superior *or* Sister Blank (Sister St. Teresa)
Sister	Sister Mary Magdelena St. John's High School Northfield, Maine	Dear Sister:	Dear Sister Mary Magdelena:	Respectfully,	Sincerely yours,	1. Sister Mary Magdelena 2. Sister Mary Magdelena

[2] The address for the superior of a Brotherhood depends upon whether or not he is a priest or has a title other than superior. Consult the *Official Catholic Directory*.

[3] The address of the superior of a Sisterhood depends upon the order to which she belongs. The abbreviation of the order is not always used. Consult the *Official Catholic Directory*.

CHURCH DIGNITARIES / CATHOLIC FAITH *continued*

Personage	Envelope and Inside Address	Formal Salutation	Informal Salutation	Formal Close	Informal Close	1. Spoken Address 2. Informal Introduction or Reference
Mother Superior of a Sisterhood (Catholic or Protestant)	The Reverend Mother Superior, O.C.A. Convent of the Sacred Heart Sacramento, California	Dear Reverend Mother: *or* Dear Mother Superior:	Dear Reverend Mother: *or* Dear Mother Superior:	Respectfully,	Sincerely yours,	1. Reverend Mother 2. Reverend Mother
Member of Community	Mother Mary Walker, R.S.C.J. Convent of Mercy	Dear Mother Walker:	Dear Mother Walker:	Respectfully,	Sincerely yours,	1. Mother Walker 2. Mother Walker

CHURCH DIGNITARIES / JEWISH FAITH

Rabbi	*With scholastic degree* Rabbi William R. Blank, Ph.D. *or* Dr. William R. Blank	Sir:	Dear Rabbi Blank: *or* Dear Dr. Blank:	Respectfully,	Sincerely yours,	1. Rabbi Blank *or* Dr. Blank 2. Rabbi Blank *or* Dr. Blank
	Without scholastic degree Rabbi William R. Blank	Sir:	Dear Rabbi Blank:	Respectfully,	Sincerely yours,	1. Rabbi Blank 2. Rabbi Blank

CHURCH DIGNITARIES / PROTESTANT FAITH

Personage	Envelope and Inside Address	Formal Salutation	Informal Salutation	Formal Close	Informal Close	1. Spoken Address 2. Informal Introduction or Reference
Archbishop (Anglican)	To His Grace The Lord Archbishop of Canterbury Canterbury, England	Your Grace: *or* My Lord Archbishop:	My dear Archbishop:	Respectfully yours,	Sincerely yours,	1. Your Grace 2. Not introduced (His Grace or The Archbishop)
Presiding Bishop of the Protestant Episcopal Church in America	The Most Reverend William R. Blank, D.D., LL.D. Presiding Bishop of the Protestant Episcopal Church in America Northwick House Northwick, Connecticut	Most Reverend Sir:	Dear Bishop: *or* Dear Bishop Blank:	Respectfully yours,	Sincerely yours,	1. Bishop Blank 2. Bishop Blank
Anglican Bishop	The Right Reverend The Lord Bishop of London London, England	My Lord Bishop:	My dear Bishop:	Respectfully yours,	Sincerely yours,	1. Bishop Blank 2. Bishop Blank
Methodist Bishop	The Reverend William R. Blank Methodist Bishop Phoenix, Arizona	Reverend Sir:	Dear Bishop Blank:	Respectfully yours,	Sincerely yours,	1. Bishop Blank 2. Bishop Blank

CHURCH DIGNITARIES / PROTESTANT FAITH *continued*

Personage	Envelope and Inside Address	Formal Salutation	Informal Salutation	Formal Close	Informal Close	1. Spoken Address 2. Informal Introduction or Reference
Protestant Episcopal Bishop	The Right Reverend the Bishop of Denver *or* The Right Reverend William R. Blank, D.D., LL.D. Bishop of Denver Denver, Colorado	Right Reverend Sir:	Dear Bishop Blank:	Respectfully yours,	Sincerely yours,	1. Bishop Blank 2. Bishop Blank
Angelican Archdeacon	The Venerable William R. Blank The Archdeacon of Baltimore Baltimore, Maryland	Venerable Sir:	My dear Archdeacon:	Respectfully yours,	Sincerely yours,	1. Archdeacon Blank 2. Archdeacon Blank
Protestant Episcopal Archdeacon	The Venerable William R. Blank, D.D. The Archdeacon of Wilmington Wilmington, Delaware	Venerable Sir:	My Dear Archdeacon:	Respectfully yours,	Sincerely yours,	1. Archdeacon Blank *or* Dr. Blank 2. Archdeacon Blank *or* Dr. Blank
Dean[1]	The Very Reverend William R. Blank, D.D. Dean of St. John's Cathedral Chicago, Illinois	Dear Dean Blank:	Dear Dean Blank:	Respectfully,	Sincerely yours,	1. Dean Blank *or* Dr. Blank 2. Dean Blank *or* Dr. Blank

Protestant Minister	*With scholastic degree* The Reverend William R. Blank, D.D., Litt.D. Delta, Mississippi	Dear Dr. Blank:	Dear Dr. Blank:	Very truly yours,	Sincerely yours,	1. Dr. Blank 2. Dr. Blank
	Without scholastic degree The Reverend William R. Blank Rochester, New York	Dear Mr. Blank:	Dear Mr. Blank:	Very truly yours,	Sincerely yours,	1. Mr. Blank 2. Mr. Blank
Episcopal Priest (High Church)	*With scholastic degree* The Reverend William R. Blank, D.D., Litt.D. All Saint's Cathedral Hartford, Connecticut	Dear Dr. Blank:	Dear Dr. Blank:	Very truly yours,	Sincerely yours,	1. Dr. Blank 2. Dr. Blank
	Without scholastic degree The Reverend William R. Blank St. Paul's Church Houston, Texas	Dear Mr. Blank: *or* Dear Father Blank:	Dear Mr. Blank: *or* Dear Father Blank:	Very truly yours,	Sincerely yours,	1. Father Blank *or* Mr. Blank 2. Father Blank *or* Mr. Blank

COLLEGE AND UNIVERSITY OFFICIALS

Personage	Envelope and Inside Address	Formal Salutation	Informal Salutation	Formal Close	Informal Close	1. Spoken Address 2. Informal Introduction or Reference
President of a College or University	*With a doctor's degree* William R. Blank, LL.D., Ph.D. *or* Dr. William R. Blank President, Amherst College Amherst, Massachusetts	Sir:	Dear Dr. Blank:	Very truly yours,	Sincerely yours,	1. Dr. Blank 2. Dr. Blank
	Without a doctor's degree Mr. William R. Blank President, Columbia University New York, New York	Sir:	Dear President Blank:	Very truly yours,	Sincerely yours,	1. Mr. Blank 2. Mr. Blank *or* Mr. Blank, President of the College
	Catholic Priest The Very Reverend William R. Blank, S.J., D.D., Ph.D. President, Fordham University New York, New York	Sir:	Dear Father Blank:	Very truly yours,	Sincerely yours,	1. Father Blank 2. Father Blank
University Chancellor	Dr. William R. Blank Chancellor, University of Alabama University, Alabama	Sir:	Dear Dr. Blank:	Very truly yours,	Sincerely yours,	1. Dr. Blank 2. Dr. Blank

Dean or Assistant Dean of a College or Graduate School	Dean William R. Blank School of Law *or* (If he holds a doctor's degree) Dr. William R. Blank, Dean (Assistant Dean), School of Law University of Virginia Charlottesville, Virgina	Dear Sir: *or* Dear Dean Blank:	Dear Dean Blank:	Very truly yours,	Sincerely yours,	1. Dean Blank 2. Dean Blank *or* Dr. Blank, the Dean (Assistant Dean) of the School of Law
Dean of a College for Women	Dean Mary Louise Blank Smith College *or* (If she holds a doctor's degree) Dr. Mary Louise Blank Dean, Smith College Northhampton, Massachusetts	Dear Madam: *or* Dear Dean Blank:	Dear Dean Blank:	Very truly yours,	Sincerely yours,	1. Dean Blank 2. Dean Blank *or* Dr. Blank, the Dean
Professor	Professor William R. Blank *or* (If he holds a doctor's degree) William R. Blank, Ph.D. Yale University New Haven, Connecticut	Dear Sir: *or* Dear Professor (Dr.) Blank:	Dear Professor (Dr.) Blank:	Very truly yours,	Sincerely yours,	1. Professor (Dr.) Blank 2. Professor (Dr.) Blank
Associate or Assistant Professor	Mr. William R. Blank *or* (If he holds a doctor's degree) William R. Blank, Ph.D. Associate (Assistant) Professor Department of Romance Languages Williams College Williamstown, Massachusetts	Dear Sir: *or* Dear Professor (Dr.) Blank:	Dear Professor (Dr.) Blank:	Very truly yours,	Sincerely yours,	1. Professor (Dr.) Blank 2. Professor (Dr.) Blank

COLLEGE AND UNIVERSITY OFFICIALS *continued*

Personage	Envelope and Inside Address	Formal Salutation	Informal Salutation	Formal Close	Informal Close	1. Spoken Address 2. Informal Introduction or Reference
Instructor	Mr. William R. Blank *or* (If he holds a doctor's degree) William R. Blank, Ph.D. Department of Economics University of California Berkeley, California	Dear Sir: *or* Dear Mr. (Dr.) Blank:	Dear Mr. (Dr.) Blank:	Very truly yours,	Sincerely yours,	1. Mr. (Dr.) Blank 2. Mr. (Dr.) Blank
Chaplain of a College or University	The Reverend William R. Blank, D. D. Chaplain, Trinity College Hartford, Connecticut *or* Chaplain William R. Blank Trinity College Hartford, Connecticut	Dear Chaplain Blank: *or* (If he holds a doctor's degree) Dear Dr. Blank:	Dear Chaplain (Dr.) Blank:	Very truly yours,	Sincerely yours,	1. Chaplain Blank 2. Chaplain Blank *or* Dr. Blank

THE UNITED NATIONS

Personage	Envelope and Inside Address	Formal Salutation	Informal Salutation	Formal Close	Informal Close	1. Spoken Address 2. Informal Introduction or Reference
Secretary General	His Excellency, William R. Blank Secretary General of the United Nations New York 16, New York	Excellency: [2]	Dear Mr. Secretary General:	Very truly yours,	Sincerely yours,	1. Mr. Blank *or* Sir 2. The Secretary General of the United Nations *or* Mr. Blank
Under Secretary	The Honorable William R. Blank Under Secretary of the United Nations The Secretariat United Nations New York 16, New York	Sir:	Dear Mr. Blank:	Very truly yours,	Sincerely yours,	1. Mr. Blank 2. Mr. Blank
Foreign Representative (with Ambassadorial rank)	His Excellency, William R. Blank Representative of Spain to the United Nations New York 16, New York	Excellency:	Dear Mr. Ambassador:	Very truly yours,	Sincerely yours,	1. Mr. Ambassador *or* Mr. Blank 2. Mr. Ambassador *or* The Representative of Spain to the United Nations (The Ambassadòr *or* Mr. Blank)

[1] The six principal branches through which the United Nations functions are The General Assembly, The Security Council, The Economic and Social Council, The Trusteeship Council, The International Court of Justice, and The Secretariat.
[2] An American citizen should never be addressed as "Excellency."

THE UNITED NATIONS *continued*

Personage	Envelope and Inside Address	Formal Salutation	Informal Salutation	Formal Close	Informal Close	1. Spoken Address 2. Informal Introduction or Reference
United States Representative (with Ambassadorial rank)	The Honorable William R. Blank United States Representative to the United Nations New York 16, New York	Sir: *or* Dear Mr. Ambassador:	Dear Mr. Ambassador:	Very truly yours,	Sincerely yours,	1. Mr. Ambassador *or* Mr. Blank 2. Mr. Ambassador *or* The United States Representative to the United Nations (The Ambassador or Mr. Blank)
United States Representative to the Economic and Social Council	The Honorable William R. Blank United States Representative to the Economic and Social Council of the United Nations New York 16, New York	Sir:	Dear Mr. Blank:	Very truly yours,	Sincerely yours,	1. Mr. Blank 2. Mr. Blank
United States Representative to the Trusteeship Council	The Honorable William R. Blank United States Representative to the Trusteeship Council of the United Nations New York 16, New York	Sir:	Dear Mr. Blank:	Very truly yours,	Sincerely yours,	1. Mr. Blank 2. Mr. Blank
Senior Representative of the United States to the General Assembly	The Honorable William R. Blank Senior Representative of the United States to the General Assembly of the United Nations New York 16, New York	Sir:	Dear Mr. Blank:	Very truly yours,	Sincerely yours,	1. Mr. Blank 2. Mr. Blank